D0457098

Renegade Regimes

Renegade Regimes

Confronting Deviant Behavior in World Politics

Miroslav Nincic

COLUMBIA UNIVERSITY PRESS   NEW YORK

Columbia University Press
Publishers Since 1893
New York   Chichester, West Sussex
Copyright © 2005 Columbia University Press
All rights Reserved

Library of Congress Cataloging-in-Publication Data

Nincic, Miroslav.
    Renegade regimes : confronting deviant behavior
in world politics / Miroslav Nincic.
       p.   cm.
    Includes bibliographical references and index.
    ISBN 0–231-13702-8 (cloth : alk. paper) —
    ISBN 0–231-51029-2 (electronic)
    1. Security, International.   2. Power (Social
sciences)   3. International relations.   4. World
politics — 1989–   I. Title.

JZ5588.N56 2005
327.1'17 — dc22
                                        2005049352

Contents

Tables and Figures   *vii*
Acknowledgments   *ix*

1 From Power Politics to International Deviance   1
2 The Logic of Renegade Regimes: A Theoretical
   Framework   18
3 Recognizing Renegades   46
4 Primary Renegades and the Genesis of Deviance   73
5 Secondary Renegades and Nonmilitary Responses   107
6 The Value of Military Coercion   133
7 Closing Thoughts   167

Notes   *183*
Index   *209*

Tables and Figures

Tables

3.1 States Possessing or Seeking Chemical or Biological Weapons Since 1989   56

3.2 State of Nuclear Proliferation Since 1989   57

3.3 Interstate Conflicts Since 1989   59

3.4 Renegade Regimes   64

3.5 The Structure of Causation   66

4.1 Truth Table for the Genesis of Renegades   101

4.2 Primary Renegades and Ideational Drives   102

4.3 Primary Renegades and Economic Strategies   104

4.4 Primary Renegades and Direct Links   104

4.5 Primary Renegades: Necessary and Sufficient Conditions   105

5.1 Targets of Comprehensive and Partial Sanctions   109

5.2 The Effectiveness of Comprehensive and Partial Sanctions   109

5.3 A Profile of Secondary Renegades   127

5.4 The Impact of Ideational Boosts   127

5.5 The Impact of Rent-Seeking Interests   128

5.6 The Impact of Political Positioning   128

5.7 Ideational Boosts and Severity of Sanctions   129

5.8 Rent-Seeking Interests and Severity of Sanctions   129

5.9 Political Positioning and Severity of Sanctions   130

6.1   Primary Objectives of Military Coercion   135
6.2   The Correlates of Military Threats   146
6.3   Military Threats and the IO Model   146
6.4   Military Threats and the IR Model   147

Figures

4.1   Genesis of Renegades   106
5.1   Who Is Most Responsible for Serbia's Predicament?   123
5.2   Economic Retribution and the Likelihood of Compliant
       Renegades   131
6.1   Positive Ratings of Milosevic   153
6.2   Who Is Responsible for NATO's Intervention?   154

Acknowledgments

I have benefited from the advice and assistance of a number of scholars. In particular, I would like to thank Donald Rothchild, Jack Snyder, Jennifer Ramos, Donna Nincic, Idin Eftekhari, Monti Datta, and Gregg Garbesi.

Renegade Regimes

1 From Power Politics to International Deviance

Global society has changed more profoundly than scholarship addressing its nature and motions. The traditional conception of a world where relations among states are dominated by peers, or approximate peers, jockeying for power and position is no longer as appropriate as it once was. International relations is now characterized as much by a clash pitting most of international society, including its leading powers, against a few actors that, their lack of conventional power notwithstanding, challenge the majority's interests and values.

Much of international history was dominated by the struggle for power among plausible contenders for international position, and academic work mirrored this fact: by and large, theories of international relations and foreign policy were theories of power politics (i.e., theories of politics among "powers"), concerned with security and with the management and structuring of power among those claiming a share of it. The matters that now head the agenda include terrorism (often abetted by states); they encompass the proliferation of nuclear, chemical, biological, and radiological weapons to weak nations; they extend to domestic transgressions of certain regimes (such as ethnic cleansing and other genocidal practices), especially when they carry international consequences. Such issues now dominate headlines and the attention of governments, and they are substantially different from those around which international politics traditionally revolved. Academics do tackle these problems, but as discrete questions (e.g., combating terrorism) rather than as the manifestation of a more profoundly altered character of global politics, now governed by the threat posed by a limited number of seemingly weak states and social movements to the values, interests, and norms that most others, especially those at the pinnacle of the global hierarchy, have come to embrace. Such threats may wax and wane, they may acquire different forms, but, for the foreseeable future, they are likely to dominate the international agenda.

These challenges cannot easily be studied within the usual terms of reference of international relations scholarship; they may be more adequately characterized by the vocabulary of sociological analysis, for they are akin to what sociologists define as *deviant* behavior. Much as deviance within societies refers to a defiance of commonly accepted societal norms, international deviance, as the term is used here, refers to a flouting of key norms of conduct espoused by the global community, or at least by those who have asserted a credible right to speak for it. Norms, in turn, are rules of behavior with some level of general applicability; in political life, they reflect the values and interests embodied in and promoted by these rules. They are, in particular, a reflection of the needs of those who are best positioned to define them, generally the community's most influential members. Under the circumstances, the foreseeable future may not pit one major power against another, one military-ideological bloc against another, but a preponderant portion of the global community against occasional though significant threats from actors of a different scale and with largely incompatible, and externally nonmalleable, incentives. They are labeled "outlaws," "backlash states," "rogues," and "renegades"; the challenge they present has, partly at least, supplanted classical power politics as the distinctive feature of international relations.

The common denominator of the agents of such threats is that they are weak by most conventional standards, while nevertheless rejecting core, internationally accepted norms of behavior. This book seeks to shed new analytic light on these challenges to world order, and on the manner in which they are molded by the international responses they provoke.

Conventional Perspectives and Changing Realities

Traditionally, scholarship has addressed the dealings, often confrontational, between "powers" (nations or aggregates of nations), which, by their political significance and coercive capabilities, shape the course of international relations. This produced a corpus of theory that could be subsumed under the heading "power politics." With certain exceptions (e.g., colonial conflicts), the literature on conflict and conflict prevention dealt with the interests and calculations of similarly capable parties; and it sought ways of establishing power equilibriums between them, such that none could be confident of its ability to engage the other without unacceptable harm to itself. Although there have been debates within the literature, for example, on the sources and proper measurement of power,[1] or on the relative merits of multipolarity or bipolarity,[2] the defining concern was relations between powers.

All of this was a natural reflection of the world that scholars responded to, a world that (with some simplification) had three important attributes. The first was an approximate parity among its leading players, who, because of roughly comparable capabilities or the play of shifting alliances, could credibly threaten each other's positions. The rest of the world was viewed chiefly through the prism of their relations and rivalries — as, for example, in the context of colonial competitions, the struggle for spheres of political-military influence during the Cold War, and so forth. Under the circumstances, the focus of scholars has been on situations involving equilibrium among nations, on the conditions that make this possible, and on the consequences of disequilibria. Situations of vast power asymmetry have not been extensively considered. An exception was provided by the *dependency* school, which examined the manner in which the wealth of some societies interacts causally with the poverty of others, but it had a short life.[3] Even theories of hegemonic stability[4] are consistent with the study of challenges to a hegemon's position from rivals capable of mounting such challenges, or with competition among regional hegemons for imperial dominance.

The second attribute was a combination of shared and discrepant interests between powers, within which the discrepant were of particular concern to government leaders and analysts. The lack of a common international authority (i.e., the fact of international anarchy[5]) made potential threats among powers weigh more heavily than possibilities for cooperation. Given the implications of these threats, security was at the forefront of national concerns. As power acquired with a view to ensuring one's own security can be viewed as threatening the security of others, it has often been assumed that dominant nations worry more about *relative* gains than about *absolute* gains,[6] implying a fixed-sum quality to their relations. Under the circumstances, security dilemmas were thought to pervade international politics,[7] and their study became the intellectual fulcrum around which much scholarship revolved. The perils and dynamics of arms races, the prospects for collective security, and the logic of nuclear and conventional deterrence were the sort of subjects studied under this general heading.

The third attribute was the presence, along with a combination of discrepant and shared interests, of a commonly accepted continuum along which these interests and values could be scaled, implying that incentives for conflict and cooperation (e.g., economic gain, accretion of military capacity) had similar meanings to the parties, making it possible, in principle, to reach compromise by reducing the distance along that common continuum. As illustrations, the conflict between capitalism and communism (involving a left-right continuum) could, theoretically, have been compromised by accepting socialism; border disputes could be resolved by drawing frontiers at some territorial midpoint; and so forth. Thus, scholarship embraced models of bargaining and negotiation, of perceptions and misperceptions among adversaries, of crisis escalation and management, and so forth, all of which assumed that an area of common interest and meaning could be found somewhere between the parties' initial positions: the challenge was to discover it.

None of these assumptions applies as well to current international circumstances. First, a credible parity of power at the pinnacle of the international system no longer exists. For the first time, one country has emerged as the world's only meaningful pole of power. Partly, this is a consequence of the collapse, due to overwhelming failures of its political and economic system, of the Soviet Union and its immediate allies, leaving the world with no credible counterweight to U.S. military might. Partly, too, this stems from the immense success of the U.S. economy and its ability to push the boundaries of science and technology much further than other nations have managed, resulting in more leverage over the fate of most nations than any other country has yet had. Finally, this is also because of U.S. "soft" power[8] flowing from the geographically far-flung appeal of America's popular culture and consumer values. Independently, then, of what might be true at the narrowly regional levels, there are no other contenders for global power and influence. The quasi-hegemony of the United States invites challenges of a sort not adequately encompassed by theories of power politics: they originate from quarters other than leading (if secondary) powers, and they are fueled by drives other than the conventional incentives of external security and domestic prosperity. Moreover, the emergence of a unipolar world has given the United States and its immediate allies the ability to mobilize a significant portion of the world's attention and resources to combat those who would threaten their values and interests. The implications are not naturally encompassed by classical models of international relations.

Second, in their mutual relations, major nations no longer are driven by a combination of incentives within which clashing values and interests weigh more heavily than those that are shared. There still is a combination of the shared and discrepant, but, at least among powers, the balance has shifted decisively toward the former. This springs from the evolution of both interests and values. Economic globalization has created something approximating an integrated international marketplace. Barriers to trade have declined substantially, the multinationalization of investment has proceeded further than ever before in the century, and consumption patterns have converged across nations to an unprecedented extent.[9] Economic interdependence had been increasing for some time, but many of its greatest leaps have occurred in recent decades. These trends, while globally discernible, have been particularly pronounced within the upper reaches of the international hierarchy. For example, nearly two-thirds of the total volume of international currency flows through the banking systems of just four countries (the United States, the United Kingdom, Germany, and Japan). Moreover, the collapse of communism has led to the absorption of what used to be a rival military-ideological bloc into the structures of global capitalism — even China, the sole remaining nominally communist power, has become a major participant in this economic system.

Related to economic globalization, a broader uniformity of political values has emerged, especially among the more developed nations. The clearest expression is the increased acceptance of democracy as the proper basis for government — especially by powers that previously had embraced rival political systems: fascism, communism, and varieties of left- and right-wing authoritarianism. Liberal democracy has not taken root everywhere, but even regimes that have not yet fully embraced it generally feel compelled to invoke it as a legitimizing basis for their rule. The implications for traditional conceptions of international relations are still being examined, but one important consequence is that, as far as is known, democracies do not fight each other[10] — allowing much of the international system to transcend security dilemmas and the need for the deterrent and balancing mechanisms of power politics.

In tandem with democracy's spread, an international consensus has emerged on a core of inviolate human rights and on the need to restrict the concept of sovereignty — perhaps the dominant norm in international relations since the Treaty of Westphalia — so as to remove a shield behind which egregious violations of human rights can hide. The concern to prevent such violations seems to be a consequence both of the spread of democratic values and of the widespread eruption of ethnic strife after the Cold War, strife that has produced particularly brutal assaults on human rights with broad international implications.

A further implication of expanding interdependence and normative accord within the international community[11] has been a developing consensus on the permissible means of foreign policy. The broad condemnation of terrorism, a condemnation that in the post–Cold War era cuts across a variety of differences in political culture, reflects an expanding determination that innocent civilians should not be the victims of radical crusades, of the realization that too many regimes may be the targets of unchecked terrorism, and of the appreciation, associated with democracy, of structured procedures for resolving differences. In a parallel normative development, there appears to be more support now than several decades ago for arresting the proliferation of weapons of mass destruction. The consensus on biological and chemical weapons has become just as firm.

If critical differences of values and interests exist in today's world, they no longer separate its most influential members to the degree they once did; rather, they divide the bulk of the international community from a small subset of actors (regimes and movements) of a different scale and with very different interests and values.

Growing normative consensus does not imply a regimented uniformity of values and priorities even among the world's dominant nations. But it does mean that disagreements rarely involve fundamental normative assumptions. Thus, although many democracies withheld support of the 2003 U.S. invasion of Iraq, virtually all condemned Saddam Hussein's regime and opposed its then-suspected quest for weapons of mass destruction. Many nations differed with the United States on the extent of the international terrorist threat, but hardly a nation could be found that did not condemn the September 11 terrorist attacks or support the war against al Qaeda and its Taliban associates.

The evolving accord within significant portions of the global community has several consequences that cannot easily be interpreted via conventional theoretical frameworks. To begin with, this apparent convergence throws into clearer relief the values that separate a preponderant portion of the world's nations from those occasional regimes and movements that defy them: the differences simply seem sharper relative to the sum of other differences that fragment the international system. This allows challengers to offer particularly stark alternatives to the dominant normative order. Coupled with this, the progressive convergence of their values allows the bulk of the world's nations, especially its leading members, to focus their attention more powerfully on such challenges than when they had each other to worry about. Along with the unipolar distribution of international power, this elevates the confrontation to a dominant position on the world's political agenda.

Finally, the assumption of common dimensions along which interests and values can be scaled applies increasingly well within most of the international system, but not to the developing international fault-lines between the system's majority and those seemingly weak actors who challenge its core interests and values. The goals of the regimes behind these threats tend to be of a nature so qualitatively different from those sought by other members of the system that, often, there is no common continuum along which resolutions could be sought. The existence of such a continuum implies that the interests involved in the confrontation are mutually meaningful. For example, for two states engaged in a territorial dispute, the interest of either side in the disputed land is comprehensible to the other (in the sense that it could imagine itself in its adversary's position). The same would apply to struggles over geopolitically valuable allies, or, say, shares of foreign export markets. With most ideological divisions of the past, the meaning of what the one side wanted was generally understood by the other side even if it was considered pernicious, mainly because the rival ideological programs were points on a common continuum. But one could argue that ethno-nationalist goals associated with genocide are not one end of a discernible normative continuum where the values of leading democracies anchor the other end; that they represent, rather, qualitatively different dimensions of value and interest. Samuel Huntington has implied that one of the reasons why clashes between entire civilizations could be hard to resolve is the absence of a common dimension of value and meaning, making it hard to compromise differences.[12] But this difficulty extends to struggles between those, on one side, who are joined by a common core of values, interests, and rules of behavior and those, on the other side, for whom the latter carry little desirable significance; as when clashes are linked, directly or indirectly, to issues of identity. Under such circumstances, compromise becomes, not necessarily impossible, but much more difficult, whereas classical models of bargaining and negotiations, of mutual misperception, or of economic interdependence have less relevant bearing. Other approaches must be devised, and their intellectual foundations developed.

Alternative Perspectives

The flip side of the conventional literature has been a body of scholarship examining the requisites of international cooperation, denying that security dilemmas are integral to international existence or that peace must be sought in an effective equilibrium among powers. Although these critiques of traditional power politics are valuable as such, they do not necessarily improve our grasp of developing international challenges. Their purpose is to question certain inferences about the world drawn from conventional postulates, but they are of limited value when it comes to accounting for a substantially different world. Moreover, while the critics reject important tenets of the dominant paradigm, they have not dispensed with some of its other assumptions: namely, that international politics is predominantly about relations between nations that are each other's peers and among whom basic normative assumptions are not incompatible.

For example, one of the most compelling views on the emergence of cooperation among nations acting as egotists, in the context of the (presumably dominant) Prisoners' Dilemma predicament, is that cooperation flourishes best where the interacting parties adopt a strict tit-for-tat strategy, directly reciprocating each other's cooperative and noncooperatives gestures, with an expectation of extended future interaction (i.e., a "shadow of the future").[13] While assuming that meaningful cooperation is possible, the model's relevance to relations among internationally deviant regimes and the rest of the world is doubtful. To begin with, the ability to reciprocate acts of cooperation and confrontation in a meaningful pattern of tit-for-tat assumes that the parties have an approximately comparable ability to punish and reward each other — an assumption rarely consistent with vast disparities of power. Further, characterizing relations as a Prisoners' Dilemma implies that both sides accept a similar rank-ordering of the game's possible outcomes, but this need not be the case where they are guided by vastly different value systems — specifically, when they have quite different conceptions of the worst possible outcome. Finally, the logic of Axelrod's theory implies that the parties at least approximately share expectations of future interaction. If, however, one side believed (for religious, ideological, or other reasons) that its adversary's days were numbered, while the adversary believed nothing of the kind, a symmetrical shadow of the future would not exist. The theory may apply to other aspects of international cooperation, but not to relations between the international community and those currently considered its leading reprobates.

Other critics of the conventional paradigm, most influentially Robert Keohane and Joseph Nye,[14] stress possibilities of transcending power politics via economic interdependence. Prosperity, not only security, shapes national incentives, and, as countries come to depend on each other for their economic performance, they are less likely to accept conflictual relations. The key, then, is to enhance the economic sensitivity of nations to each other.

At times, this will be accompanied by the development of international regimes (loosely defined by common rules and institutions) designed to further encourage cooperation. While the theory clearly is pertinent to certain areas of developing cooperation — most notably among the world's wealthy trading nations — one doubts its full applicability to relations with deviant members of the global system. Few renegades have economies sufficiently developed and differentiated to make them successful trading partners of the richer countries, and few seem to rank economic welfare as highly as do the more compliant members of the international community. Under the circumstances, hope that their conduct might be constrained by economic incentives seems vain.

Thus, neither the dominant model of power politics nor its challengers within theories of international cooperation appear particularly useful when it comes to accounting for delinquent behavior or for suggesting effective ways of dealing with it.

Because of the discontinuity between past and present, academic models traditionally used to capture the essence of international relations fail to encompass evolving reality. The paradigms that are needed are not those of power politics, nor those that criticize power politics while retaining some of its cornerstone assumptions.

Not only do conventional theoretical perspectives fail us in the context of evolving reality, lessons of history are hard to draw from previous instances of deviance. While individual actors have sometimes challenged key values and interests accepted by dominant groups of nations, and thus defied the norms they defended, credible parallels with current circumstances cannot be drawn.

Deviance in History

Some notable instances of deviance in international relations have been linked to major social and political revolutions, revolutions rejecting basic assumptions of domestic political organization as well as of the international order upon which these arrangements rested. The French Revolution, which ousted the monarchy and rejected the balance of power system — on which European stability reposed since the Treaty of Utrecht (1713) — and even challenged dominant religious beliefs, was considered dangerously deviant by the European powers, who sought to check the threat. The king of Prussia and emperor of Austria proclaimed in the Declaration of Pillnitz (1791) an obligation for European monarchs to restore order and the monarchy in France. When the French Assembly voted for war with Austria while the Jacobin manifesto offered French aid to revolutionaries throughout Europe, France became not only the home of political apostasy but also its major exporter. Eventually, a coalition led by England, Spain, and Portugal joined Austria and Prussia in the war against France, a war that continued during the Napoleonic years, with a two-year hiatus, until 1815. Following Napoleon's defeat, the Congress of Vienna set as its mission to restore the principle of "legitimacy" (i.e., dynastic rule) as the basis for domestic rule and the balance of power as the pillar of international order.

The triumph of the Bolshevik Revolution was greeted with shock and horror by the United States and most other democracies. Whereas the czarist regime had merely been considered distasteful, the Bolshevik regime was perceived as a direct threat to Western values and interests: as a force striving to subvert that for which the capitalist democracies stood, and claiming, with haughty confidence, to have history on its side.[15] In addition, by signing a separate peace with Germany, the Bolsheviks had violated a covenant to fight the Germans that others considered binding. Accordingly, Japanese intervention against the regime in Siberia met with considerable approbation in the Western world, and when President Wilson dispatched two battalions of U.S. troops into the Russian fray, the only criticism in the popular press was that he should have sent more.[16]

Few regimes were as broadly condemned as Nazi Germany's, but this opposition took some time to crystallize. Despite Hitler's disdain for the Versailles principles, despite his occupation of the demilitarized Rhineland, despite the Austrian Anschluss and claims on the Sudetenland, most Western democracies, apparently deeming acceptable a desire to unite German-speaking peoples and eager to avert a major European war, did little to brand the Hitler regime as an outlaw to be dealt with decisively. Only after the invasion of Czechoslovakia made it apparent that Hitler's ambitions extended to grabbing much of Eastern Europe and subjugating non-Germanic people were the democracies galvanized to action, and only after the invasion of Poland were Britain and France led to war (while other democracies were even slower to respond). However, once opposition galvanized, it developed into a broad and vigorous international struggle against both the internal practices and external aggression of Nazi Germany.

The Cold War, dividing the international community on ideological lines coextensive with the power blocs anchored by the United States and the Soviet Union, precluded a meaningful concept of deviance on a broad international scale but sharpened its meaning *within* the rival political-military communities. Yugoslavia, because of departures from Soviet-style politics in 1948, as well as an unwillingness to recognize Moscow's control over other communist countries, was declared a reprobate by the Kremlin[17] and subjected to pressures ranging from economic sanctions to threats of armed intervention. Actual military action was taken to keep Hungary in the Soviet fold in 1956 and to crush the Prague Spring of 1968. Similarly, within the U.S. sphere of Cold War influence, the slightest movement in the direction of socialism, especially for a developing nation, the slightest hint of sympathy for the Soviet Union, often sufficed to justify intervention by covert or military means — as evidenced in Guatemala, Lebanon, the Dominican Republic, Chile, Grenada, Nicaragua, and elsewhere.

Although individual states or groups of states have, in the past, threatened core norms embraced by significant segments of the international system, parallels do not sustain generalizations to the present. During most of history, and largely as a result of the manner in which the international system was structured, consensus on core norms was restricted to a small portion of the international community and to particular periods in the development of nations and interstate relations. With the partial exception of the latter years of the anti-Hitler coalition, an authentically international concept of deviance could not be assumed. As a rule, the defied norms were those of restricted subsets of global society; they did not even include nations within the upper tiers of the international hierarchy. Since we have come to approximate a more widely embraced system of interests and values than ever before, and a correspondingly more uniform set of principles expressing them, the norms defied have never had as broad a set of defenders. One implication is that, having few major sources of foreign support on which to draw, the methods by which challenges are mounted have acquired a novel character, as have the ways they are dealt with. Another important difference is that actors once regarded as deviant generally could be considered the international peers of those they defied. France was no less a power than the monarchies it challenged. Bolshevik Russia had, in many relevant ways, a weight comparable to that of the countries whose political order it sought to undermine. Hitler's Germany was easily the peer of the countries it fought. Only in the case of those who, within or potentially within a Cold War bloc, were deemed miscreants by either superpower was a substantial disparity of power evident.

Some parallels may be appropriate, but differences between the past and present mean that a search for currently applicable insights via a scrutiny of earlier history is of limited value when it comes to understanding the current world.

Renegades and Rogues: A Terminological Note

When speaking of deviance, I refer to conduct that flouts key, internationally accepted norms of behavior. But how to characterize those guilty of such behavior? One convention refers to them as "rogue states," but, though this designation includes a core of relevant meaning, its analytic utility has suffered from overuse and misuse. The moniker "rogue states" gained currency, within the United States and elsewhere, to describe nations against which national indignation and military planning should be directed. The countries so designated have included Iraq, Iran, Syria, Libya, North Korea, and, occasionally, Cuba and Yugoslavia. According to former Secretary of State Albright, "dealing with the rogue states is one of the greatest challenges of our time."[18] In search of greater policy flexibility, the Clinton administration later replaced the term "rogue states" with the blander "states of concern," but the term was revived by President Bush, especially with respect to states constituting, in the administration's view, an "Axis of Evil."

Nevertheless, the concept of rogue states does not adequately cover our needs. While we are interested in the violation of core norms of international conduct, states that have been designated as rogues were mainly guilty of threatening U.S. interests, and the two classes of behavior do not fully overlap. For example, although Syria is known to have supported terrorism and sought chemical weapons, it has generally been left off the U.S. list of rogue states — the hope that President Hafiz al-Assad could be led to support the Middle East peace process explaining the disinclination to vilify him. In Robert Litwak's view, Cuba's presence on the list stemmed primarily from the demands of domestic U.S. politics, not from anything specific about its international behavior,[19] and one can question whether, in the relevant past, Cuba has been guilty of internationally deviant actions. It is especially interesting that Afghanistan's Taliban regime, against which the United States waged a full-scale war because it harbored Osama bin Laden and the al Qaeda terrorist training camps, did not make the rogue list: not even the list of states supporting terrorism. One explanation is that U.S. leaders hoped the Taliban could be induced to turn over bin Laden by holding out the threat of such listing if it did not.[20]

Beyond the specific use to which the term is put by the United States, it has been employed widely, sometimes capriciously, as an expression of dis-approbation for any disliked countries. Thus, Greece has been designated a rogue state by one editorialist because of its allegedly anti-NATO and anti-U.S. attitude.[21] The pan-African New Partnership for Africa's Development castigated as rogue states those within its membership who flout their obligations to that institution.[22] And so forth.

The term used here will be that of "renegade regimes," eschewing the U.S.-specific term "rogue," and replacing the notion of "state" with that of "regime." This invites a brief discussion of the term regime, especially as it is distinguished from the related concepts of state and government. A state should be viewed as "the community organized for political purposes";[23] it is, in other words, political authority applied to a specific community irrespective of its rules and substance, The community may, but need not, also be a nation. The state is the ultimate legitimate source of coercive power within the community. The regime defines the norms that follow from its definition of state interests and determines, in broad outline, who should be in charge of pursuing them, and how this should be done. Government is the regime's agent — it concretizes and applies regime rule — and it is embodied in a set of individuals embedded in institutional settings. Another way of distinguishing between these forms of political organization is to conceive of states as being largely defined by *whom* they govern, governments by *who* is governing, and regimes by *how* and *why* a government governs. More specifically, regimes are defined by three attributes: (1) characteristic methods of rule, (2) characteristic policy goals, and (3) characteristic principles of legitimacy. If the regime is considered a renegade it is because its methods of rule and/or its goals violated norms embraced by the bulk of the international community.

Regimes are located between state and government.[24] They may change while the state persists; for example, the Iranian state encompassed both the regime of the shah and that of the ayatollahs. Governments may succeed each other under the same regime (the governments of François Mitterand and Jacques Chirac represent, by most standards, the same regime). The implication is that governments formed under the same regime are of a largely similar nature.[25] In many developing polities, regimes and governments are tightly intertwined, with change of the latter implying change of the former, a fact that does not affect the conceptual distinction. A regime can be thought of as a structure, but it can also be considered an agent — the acting structure of rules. When the term is used in the latter sense, it goes beyond the notion of government, since a regime can include a succession of different governments. It is clear, too, that a social movement cannot, in and of itself, be equated with a regime.

The reason not to focus on states is that, not being the source of particular policy choices, the state is not the agent of renegade conduct. The reason to focus on regimes rather than governments is that, as long as a regime persists, a change of government may not alter the renegade behavior.

Purpose and Outline of This Book

The altered character of international politics requires efforts to encompass the changes intellectually. It is as if, to seek an analogy within another social science, a world where firms once competed lustily for market shares was replaced by one in which the competition had been resolved (perhaps, because one firm emerged as the unchallenged market "hegemon," while willingly parceling out some portion of its market share to would-be competitors) and in which the erstwhile rivals had, instead of competing, pooled their resources to tackle an illicit threat to their joint interests. It is as if, to use a specific example, members of the recording industry had ceased worrying about competition among them, deciding rather to direct their energies at jointly dealing with those who would pirate their products. The response of academic economists might then be to shift their efforts from devising dynamic models of market equilibrium to contriving theories of oligopolistic responses to deviant challenges. The difference, of course, is that the world economists observe is unlikely to change in the manner indicated above, while the world of international relations pretty much has.

A better scholarly understanding of renegade regimes has little existing foundation on which to draw: it is a matter of starting with a blank slate and trying to trace a logically credible and empirically founded sketch of the major mechanisms behind the genesis and course of such regimes. Chapter 2 lays the theoretical foundation on which the subsequent edifice will stand. It begins by discussing the notion of deviant conduct as internationally consequential norm-breaking conduct, and of defining the conditions under which international norms can be spoken of meaningfully. It then develops the assumptions from which the empirical investigation will proceed, the leading postulate being that the behavior of renegade regimes is positively related to an externally apprehensible purpose, that purpose being to maintain and strengthen their hold on power, that is, to consolidate their domestic position. In turn, the regime's domestic position is largely dependent on its ability to provide crucial groups of supporters certain ideational and economic gratifications, an ability that can be affected by internationally delinquent behavior. In this regard, two further core propositions are developed. The first is that the link between objectionable conduct and domestic gains can be direct or indirect: in the former case, the benefits to the regime stem expressly from defiance of the international community and from the responses this provokes; in the latter case, the benefits of misbehavior are causally unrelated to their external impact, and the fact that they flout basic international principles is a largely unintended side effect of policies devised with another purpose in mind. A final, related, assumption is that the precise logic of renegade behavior depends on whether the international system has, or has not yet, labeled the behavior as deviant and responded accordingly; different forces shape the behavior in the two instances, so deviance should be examined as a two-stage process.

Chapter 3 provides the specific operational criteria allowing us to designate certain regimes as renegades. We begin by asking what forms of behavior violate key currently accepted norms, finding that four matter most. The first is the pursuit of weapons of mass destruction — a quest that, while always broadly criticized, has become particularly incompatible with international norms since the end of the Cold War. The second is the support of, or active engagement in, acts of terrorism. The third is a vast assault on human rights with externally harmful consequences. The fourth is outright territorial aggression. In addition, since certain of the above behaviors (especially the acquisition of weapons of mass destruction) have been deemed relatively nonthreatening when involving politically transparent, democratic regimes, an additional definitional criterion for a renegade regime is that it should be unambiguously nondemocratic. Given the latter, necessary, condition any subset of the four forms of behavior constitutes sufficient conditions for renegade status.

On the basis of the theoretical framework and empirical criteria offered in the previous two chapters, chapter 4 examines the genesis of renegades, asking how a regime's domestic standing might be affected, beneficially or not, by renegade conduct. The assumption at this stage is that other nations have not yet responded to the misbehavior, and that indirect links between regime behavior and domestic position explain more than do direct links. Accordingly, the chapter focuses on ways in which a regime's attempts to gratify its supporters' ideational and economic desires may, incidentally, produce internationally unacceptable policies. We then contrast the conditions behind the origin of deviance to circumstances proper to a comparison set of regimes fulfilling certain necessary conditions for, yet not guilty of, renegade behavior.

Chapter 5 follows the trajectory of renegade regimes to the point where they are stigmatized as such by the international community and treated accordingly. In contrast to the previous phase, the most important effects, here, are direct, whereas economic (rather than ideational) considerations dominate regime calculus. In this chapter, we ask how delinquent behavior is affected by nonmilitary responses; as the most frequent punishment involves economic sanctions, we focus on their effects. Two models are considered as a further development of the notion of direct links between regimes' domestic position and delinquent behavior. The first, the "incentives offsetting" (IO) model, assumes that sanctions are an additional consideration for the regime, one that is independent of other incentives and that counteracts existing stakes in deviance, encouraging, in principle, improved behavior. The second, the "incentives restructuring" (IR) model, assumes that sanctions do more than counter the regime's renegade incentives: they actually reconfigure existing interests and values; by so doing, they may produce counterproductive results.

Chapter 6 examines the impact of military responses and their two possible purposes: to oust the regime or to modify its behavior by altering its incentives. The former generally implies full-scale resort to force; the latter is associated with threats of force or with its measured application. We discuss the conditions under which regimes may actually be removed through foreign intervention, and we inquire how the controlled use of actual or threatened violence may affect their incentives (and capability). As in the previous chapter, we consider these effects through the prism of both the IO and IR models.

Chapter 7 draws the implications suggested by the previous chapters, summarizing the elements of an empirically grounded theory of the origin and development of renegade regimes and of the manner in which this is shaped by their interaction with the global community or, at least, its principal norm-setters. The chapter dwells on further theoretical and policy implications suggested by the preceding analysis.

The temporal framework for this study is the post–Cold War era, dated here from the fall of the Berlin Wall in 1989. The examination of major assaults on core norms accepted by the global community requires, as suggested earlier, sufficient normative convergence at the international level. Moreover, since current responses to culpable regimes are very much affected by the quasi-hegemonic position of the United States, it is useful to focus our study on the period during which this position was attained. The restriction, then, is that the regimes qualifying as deviant within the context of this study should have so qualified after the end of the Cold War, without implying that the behavior must have originated then. In other words, it is possible that a nation considered a renegade during the post–Cold War era, because, say, of its chemical or biological weapons programs, would have initiated this program earlier. Thus, in order to study the responses of the international community to renegade behavior in a meaningful fashion, we focus on regimes that were renegades after the Cold War. At the same time, examining the origins of that behavior may take us to a prior period.

One final prefatory observation: the goal here is a study in which desirable norms of scholarship and relevance meet. The purpose of the social sciences should be to illuminate the range of the possible and the implications of various courses of action, particularly with respect to issues that are both intellectually intriguing and practically consequential. Moreover, as I have argued elsewhere,[26] relevant scholarship is apt to be superior qua scholarship than is work whose purpose rises no higher than providing a foil for academic debate and a vehicle for the promotion of academic careers. Consequently, this study aims to illuminate rigorously a matter of both intellectual and political import, and to do so with a view to informing practical policy.

2   The Logic of Renegade Regimes

A Theoretical Framework

This chapter offers a theoretical framework within which to structure our investigation of renegade regimes. The purpose is not to generate a full-fledged theory, in the sense of a structured set of propositions linked by relations of deductive implication — which would require much more of an existing foundation than is available. Rather, the goal is to develop a conceptual framework and set of expectations illuminating the research by suggesting questions to ask and answers to expect. Since there is little to draw upon within the discipline of international relations itself, I follow a more elliptical path: relying on inferences drawn from a few foundational assumptions, and, where useful, on cues from other disciplines such as the sociological study of deviance.

The chapter has four parts. The first places the issue of renegades in the context of an international system of norms. The second outlines four assumptions on which the theoretical framework rests. The third and fourth sections discuss, respectively, the set of incentives by which renegades are driven and how they condition behavior at two distinct stages of renegade development. The starting point is provided by the existence of core international norms and by the renegades' posture with regard to these norms.

Norms and Renegades

Because renegade regimes are deviant members of the international community, norm-breaking is their key defining feature, and a focus on norms is the foundation upon which understanding of such regimes must build.

Norms and the International System

Norms are shared assessments about appropriate conduct: they furnish standards that constrain and channel behavior in conformity with expectations and aims transcending individual preferences.[1] While no set of international norms has ever enjoyed universal acceptance, they have played an important role in world politics — accounting for the aims of many states, the limits on their policy options, and the sense of common purpose they often experience. Norms of sovereignty, of diplomatic immunity, of the freedom of the seas, have all placed predictable limits on national foreign policies, improving the scope of international cooperation.

Despite the role of norms within any social system (subnational, national, or international), realist and neorealist perspectives on international relations have caused them to be "viewed as by-products of, if not epiphenomenal adjuncts to, the relations of force and the relations of production."[2] But not all have considered this appropriate. Edward H. Carr, a leading political realist, had recognized the costs of ignoring the role of social purpose and ethical principle in world politics,[3] and a number of scholars have sought to elevate ideational considerations and other normative considerations to a role comparable to that of the positional concerns dominating realist models.[4] Better clarity on the manner in which norms function as part of the mechanisms of world politics has produced two benefits: an improved understanding of the manner in which norms evolve and a better grasp of how they constrain behavior.

A clear and credible picture of the pattern of norm evolution is beginning to emerge. Recognizing that, contrary to realist claims, notions of goals worth pursuing respond to developing international values and expectations, an evolutionary approach to norms has gained currency. Based on analogy with population genetics, it suggests when one or another set of competing norms will prevail at any given time.[5] Similarly, the spread of norms has been viewed as a three-stage process.[6] A first stage, one of *emergence*, sees a number of actors (individuals, groups, states) acting as "norm entrepreneurs," striving to convince others of the value of certain normative principles. Once a critical mass of other nations is so convinced, a "tipping point" is reached and a second stage, one of *norm cascade*, appears as pressure for conformity leads to the norm's accelerated acceptance. Eventually, a third stage — *internalization* — may be attained, at which point acceptance of the norm is so broad that it no longer is the object of meaningful debate.

At the international level, new norms are most broadly introduced when the structure of international power undergoes profound change — for example after major wars or other systemic transformations — and it is at such times that norm entrepreneurs are most effective and cascades most dramatic. This is because the norms espoused by the winners, and partly at the source of the contention, no longer encounter the opposition they once faced. It is also because norms that did not rank highly enough with the winners at the time of the conflict rise, once the conflict has been won, to a more exalted position within their normative hierarchies. Thus, the post–Cold War world has witnessed, and continues to witness, a higher value placed on human rights, a declining importance accorded to sovereignty, a somewhat higher value on international environmental protection, and so forth.

In addition to a better grasp of the life cycle of norms, we are also gaining a better appreciation of how they condition the conduct of states. Partly, they do so via their link to the identity of states and nations. Identity is an integral part of statehood and nationhood, which, as social constructivists have argued, guides state behavior.[7] It is reflected in the social category to which a group belongs, whereas part of what defines social categories is that its members follow similar rules.[8] Moreover, a state's ability to derive its full share of benefits from interacting with other nations depends on its reputation within that community, and the trust and credibility it enjoys. A good reputation, in turn, hinges on the observance of shared norms — some of an evaluative nature, others of a strictly regulative character[9] — providing what Robert Axelrod calls "social proof" that they "belong."[10] Finally, observance of widely accepted international norms may contribute to a regime's domestic acceptance because citizens judge their own regime's legitimacy, in part, by how other nations treat it, which in turn depends on the regime's adherence to common rules and expectations.[11]

Given the apparent benefits of adhering to major international norms, we must ask why some regimes embark on their large-scale rejection. These have been called rogues, outlaws, and backlash states; their threat to policymakers is matched by the challenge they pose to scholars.

Deviants, Renegades, and Norm Defiance

Although threatening and disruptive, some level of norm-breaking (deviance) may also be beneficial. More than a century ago, Durkheim argued that such behavior helps society recognize and sharpen its common values, infusing them with increased vigor[12] — a view later adopted by a number of functionalist sociologists. A similar claim could be made with regard to international society, where it is even harder for common values to crystallize. One might, for example, argue that the growth of international terrorism in the late twentieth century, culminating in the attacks of September 2001, galvanized a sense of common purpose among a disparate community of nations threatened by terrorism.

To perform its beneficial functions, however, deviance must be opposed, and this requires some consensus on the norms whose disregard amounts to deviance and on the regimes guilty of such conduct. For the greatest part of history, anything approaching normative agreement could be found only within some regional subsystems of global society, not at the global level. But this may be changing: while its outlines are not yet very firm, a broad consensus regarding some core norms of political behavior appears more apparent now than at any time before.

Not all members of any society (subnational, national, or international) embrace its major normative assumptions, which do not tally equally with the interests and values of all. Rather, patterns of normative consensus are related to the structure of the society, in the sense that, absent major ideological rifts at the apex, dominant social norms are more likely to originate within the upper tiers of the social hierarchy than at its base. Within the parameters of the normative consensus, deviant behavior is not identified by wholly objective criteria since, even if abstract norms are widely agreed upon, considerable scope remains for subjective assignment of the label "deviant" to *specific* sorts of conduct.

Hierarchical Nature of Normative Consensus   A social system's normative consensus usually reflects a hierarchical pattern of belief propagation, where norms espoused by the most influential members come to be accepted by those of lesser power and consequence. No doubt, this is because normative assumptions are closely entwined with interests,[13] whereas the powerful are best positioned to encourage a definition of common interests that reflects their own. This is also because normative assumptions are embedded in cultures, and the cultures of leaders often are those to which others aspire. Thus, at the international level, those whose influence places them at the apex of a regional (or global) hierarchy tend to be the principal source of the assumptions behind whatever normative accord can be found: they are its *norm-setters*.

It is also natural that, within the traditional subsystems of global society, normative consensus has typically been more solid within the upper tiers of the regional hierarchy than at its lower layers, and to the extent that something approaching a universal normative order can now be conceived, agreement appears strongest among the system's top dogs. This does not mean that some level of commitment to common norms cannot be found throughout the system, but it tends to be firmer at the top than at the bottom.

Correspondingly, the likelihood of being considered deviant, both within societies and at the international level, is related to position in the applicable social hierarchy. For example, the probability that a regime developing weapons of mass destruction would be stigmatized depends on whether the nation is a major power (for example, no permanent member of the Security Council is considered a renegade). Nations best positioned to mold the substance of international norms also tend to determine when a violation has occurred. Accordingly, within global society, some countries function as norm-setters, membership in this select group requiring high international power-ranking.

A *Socially Constructed or Objective* Concept   Some controversy remains over whether international deviance involves the objective conduct of regimes, independently of any vagaries of subjective content attributed to that behavior by others, or whether its meaning flows predominantly from the significance that others, the system's norm-setters in particular, attribute to the behavior, and from the manner in which, given the assigned meaning, they respond. At first blush, it may seem that the former must be the case: that, as there is a growing international accord on core norms of political behavior, so is there a broad consensus on a checklist of characteristics behind an operational definition of deviance. In other words, one could assume that any dominant consensus on key norms also encompasses empirical criteria that, when met, automatically qualify a state as deviant, naturally invoking certain external responses. But a different view has it that the meaning of deviance is not so much intrinsic as extrinsic to behavior: the label is attached by those with whom the reprobate interacts in a way that reflects the meaning they *choose* to attach to the behavior. This meaning, in turn, depends on properties of the responders and of the type of interaction they have established with the agent. "The label [deviant] becomes attached to behavior during the course of social interaction. . . . Behavior has to be interpreted and meanings assigned before labels are applied."[14]

The likelihood of being considered deviant may be culturally or historically determined — external aggression was not always frowned upon, nor was, say, the practice of ethnic cleansing. But the point is not so much that norms change, or that the meaning of a given norm (e.g., social equality) varies in time or space, but that norms on which there is a conceptual consensus may leave room for subjectivity when it comes to determining whether it is violated by the specific behavior of a particular agent. Subjectivity may intrude because the conceptual meaning of norms is fuzzy at the margins (for example, does the right of states to self-defense, guaranteed by the Charter of the United Nations, imply a right to preemptive attack if aggression is expected, and, if so, how unambiguous must the evidence be?). But usually it is because vagaries of interest, perception, or position encourage different responses to similar behavior, or identical responses to dissimilar behavior. This may depend on what sociological study of deviance terms "contingencies": circumstances that have no direct connection to the objective features of deviance, and that theoretically should not influence the labeling process, but actually do.

As an example of a contingency, it has been observed that the availability of mental care facilities might determine whether a rural doctor does or does not diagnose a patient as being mentally ill.[15] Similarly, the likelihood that a state would be labeled a "rogue" by the United States during the 1990s was at least partly linked to domestic political considerations and U.S. foreign policy strategies: it was not always a direct and objective reflection of that state's behavior. Both examples suggest that the same objective behavior may or may not be defined as deviant. A growing international normative consensus does not preclude the operation of such contingencies — it simply means that there will be less scope for *competing types* of contingencies.

Before considering specific responses, we must ask why, despite considerable incentives to conform, certain regimes flout prevailing norms on a grand scale.

The Four Assumptions

Though there may be no plausible, nontrivial, axioms and theorems on which a fully deductive analysis of renegade regimes could build, certain assumptions can usefully guide what I intend as a predominantly inductive analysis.[16] They will organize the inquiry by providing concepts, questions, and, especially, empirical expectations. These assumptions are not presented as "useful fictions," which whether true or not may have predictive value. Rather, they *are* deemed true statements, and thus a basis for eventual explanation, not mere prediction. Let us begin, however, with an observation: namely, that deviant regimes are not crazy regimes.

The emergence and trajectory of deviant regimes (renegades) depends on their motivations and on the context of opportunities within which these are acted upon. If their behavior is at all predictable, this is because they are purposeful actors whose policies are related to understandable objectives and based on discernible, if sometimes loosely performed and ill-articulated, calculations. Their goals may set them apart, their tolerance for risk may exceed that of other nations, but within these limits, they are not irrational or "crazy" states.[17] This does not mean that they engage in the extensive calculus of options, probabilities, and utilities implied by formal rational choice theory; rather, the expectation is that their conduct is guided by more plausible mechanisms of "limited information rationality." Since Herbert Simon's pioneering work on the subject,[18] we appreciate that, via cognitive shortcuts and "mini theories," elementary premises are formed via which behavior is related to goals.[19] These premises may rest on such simple cognitive cues as benchmarks and analogies, and policy decisions may be based on how a policy is reckoned to affect a single goal or value, although several may be at stake. In any event, the basic structure of the goals and their relation to chosen courses of policy are accessible to analysts. Beyond this observation, four assumptions guide our investigation.

Assumption 1: Regimes care most about the security of their domestic position

Not only are renegade regimes purposeful in the pursuit of their interests, but these interests are not very different, at a general level at least, from those encountered elsewhere. Every regime's primary purpose is to maintain and solidify its position. This requires tending to the interests of those who most directly control access to power; it also means discrediting those who would challenge the regime's right to rule, and it means establishing a plausible, hopefully compelling, case for this right with the country's population. Accordingly, to understand renegades we must appreciate the priority that such regimes attach to their domestic position and the implications they draw for their political behavior. In this regard, renegades are no different from most other regimes.

That regimes take their own domestic position as a point of departure does not imply that they are cynically indifferent to broader objectives and values, since these cannot be effectively pursued if their political position is precarious. Their grip on power, in turn, hinges on symbolic and practical achievements that matter to politically potent segments of society; it also depends on undermining the position of political rivals. In a democracy, regime interests would, of course, reflect the need to conciliate the support of the electorate, a need that does not apply to most renegades, since (with the partial exception of the Tehran and Milošević regimes) they tend not to be electorally based regimes (and, when they are, do not qualify as full democracies). Yet, even where power does not rest on an electoral mandate, it requires the support, or at least the passive forbearance, of politically consequential groups or combinations of groups.

The key, then, to understanding renegade regimes is to fathom how their behavior is connected to expected consequences for their domestic security, asking how this may be affected by decisions to embrace or defy core international norms. The latter resolves into the question of how behavior with regard to these norms may produce *stakes in compliance* or *stakes in deviance* — in the first case, because of an expectation that compliance with norms will bolster the regime's domestic position; in the second case, because flouting these norms will do so more effectively. The relative weight of these two kinds of stakes illuminates the decisional calculus of renegade regimes.

Assumption 2: The link between regime position and renegade behavior may be direct or indirect

Renegade behavior could affect a regime's political standing in two ways. To begin with, its position might benefit from policies that appeal to significant domestic constituencies but are, incidentally, offensive to much of the international community. A domestic audience's partiality to the policies accounts for their adoption — the clash with other nations is a secondary effect, one that may not be expected or explicitly desired. In this sense, the link between the regime's intentions and its renegade status is *indirect*. In a second model, the regime anticipates direct political benefits from the very fact of its collision with the outside world, expecting that this clash may alter the structure of domestic interests and the context of domestic political discourse in a manner beneficial to it. For example, externally beleaguered governments often encounter rally-round-the-flag sentiments; these sentiments may encompass those who, under different circumstances, would oppose the government or regime. A we-they feeling vis-à-vis other nations solidifies, as does a sense that the regime, for all its imperfections, is at least one's own, as are the values it claims to represent. A conflict with outside forces allows those who will not rally to be portrayed as lackeys to foreign interests and values: traitors to the nation. In short, the fact of renegade behavior may allow the regime to restructure domestic political interest and discourse in a manner helping its own standing. Because the regime benefits expressly from the fact of the external hostility, the link is *direct*.

Assumption 3: There are two, analytically separable, stages of renegade behavior

To study renegade regimes is to study a sequential unfolding in which the initial causes of deviant behavior may only partially overlap with those driving it at a later stage. As Howard Becker pointed out, "it would be a mistake to assume that all factors behind deviance operate simultaneously; it is far more fruitful to consider that it develops in some orderly sequence."[20] The most important aspects of deviance may come to light after the initial norm-breaking behavior has been embarked upon, when others have decided to respond to the transgressions.

The notion that the initial sources of deviance, on the one hand, and its subsequent course, on the other hand, may be determined by somewhat different causes is rooted in the sociological literature on deviance. More than half a century ago, while arguing that the initial causes of individual deviance (e.g., criminality) often diverged from those shaping its later trajectory, Edwin Lemert distinguished *primary* from *secondary* deviance.[21] The former refers to the initial enactment of the deviant act, the latter to the consequences for subsequent deviant behavior of societal responses to the primary deviance. Secondary deviance thus reflects "how deviant acts are symbolically attached to persons and the effective consequences of such attachment for subsequent deviation on the part of that person." [22] According to Lemert, primary deviance is caused by a broad range of factors (it is "polygenic"). With secondary deviance, the original causes recede in importance, as behavior is shaped by the external responses to the primary deviance.

The distinction between the two stages of deviance is as relevant to the international as to the domestic level, and, in this study, the course of renegade regimes will be viewed as a two-stage process, each with a distinctive causal structure: (1) an initial stage, characterized by a realization that, in light of its concerns about its own position, the regime's stake in defying key international norms outweighs its stake in compliance. Regimes originating thus will be termed *primary renegades*. (2) A subsequent stage, in which behavior is molded by the regime's interaction with international system, its norm-setters in particular; the regimes thus shaped will be referred to as *secondary renegades.*

International circumstances may play a role at both stages. For example, Ayatollah Khomeini's Islamic Revolution, from which the Iranian regime joined the renegade ranks, was largely a reaction against Western influence under Shah Reza Pahlavi. But once the Islamic fundamentalists came to power, challenging key features of the international order, Iran's behavior was profoundly affected by the response of other nations, the United States especially. Though the international system may matter at both stages, external circumstances do not produce their impact on primary renegades *because* they are considered renegades: no decision to treat them as such has yet been taken. With secondary renegades, it is precisely this decision that determines other nations' responses, influencing the regime's relative stakes in compliance and deviance and, by implication, the future course of its behavior.

Whether direct or indirect links dominate depends on which of the two stages is considered. Generally, a primary renegade's main purpose is to gain domestic political advantage from the objectionable policies themselves; international outrage is an incidental by-product. Once other nations respond, however, their hostility may provide direct political benefits to the regime. A primary renegade might provoke a clash with the international community in order to structure domestic political discourse in a self-serving fashion, but indirect links dominate at this stage; at the secondary stage, they are displaced by direct links.

Assumption 4: Punishment may offset or reconfigure renegade incentives

This assumption bears particularly on secondary renegades and on the direct link between domestic political circumstances and deviant behavior. At the secondary stage, the international community (or, at least, its norm-setters) responds, in most cases punitively, to the renegade's transgressions: it does so to affect the regime's incentives or ability to misbehave. If the former are targeted, the expectation is that these incentives will be offset by

the retaliation. The regime, in its primary phase, embarks on deviant behavior to boost its domestic position. But if, it is reasoned, external punishment causes significant domestic privations, the boost in support may be offset
by anger at this hardship. As stakes in compliance come to outweigh stakes
in deviance, the regime's political calculations lead it to modify its behavior.

This model informs most international punishment, but frequently a
wide gap separates expected from actual consequences. This is because the
assumption of fixed incentives, for which countervailing disincentives must
be created, can be very wrong. Often, the original drives are drastically reconfigured by the punishment, implying that the incentives to be offset are
no longer what they used to be. If so, the increased costs and hardships may
fail to change the behavior because, now, other things are propelling it. This
is something well known to students of intrasocietally deviant behavior.
Study of crime and delinquency often reveals that those that society punishes
acquire an altered self-perception and conception of self-interest, reconfig-
urations that may increase, not decrease, their commitment to crime. We
also observe that external punishment sometimes reinforces, in the short
term at least, a regime's commitment to the behavior that elicited the punishment — for example, because it benefits from a "rally round the flag" as
external pressure increases, or because economic interests linked to the external punishment are created.

The model of renegade responses based on the assumption that retaliation
will offset undesirable incentives will be termed the incentive-offsetting (IO)
model; the one recognizing the possibility of a counterproductive reconfiguring of incentives will be termed the incentive-restructuring (IR) model.

These, then, are the foundations on which this study builds. The observation that deviant regimes are comprehensibly purposeful is not only plausible, it also establishes a foundation from which important inferences can
be drawn, especially when coupled with the assumption that any regime's
primary concern is with its domestic political position. The key implication
is that stakes in deviance or compliance rest on the expected impact of
renegade behavior on regime security. The further assumption that renegades can benefit directly from international hostility, or produce it as a by-
product of policies directed only at a domestic constituency, means that this
impact should be viewed two-dimensionally. The assumption that there is a
difference between the causes of the behavior before and after others have
branded the regime a renegade and responded accordingly provides a framework through which time-dependent influences become part of the analysis.
Finally, the assumption that renegade incentives may be either offset or

reconfigured by the retaliation suggests that, under some circumstances, punishment may be counterproductive.

Assuming that decisions to embrace or defy core international norms depend on the expected implications for the regime's domestic position, we require a clear description of the pillars on which domestic position stands: only when this is provided can we ask how domestic position and deviant behavior are connected — directly or indirectly, within primary or secondary renegades. The following section describes the foundations of regime security; subsequent sections suggest how they may shape behavior at different stages of renegade development.

Domestic Political Foundations of Renegade Behavior

Regimes and governments are always concerned with "providing an answer to that most immediate of political questions: who are you that I should obey you?"[23] The answer is either because I am forced to, or because, given a free choice, I would chose to in acknowledgment of the benefits you provide. In the latter case, obedience flows, not from coercion, but from legitimacy based on performance.

The role of coercion for the security of transitional regimes is well documented and widely recognized, and no regimes seeking a new foundation of legitimacy are so confident in their ability to furnish the gratifications society desires that they foreswear military and police forces.[24] Nevertheless, the effectiveness of coercion, especially in the long run, should not be overestimated,[25] since it is costly and encourages the creation of countercoercive capabilities — sometimes in the form of violent resistance. Coercive or not, no regime can survive very long unless those it governs regard it as legitimate, whereas a "regime is legitimate to the extent that it can induce a measure of compliance from most people without resort to the use of physical force."[26] Neglecting, for the moment, the gossamer quality of leadership charisma, legitimacy must be based on the regime's ability to furnish those whose support it needs with what they value and expect as their due. This requires performance on two planes: ideational and material. Ideational values are the nontangible, often moral, aspirations of important segments of society — aspirations the regime is expected to promote. Material values involve the tangible, particularly economic, goals upon which support for any regime rests. Calculations with regard to both drive major domestic and foreign policy initiatives.

Ideational Values

Any regime's character and support is shaped by the link between its policies, on the one hand, and societal ideals, values, and worldviews, on the other. These define the society's objectives, provide guidelines for resolving tradeoffs between wholly or partially incompatible goals, help define friends and foes, furnish interpretations of historical causality, and constitute an emotionally laden basis for the society's identity. By virtue of these functions, ideational systems on which regimes base their legitimacy portend the policies they select. Three broad ideational categories dominate a society's purpose and identity, and when they display certain attributes, the probability of renegade behavior increases markedly.

Behavioral excesses often are associated with regimes seeking domestic acceptance based on the *ethno-nationalist* values they represent. National or ethnic identity draws a boundary between in-group and out-group — providing the former with dignity, possibly glory, usually at the expense of the latter. Contrary to many earlier expectations, increasing international communications and economic interdependence have not loosened nationalism's emotional hold. The grip of nationalist/ethnic values on many societies comes from their ability to provide a group with a common symbolic patrimony, situating it geographically and historically, making it a culturally (possibly racially) distinct entity, and contributing, from the individual's point of view, to a sense of belonging and location. Emotions rooted in nationalism can powerfully counterpoise "us" and "them," the virtues of the former being contrasted with the iniquities of the latter, who can be blamed for present hardships, often on very slim evidence. The concept of nationalism with the strongest implications for the emergence of renegade regimes, is linked to the "primordialist" view of a nation,[27] a view that considers the "nation" as a natural and organic creation, with ethnicity and its attendant emotional bonds at its base. This view is distinguished from the "civic," or "situationalist," conception of nationalism, where a common purpose rather than common ethnicity forms the dominant bond.[28]

In either case, the defense or promotion of radical ethnonationalist goals often animates internationally censured behavior, and there are two paths that can lead to that outcome: first, when a sense of injured national dignity invites bold acts intended to affirm the community's position and worth, acts can occur whose extremity and potentially violent nature breach norms of permissible behavior; second, when a sense of injustice suffered at the hands of another ethnic group leads the regime to actions against that group that are inconsistent with internationally accepted principles. The latter case usually assumes a multiethnic society; the former need not.

Religion may also provide the basis for a regime's claim to rule while encouraging internationally transgressive conduct. Religion combines intense emotional meaning with a sense of belongingness (the exalted community of "believers"). Sometimes (as in the Serbian case) it functions as a component of nationalism, providing an important basis for ethnic/nationalist identification. More often, it goes beyond nationalism, implying membership in a larger, transcendental, community — addressing, therefore, far broader identification needs. Unlike ethnonationalism, religion locates the individual *metaphysically*, within a system of meaning that rises above the referents of daily life and that "defines the contours of the broadest possible range of relationships — to self; to others near and distant, friendly and unfriendly; to the non-human world; to the universe and to God, or that which one considers ultimately real or true."[29] Acting on behalf of God elevates the regime, in its own eyes and those of its public, providing a justification for its unquestioned support by all but the benighted. When the tenets of the True Faith are threatened, the community that comes to their defense is ennobled, as is the regime undertaking that mission. If religion's enemies are sufficiently evil and perfidious, they may be dealt with with appropriate roughness, even if the international community deems this delinquent.

Political ideology offers a final category of ideational objectives — less powerful than ethnicity or religion, but more easily tailored to regime ends. Political ideals may place a person on the side of justice and virtue, but this is more effectively achieved via religious values (which, as in the Islamic case, may also carry profound implications for social and political life); and ideology does not provide for the same sense of identity as ethnicity/ nationalism, probably accounting for its weaker emotional grip. The success of Fascism and Nazism can largely be attributed to the extreme nationalism in which they were grounded, while communist doctrine, except in its very early phases in a few countries, never managed to trump religious and nationalist attachments. Its limitations notwithstanding, political ideology can produce a coherent vision of justice and virtue, and this is not irrelevant to popular and group loyalties.

As importantly for our purposes, ideology is more easily tailored to regime objectives than the other two categories. Regimes can latch onto religion in a quest for legitimacy, but it is difficult to *mold* religious symbols and tenets to regime needs, since these typically are rooted in the revelations of sacred texts, and since responsibility for interpretation usually is vested in professional clergy. Political authorities can manipulate ethnic and nationalist symbols, seeking to intensify their public salience, but they cannot easily create or extinguish symbols rooted in the group's historical experiences. With ideology — i.e., with symbols and principles related to sociopolitical organization — there is greater latitude for creative tailoring, as they are grounded neither in divine scriptures nor in history. The empirical generalizations from which they flow generally are soft, and their axiomatic foundations, if any, rather arbitrary. In this sense, ideology is more plastic than religion and ethnic identity, giving the regime greater autonomy in shaping its message and meaning to suit objectives of policy and legitimacy (thus, for example, Qaddafi's Green Book, or Kim Il-Sung's *Juche* ideology). Ideology provides cues to identifying the good and the bad in social life, as well as those guilty of iniquity and other grievances experienced by the community. Regimes responding to the demands of ideology have occasionally committed excesses that the international community at the time, and history in retrospect, have denounced.

Where ideational fervor spurs renegade conduct, it typically rests on the conviction that a grievous wrong has been committed against nationalist, religious, or ideological values. Intense outrage surrounds the injured values, its defenders are virtuous, its enemies evil, and emotions are not structured by dry and dubious facts. The depth of the wrong and the perfidy of the enemies justify redemptive measures whose extremity may violate constraints on permissible behavior promoted by the international system and its norm-setters.

Feelings of indignity and injustice produce febrile emotions, whereas emotion, like cognition, shapes attitudes and conduct: it helps actors interpret information and mobilize resources, and it sheds light on dimly understood aspects of collective behavior and political decision-making.[30] In any event, emotionally fraught ideational claims frequently lie at the basis of a regime's assertion of its right to rule.

Economic Objectives

While legitimacy may benefit from the fanned embers of nationalist, religious, or political fervor, from indignation at real or imagined wrongs and gratitude to those ready to right them, few regimes enjoy long-term stability that consistently fail to meet a society's material aspirations. Even short-term regime security may depend on gratifying the economic interests of those whose support most matters. In any case, the sort of regime a nation has is, to some extent, economically determined. The literature on political development almost unanimously sees a correlation, on the one hand, between regime type and level of national wealth, and, on the other hand, between economic performance and political stability. Since Seymour Martin Lipset's trail-blazing work on the matter,[31] it has been understood that democracy cannot prosper in poverty, that its prospects improve with development. The generality of this claim has since been qualified, often with the argument that the economics-democracy link is mediated by social and historical circumstance.[32] A current view is that, if economic growth is to encourage democracy, it must transform the society's class structure, expanding the middle and working strata, promoting their self-organization, and weakening the landed upper class, democracy's principal opponent.[33]

The important point is not just that certain regime types rest on particular economic foundations, but that the stability of *any* regime is imperiled by economic hardship. Przeworski and Limongi found that the probability of transition to democracy increases with GNP per capita up to $6,000; beyond that, dictatorships enjoy increased stability. They also concluded that all regimes are imperiled by economic downturns — poor democracies being the most vulnerable.[34] Similarly, Londregan and Pool report that the probability of a military coup is affected by levels of economic well being, and that authoritarian regimes, like democratic regimes, face the prospect of removal by force if economic performance disappoints.[35] The link between political instability and state of the economy has been confirmed in other studies,[36] and there is little doubt that governments and regimes are alert to the political implications of their economic performance, usually tailoring their policies accordingly.

Economic performance, in turn, fares better with full integration into the international economy, as the success of many export-led economies has demonstrated. The dependency literature of the 1970s, warning developing countries against extensive involvement with the international capitalist economies,[37] finds very few adherents today. Although an updated form of dependency theory may provide a part of the explanation for a number of development choices and their social implications,[38] few regimes eschew foreign trade and investment. Similarly, the more recently observed perils of globalization have not deterred most nations from chasing its rewards. Critics of economic globalization[39] argue that its collateral ills range from corruption, to disruption of labor markets, to environmental damage. It is also understood that the most vulnerable parts of society are often hurt in a newly opened economy adhering to market principles. Nevertheless, and although some selectivity may characterize participation in global economic flows, far more countries complain of barriers to participation than of its consequences.

Because regimes and governments are held accountable for their nation's economic performance, which, in turn, generally benefits from integration into the global economy, economic concerns should provide a stake in compliance, discouraging internationally deviant behavior. Why, in the case of renegades, does it not?

Primary and Secondary Renegades: Patterns and Mechanisms

To appreciate stakes in deviance and compliance, we must distinguish between primary and secondary renegades.

Primary Renegades: The Genesis of Renegade Regimes

At the primary stage, a regime emerges whose objectionable policies may include egregious and externally consequential abuses of its own population, efforts to acquire weapons of mass destruction, outright territorial aggression, terrorism, and so on. This conduct is not conditioned by the reactions of other nations, for the latter have not yet labeled the regime a renegade and dealt with it as such. We expect, then, that part of what distinguishes primary from secondary renegades is that, for the former, most of the political benefits flow from the behavior's link to ideational and material pursuits, not from a confrontation with other countries. For primary renegades, then, the link between misconduct and political needs is more often indirect than direct. With secondary renegades, either link may be present, but their relative weight is reversed: now, a large part of the political advantages to the regime is expected to flow directly from its collision with significant segments of the international community.

How, specifically, may the regime's quest for performance-based domestic support account for the genesis of renegades?

Ideational Performance   Ethno-nationalism often spurs renegade behavior: it excites popular passions, and it has proven relatively easy for power-seekers to charge that the nation or ethnic group has been slighted or threatened by others, that only extreme measures can set things right. A potential renegade may have ridden to power on a claim that the previous regime had jeopardized nationalist/ethnic values, that it is now imperative to redeem these values, elevating then to the heights they merit. By promising to reassert in-group prerogatives at the expense of out-groups, regimes may adopt policies that, via the extremity of their methods or consequences, qualify them as renegades. Massive ethnic cleansing, terrorist support for irredentist groups abroad, pursuit of nuclear weapons as a symbol of national achievement, and violent territorial expansion to reclaim national territory all may breach key international norms.

Similar reasoning applies to religious values and identity; in fact, here, the call to action may resonate more powerfully, and the scope of the behavior justified by service to God may be even broader than with ethnonationalist values. If others at home or abroad can be portrayed as infidels and the regime as Defender of the Faith, its claim to rule is especially strong, few challenging its right to take extreme measures to protect the True Religion.

It is hard to believe that any contemporary variant of political ideology could provide a foundation for renegade behavior, but there was a time when this was so. The vision of a new and better sociopolitical world fueled the fervor surrounding the French Revolution and its challenges to the order defended by Europe's established monarchies. There was a time when Marxist ideals roused the passions of many of the world's dispossessed. Under current circumstances, millennial ideologies have been badly tarnished, and few serious ideological challenges to key democratic tenets appear capable of generating mass enthusiasm. Now, ideology is likely to play its role, if any, as a component of broader religious doctrines (as in the case of radical Islam), and, perhaps (though more remotely) as part of an ethno-nationalist doctrine. Even so, ideology provides scope for regime creativity in arguing its own legitimacy and, if associated with certain policies, could be a source of renegade conduct.

In very many, probably most, instances of ideationally-prompted misconduct, the benefits to the primary renegade stem from the way the behavior appears to advance the values pursued. The political gains from the repugnant behavior do not necessarily assume external opposition. Thus, domestic political advantages expected by Milošević from his policies of ethnic repression did not, at the outset, require any response from the international community. Similarly, the Pakistani nuclear and missile programs were arguably driven by domestic demands to acquire the means with which to confront India; denunciations from abroad were not a supplemental source of political benefit.

Sometimes, however, additional political advantage may be gleaned by emphasizing the conflict with foreigners, grafting a direct connection onto the indirect links. If the rift with other nations becomes a central political fact, domestic opponents of ethno-nationalist policies can be branded as quislings, those who oppose religious extremism may be deemed traitors in the service of alien faiths, and so forth. The terms of the domestic political discourse can be biased against the regime's political rivals; coercive measures are more easily justified if the latter can be charged with treasonous loyalties. Thus, North Korea's claim to stand for socio-political ideals far superior to those of the rest of the world gained some credence from the international hostility the country has encountered. The direct link between regime benefits and external conflict is less endemic to primary than secondary renegades because, in the former case, other nations have not yet responded to the egregious conduct; in the latter case they have, providing grounds for structuring domestic politics accordingly. As an illustration, Milošević's ability to deal coercively with his opponents after 1992, profited from their apparent association with foreign powers punishing Serbia. Khomeini's regime benefited in its early years from the fact that both the United States (the Great Satan) and the godless Soviets were hostile to it.

In this way, strong ideational commitments can play a dual role in the genesis of primary renegades (1) by justifying the extreme policies that brand the regime a renegade (the indirect link), and, (2) by structuring the domestic political climate such that the regime's position benefits from an assumption of external enmity (the direct link). This twofold impact accounts for the causal potency, at this stage, of the ideas and values the regime claims to champion.

Plainly, not every quest for ideationally based support spawns renegade behavior. Rather, the ideational program must display certain attributes, and the behavior may take root only where the gap between values sought and those rejected is great enough. In other words, conditions of sufficiency and of necessity may differ simply in the matter of *degree*. But there is more to it, and regimes whose ideational agendas fuel renegade policies satisfy additional conditions. For example, extreme repression may be rationalized by domestic threats to the values involved; in which case, significant domestic divisions implying credible challengers to these values must exist within the country. The greater the domestic divisions, the greater the likelihood of renegade conduct. Second, if renegade behavior springs from a need for foreign scapegoats or foes around which to galvanize "rally-round the-flag" sentiments, there must be a credible basis for external enmity. The more it appears that other nations oppose the new values, the greater the disparity between the values championed by the regime and those preferred by the norm-setters, the more likely it is that the regime seeking a new basis for ideational legitimacy would defy the principles on which the international order rests. Most importantly (given our assumptions), the ideational drives may be curbed by worries about the economic consequences of renegade conduct.

Economic Needs   As renegade behavior is most predictably punished by economic isolation,[40] the natural expectation is that economic interests create stakes in compliance — offsetting the stake in deviance that other calculations may produce. The task is to explain why, in the case of primary renegades, the threat of international economic punishment does not deter objectionable behavior.

One tack would be to argue that economic sanctions are not always or uniformly applied or enforced, that this depends on a variety of circumstances partly independent of the regime's conduct, and that those who fail to be deterred by the prospect of sanctions think it unlikely that they would be applied in their case. From this perspective, and assuming other incentives to renegade behavior, the regime's estimate of the *probability* of external punishment determines whether it would be deterred, the analytic challenge being to discover how this probability is reckoned. But, as we will see, no renegade has escaped some form of economic punishment.

Another tack assumes that the likelihood of economic retaliation generally is deemed high, and that a regime's readiness to act on its incentives depends more on how it estimates the *consequences* of the international response. If so, deterrence hinges on how effectively the regime feels it can mitigate the impact of sanctions upon its domestic position. Two strategies suggest themselves. In the first, the regime seeks to control the political risks of externally induced hardship by downplaying the importance of economic advancement, relative to the other, presumably ideational, goals. Although few within the nation may be brought to believe that economic betterment does not matter, they may accept that it is less important than, say, the religious or nationalist objectives that risk punitive responses; that, in fact, the regime should be rewarded for maintaining its priorities. Obviously, this strategy requires powerful ideational drives, indicating how important ideas and values are at this stage. The second strategy is to favor the economic position of key societal groups, so that, conscious of their protected position, they would support the regime despite the overall hardship caused by potential sanctions. By strategically structuring patterns of relative privilege, the regime might hope to weather economic difficulties while retaining the political benefits associated with its nationalist, religious, or ideological programs.

Neither approach is likely to be effective in the long term. Ideational fervor wanes in the face of prolonged economic privations, and over the long haul it is hard to convince people that living standards do not matter. Although the preferential treatment of certain groups may ensure their support while economic sanctions are but a prospect, a *relatively* favored status may not console those whose fortunes suffer an *absolute* decline. Nonetheless, a regime not discouraged by the possibility of economic retaliation probably considers it unlikely, or it feels that either of the two strategies might cushion the domestic political impact.[41] Thus, the null hypothesis is that economic considerations provide a stake in compliance, decreasing the likelihood that a regime would become a primary renegade, but that this stake stands to be weakened by policies designed to protect the regime from the political consequences of external economic retaliation.

Secondary Renegades

Contingencies and Aims of International Response   Not all deviant behavior evokes strong responses from norm-setters, and a number of conditions determine what, if any, response there will be. At the international level, the major circumstance is the responder's *national interest*: an amorphous concept capturing the notion that national foreign policies are guided more by self-serving calculations than by lofty principle.[42] Historically and geopolitically specific circumstances determine how an instance of deviance will be reckoned to affect the national interest. Depending on how it is expected to do so, different nations may react differently to the unpalatable conduct of other regimes, and a given nation may not respond identically to similar behavior by different deviants, or even to the same behavior at different points in time. In most cases, this is a path-dependent process: decisions initially taken by a nation constrain, often very significantly, its subsequent interests and options. A former U.S. foreign policy official, examining U.S. policy toward "rogue" states, lamented that early decisions constrain future policy options in a way that makes it difficult to deal effectively with them.[43]

Lessons nations draw from their historical experiences often determine the responses they consider most appropriate — thus European nations' history has induced a less Manichean concept of the world, and a preference for more flexible and nuanced responses to those transgressing international norms than has been true of the United States. In any case, domestic politics may weigh as heavily as international considerations in determining the appropriate response. (Few, for instance, would deny that internal political pressures have guided U.S. policy toward Cuba.)

When norm-setters and their associates decide to respond, the balance of direct to indirect links between regime behavior and its domestic situation shifts toward the former. External responses seek to affect the renegade's *incentives* or its *ability* to act in a delinquent manner. In the first case, the aim is to alter the balance between the regime's stakes in compliance and in deviance, by weakening or reversing the link between domestic political benefits and renegade behavior. In the second case, the goal is to make it difficult or impossible for the regime to act on its incentives: either by destroying its capacity to do so or by removing it from power. The distinction between the two aims overlaps the distinction between nonmilitary and military responses, but only imperfectly, since military action can alter a pattern of incentives and also undermine a capacity,[44] while nonmilitary pressure may be designed to cause a government's ouster (as sometimes is the purpose of economic sanctions). Nevertheless, the classification of external responses into nonmilitary and military types provides a convenient way of organizing our thinking on the manner in which international efforts to deal with such regimes may determine their nature and course.

Nonmilitary Responses Economic sanctions are the major nonmilitary response; their purpose, generally, is to alter the regime's estimate of what its domestic position requires by *rewarding* improved behavior or *punishing* continued bad behavior, making the regime either better off or worse off, relative to some baseline, depending on its conduct, and thus inducing desired policy outcomes. The baseline is important because I am not equating rewards with an easing of sanctions, or punishments with the withdrawal of earlier inducements. Both are viewed in *net* terms, in that rewards seek to improve the regime's position relative to what it was at the primary stage, while the opposite applies to punishments — though either may be pursued at any time following the initiation of policy responses to the deviant behavior.

Punishments — ranging from economic coercion to diplomatic isolation — have been the preferred response to renegades, particularly during the early phases of their development. The reasons are evident: rewards to renegades encourage warped incentives — as deviant regimes appear to profit from misbehavior, possibly encouraging others to follow their example. Also, this comes very close to *appeasement*, a term with unattractive historical connotations, and a difficult position from which to seek domestic support for the policy. Finally, there is always the chance that steps to affect the regime's calculations by harming its domestic position may, if very successful, lead to its removal. No such outcome can be anticipated from net inducements. For these reasons, while sanctions may be eased or tightened at any time, net rewards for improved behavior are rarely offered; when they are, this tends to happen late in the game — as when the prospect of improved trade was offered to Iran in the early years of the George W. Bush administration (more than two decades after Ayatollah Khomeini's Islamic Revolution). In the earlier stages, the emphasis is on punishments.

Punishments are intended to produce costs that weigh against the nationalist, religious, or ideological campaign, decreasing its appeal relative to the hardships it entails and leading people to reassess their support for the regime, thus discouraging the objectionable policies. But the punishment's impact on the renegade's political calculus may not be as expected, since the pattern of causation often is more complex than initially conceived: specifically, the punishment can bring political benefits to the misbehaving regime, wholly or partially offsetting its intended effect.

For example, although ideational zeal may provide both a basis for regime legitimacy and a source of renegade behavior, history indicates that ethnic, ideological, and even religious ardor cannot be maintained at a high pitch for very long. Religious fervor in Iran was much more muted in 1999 than during the Islamic Revolution of 1979; Serbian nationalism was less keen, even in absolute terms, in 2002 than in 1992, and so forth. Therefore, some secondary renegades may, with time, be inclined to abandon their objectionable policies simply because the drives behind them have weakened. But the situation is complicated if an added layer of direct political benefits comes to be associated with those policies, and such benefits may be created by the punitive response itself.

Foreign economic pressure may reconfigure domestic political discourse by *increasing* societal commitment to ideational goals that seem to be assaulted by hostile foreigners and by casting the regime as their protectors. If so, evidence of external hostility — particularly by norm-setters who stand for very alien values — may, contrary to expectations, offset a natural tendency for ideational ardor to wane. Moreover, political opponents who can be identified with hostile external forces are less likely to garner domestic support, while coercive measures against them are more easily justified. Under the circumstances, punishment designed to weaken the regime may actually fortify its position, at least in the short to medium term.

Interests benefiting from the confrontation with the international community and its norm-setters may also develop, providing further support for the regime whose misbehavior makes these gains possible. The purpose of economic sanctions is to cause as much pain as possible to those upon whom the regime's support depends, so that they would pressure the government to change its policies, or, failing that, they would oust it.[45] Nevertheless, sanctions rarely are effective,[46] and this may be because of the domestic interests they spawn: many segments of the nation suffer from sanctions, but some are net beneficiaries and their support bolsters the regime.

Economic closure via sanctions opens possibilities for gain to those who can profit from attendant dislocations and shortages. Sanctions may benefit those within the target economy threatened by foreign competition and who can function more profitably behind the sanctions barriers.[47] Also, black and gray markets associated with smuggling are spawned by economic isolation. The goods and services thus provided sometimes can be offered for less than it would cost to manufacture domestic substitutes — leading to rent-seeking activity,[48] often involving organized crime, possibly operating in cahoots with the regime's security apparatus to their mutual material gain.

The ability of sanctions to create interests, including rent-seeking interests,[49] has been recorded in a variety of nations. As an illustration, in Haiti, where the 1991 sanctions were meant to induce the military rulers to reinstate the democratically elected president and reestablish democracy, the expectation was that economic pain, especially of the wealthy business classes, would create the necessary domestic pressure. But black marketers, operating in association with the military itself, managed to benefit from the situation. The outcome is described by Elizabeth Gibbons, UNICEF representative to Haiti at the time:

The Haitian army, by seizing control of the black market in embargoed goods, especially fuel, was also to realize huge windfall profits, creating a strong, perverse incentive to continue sanctions. Sudden wealth also increased the military's independence from patrons in the business elite, thereby making it less susceptible to pressure emanating from that quarter. In addition, control of the black market may have helped to produce resources the army needed to create and maintain the

paramilitary group, FRAPH, which, from September 1993, was skill-
fully deployed throughout Haiti to carry out its massive campaign of
terror, rape, and murder against the population.[50]

Counterproductive economic interests can develop in other ways. When
the Rhodesian Front (RF) government issued its Unilateral Declaration of
Independence and the United Nations retaliated with comprehensive sanctions, not everybody in that country objected. Although some sectors of the
economy suffered, import-competitive domestic manufacturers benefited
from isolation. What was recorded as the "remarkable expansion of secondary industry behind the protectionist barriers of sanctions" meant that "Sit-
ting behind high tariff and sanctions barriers, many companies often preferred to produce complacently for the captive Rhodesian market rather than
aggressively seek to export to South Africa and other overseas markets."[51]
Accordingly, "The vulnerability of the manufacturing sector to a return to
free trade or a lifting of sanctions had a profound influence on its political
behavior [and it] began forging closer ties to a government that had previously been its principal opponent. By the early 1970s, the RF was receiving
considerable business support."[52]
    While some within a country may profit from its economic isolation, most
do not. Consumers tend to suffer, as do those who rely on imports, and those
who can compete on foreign markets. With the decline in economic activity,
markets atrophy and investment opportunities shrink, as do public resources.
If losers invariably outnumber profiteers, they may not have established tight
links with those who control the instruments of domestic force, while the
net consequences for the regime depend on the relative ability of winners
and losers to affect its domestic standing. Because of this, the consequences
of economic punishment for the regime's position, and consequently its
commitment to the policies that evoked the sanctions, hinge on how heavily
winners and losers weigh on its own security.
    Ultimately, then, expectations regarding the likely success of sanctions
against renegades depend on the analytic model applied. One can think of
sanctions as an independent disincentive to delinquent behavior, providing
a counterweight to existing stakes on deviance, or one can view sanctions,
not as a force offsetting existing incentives, but as one actually *modifying*
these incentives, in some of the manners suggested above. The former is
consistent with the incentives-offsetting (IO) model, the latter with the incentives-restructuring (IR) model.
    What is evident is that (a) the behavior of secondary renegades is signifi-

cantly affected by their interaction with the international community, and (b) because international pressures create a more mixed set of incentives than their authors generally anticipate, success may be elusive within a politically acceptable time frame. The challenge is to grasp the circumstances that make success more or less likely, while recognizing that, occasionally, frustrations with nonmilitary forms of coercion will increase the attractiveness of armed intervention.

Military Action   The link between incentives and behavior is perfectly direct here, and armed coercion can have several purposes. It can seek to shape the renegade's *incentives*, by adding the avoidance of direct physical pain and destruction to its stakes in compliance. To be thus effective, the actual or anticipated pain must outweigh the regime's stake in deviance. Often, the purpose is to signal that even more destructive force may be in the offing should the regime persist — pain is applied incrementally, to convey the possibility of further destruction if behavior does not improve. U.S. bombings of North Vietnam in the late 1960s and early 1970s were as much intended to decrease Hanoi's motivation to wage war as to undermine its capacity to do so.[53] Similarly, U.S. naval exercises within the Gulf of Sidra in 1981 challenging Libya's claim to the entire Gulf and resulting in the downing of two Libyan fighter planes may be viewed as a shot across Libya's bow, to encourage abandonment of its geopolitical pretensions (and its terrorist activities). As with economic sanctions, however, any attempt to influence incentives must contend with the possibility that an IR outcome may trump an IO purpose.

When armed force is directed by the system's norm-setters against a renegade, power disparities imply its eventual success, but military action can also backfire in a number of ways. Concessions by the renegade regime usually entail some political price domestically, a price that may increase as a result of foreign coercion — since it stands to compound a political sacrifice (e.g., abandoning a campaign of ethnic cleansing) with the humiliation of acceding to foreign pressure. Under the circumstances, the regime's disincentive to comply is increased, especially if its defiance of powerful foreigners can further enhance its domestic standing. Yet another reason why military force sometimes is counterproductive, especially at the point where it seems to be weakening the regime's position, is that it may restrict the latter's political maneuvering space, allowing it little room for concessions — concessions that politically stronger leaders could afford to make.[54] Thus, as with nonmilitary pressure, two models could guide analysis. With the first, actual or threatened military destruction is an independent consideration in the regime's calculations — offsetting, but not altering, the incentives to continue in the objectionable behavior. With the second, armed force actually modifies regime incentives, possibly in a manner counterproductive to its purpose, making the balance of incentives to deviance and compliance harder to predict. Paralleling the discussion of nonmilitary pressure, these may, again, be referred to as the incentives-offsetting and the incentives-restructuring models of the effectiveness of foreign punishment.

At times, however, the aim is not to modify the renegade's incentives but to impair its capacity to act on them, without necessarily expecting that it would be toppled. Thus, if the renegade is pursuing weapons of mass destruction, then the installations for producing them, or the associated research and development facilities, can be eliminated — as was done in the Iraqi case during the 1991 Gulf War. Similarly, in June 1981 Israeli warplanes bombed and destroyed Iraq's Osirak nuclear research reactor, fearing that it would be used to produce weapons-grade nuclear fuel. In August 1998 the United States launched cruise missile attacks against the al Shifa pharmaceutical plant in Sudan, claiming it was producing chemical weapons (and that it was linked to Osama bin Laden).[55] Each of these examples illustrates a use of military force aimed at impairing an adversary's military capacity: if the capacity to harm is wiped out, incentives may no longer matter.

Beyond destruction of capacity, the purpose or consequence of military action may be to oust the renegade regime. This can be done directly, by physically eliminating or forcibly removing the regime's leaders, as Soviet troops did in Hungary in 1956 and Czechoslovakia in 1968, and as U.S. armed forces did in Lebanon in 1958, the Dominican Republic in 1965, Grenada in 1983, Panama in 1989, Afghanistan in 2001, and Iraq in 2003. A similar result can also be achieved indirectly: if domestic forces decide they will no longer support the regime that has brought military destruction upon the country, or if the regime's coercive capacity is so impaired by the military action that its domestic opponents can remove it. U.S. air attacks on Taliban and al-Qaeda facilities made it possible for Afghanistan's Northern Alliance, with the subsequent help of the Southern Alliance, to overthrow a regime that had been sponsoring massive terrorist campaigns.

When contemplating a renegade's removal, our focus shifts away from the circumstances that shape its decisions (since no decisional calculus on the regime's part really surrounds its forced ouster), but the issue of a regime's domestic acceptance remains apposite. Now, we no longer ask how a renegade's concern with this acceptance affects its willingness to engage in internationally censured conduct. Rather, we consider how domestic perceptions of the military intervener, and of the regime it seeks to install, condition the transition from renegade to normatively desirable regime. We ask how the application of external force influences this perception, and how the new regime's association with a foreign military power shapes its legitimacy and, consequently, the outlook for a successful transition.

Even if the intervener persists to victory, a number of secondary consequences could discount the proximate achievement. If success was achieved at very great expense, and if key norm-setters are disinclined to endure such costs again, the threat of future force against other renegades may carry little conviction, sapping military power of its deterrent value. More subtly, and perhaps in the longer term, victory against a specific regime may weaken commitment to the international norms the intervention was designed to bolster, impairing the position of the norm-setters. A perception, by societies sharing some of the defeated renegade's values, of being besieged, their deeper alienation from the international normative order and strengthened commitment to alternative value systems, could further polarize the global system, amplifying the threat to established values and structures. The understanding of policymakers and scholars may not be up to the task of predicting whether intervention favors backlash or deterrence in every specific instance, but it may be possible to acquire a better understanding of the circumstances likely to tip the balance. Accordingly, we ask what circumstances encourage attainment of the goals that military intervention is designed to achieve, and when force may be counterproductive — with regard to either a specific renegade or, more generally, the international community's broader policy objectives.

3   Recognizing Renegades

Renegade regimes are those that defy core international norms, often with harmful consequences for other nations, but this definition does not suffice to recognize those to which it applies: further operational rules are needed to identify the specific cases to be examined. Moreover, explaining the genesis of renegades requires that they be compared to regimes that are not, so that we can evaluate our explanations by seeing how well they distinguish the two groups. Accordingly, this chapter will also propose criteria by which to select a comparison-set of nonrenegades.

Identifying Renegade Regimes

Hard and Soft Concepts

Like many terms of the social sciences, "renegade regime" represents a "soft" rather than "hard" concept. With the latter, the concept's indicators are directly contained in its definition. For example, the indicators by which economic inflation is assessed (rising price levels) directly reflect the concept's definition; no inferential leaps or additional theoretical decisions are needed. With soft concepts, links between relevant properties and their corresponding indicators are not direct, and, since agreement at one level does not guarantee agreement at the other, a supplementary level of inference is required. Thus, one might agree that democracy should be defined as a system of representative government that also respects basic freedoms and human rights but differ on what constitutes representative government or on a critical threshold of basic human rights. Decisions on the latter points are then required, involving an additional tier of theoretical reasoning, and choices of indicators reflecting the definitional properties will determine how cases are selected for analysis and shape the conclusions drawn from empirical investigation. This distinction reflects that between two sorts of measurement: *fundamental* and *derived*. The former presupposes no measurement beyond what is involved in establishing a count; the latter requires that further laws be applied to the fundamental measures, often requiring that quantitative connections be established between them.[1] Typically, hard concepts are better suited to fundamental measurement; soft concepts, to derived measurement.

Differences concerning appropriate indicators of a concept might reflect differences in values, or in the interpretation of semantic conventions, but they may also stem from discrepant assumptions about causality. For instance, and with regard to democracy, leftists and rightists might disagree on the impact of various institutions on freedom (how necessary is a multiplicity of political parties?). Similarly, conservatives and liberals are apt to offer different definitions of equal economic opportunity. In one view, the adequacy of a definition depends on the thoroughness with which the concept is examined, a thoroughness that may expand the more that is invested into the inquiry. This implies that definitions themselves may not be fixed, that they are subject to revision as inquiry deepens. For example, and in a direct challenge to epistemological trends of recent decades, a leading social scientist has argued that "Concepts are revised and refined as the boundary of the set of relevant cases is sifted and clarified. . . . [Cases] often coalesce in the course of the research through a systematic dialogue between ideas and evidence."[2]

Whether or not one is willing to accept that definitions may be subject to revision in the course of investigation, and that the set of cases is correspondingly fluid, we must recognize those concepts that can only be softly defined and acknowledge the fuzziness of the boundaries of the resulting set of the cases. While losing some of the illusion of hard science, one gains an appreciation of the differences that varying choices of indicators might have on the conduct of analysis and, possibly, on the conclusions reached. By most standards, the concept "renegade regimes" is of the soft variety.

Renegade Behavior and Renegade Regimes

We qualify regimes as renegades by identifying concrete forms of behavior that violate core norms of international conduct in which they have engaged. Two sorts of questions must be addressed. First, which forms of *behavior* are subsumed in our general definition of renegade regimes? Second, which specific *regimes* have engaged in such conduct? Both questions are important, since one might concur on the unacceptable behaviors while disagreeing on a list of culprits.

The first question may be dealt with by taking our general definition as a point of departure and developing a checklist of misbehaviors it implies. All we would be concerned with is the extent to which the definition of each form of misconduct tallies with the concept's own. However, the catalogue could not be compiled independently of the manner in which the international community, especially its norm-setters, reacts to these behaviors: it cannot be determined whether a type of conduct violates international norms unless others forcefully object to it. Evidence that certain behaviors are deviant is provided by the responses they evoke; no other manner of establishing renegade behavior is fully convincing.[3]

The second question concerns the regimes that should be labeled renegades, implying that some inconsistency might attend such decisions and the responses that follow. For instance, even if the acquisition of nuclear weapons were considered transgressive, not all guilty regimes would necessarily be labeled renegades and punished accordingly. The decision to do so or not may, as pointed out, be subject to what theorists of social deviance have termed "contingencies," that is, circumstances that should not affect labeling but in fact do. Once types of renegade behavior are identified, contingencies should reveal patterns of variation in responses, and while this may shed little light on what we have called "primary" renegades, it is central to understanding the influences that mold renegades at the "secondary" stage.

Attributes of Renegades

There is considerable agreement on behavior that can be described by epithets such as "rogue," "outlaw," "renegade," "backlash," which capture egregiously deviant characteristics. In one conception, "rogue" states "show contempt for international norms by repressing their own populations, promoting international terrorism, seeking weapons of mass destruction, and standing outside the international community."[4] According to a former presidential security adviser, "backlash" or "outlaw" states are "ruled by cliques that control power though coercion, they suppress human rights and promote radical ideologies . . . [and] exhibit a chronic inability to engage constructively with the outside world. . . . [They] share a siege mentality."[5]

More specifically, an academic analysis of the use of the terms "rogue" and "pariah" by U.S. cabinet members found that the areas that "clearly dominate" the attention of U.S. policymakers when referring to such states are "their alleged pursuit of weapons of mass destruction and the means to deliver them, their alleged support of terrorism, and the perceived threat such states pose to their neighbors and the world at large, including the United States."[6]

All of these attempts to identify renegade-like conduct refer, on the one hand, to specific unsavory activities — pursuit of weapons of mass destruction (WMD) and support for terrorism — and, on the other hand, to a general but unspecified class of policies that threaten or repulse other countries. To bring this second category into clearer focus, we must ask what, in addition to WMD and terrorism, has been considered unacceptable to other nations, evoking their condemnation and retribution. Post–Cold War history has provided us with two examples of such behavior. The first is massive internal repression, often of an ethnic group, that also threatens the interests of other countries. The second is overt aggression against another nation. These two categories of behavior, along with terrorism and acquisition of weapons of mass destruction, have characterized those regimes widely considered renegades, independently of the specific epithets by which norm-setters have described them. The reasons for the opprobrium associated with these four types of conduct are clear enough.

Weapons of Mass Destruction   Nuclear, chemical, and biological agents are the principal categories of such weapons.[7] The legitimacy of nuclear deterrence, at least from the perspective of major powers, was associated with Cold War imperatives. However, the declining reliance of both the United States and Russia on their nuclear arsenals, the limited applicability of deterrent logic to other rivalries, and a realization that regimes whose behavior deviates from international norms in other respects are especially eager to acquire such weapons explain the onus placed on nuclear proliferation and the attempts to stop it. During the Cold War, commitment to the Nuclear Non-Proliferation Treaty suffered from the double standard involved in denying developing nations access to these weapons while the superpowers pursued a headlong nuclear arms race. But the substantial reduction of U.S. and Russian nuclear arsenals since the Cold War has removed some of the appearance of hypocrisy surrounding the nonproliferation regime, bolstering the prohibition against nuclear weapons programs in other countries.

As sharp a stigma attaches to chemical and biological (CBW) weapons. Although it has been observed that the death and devastation they cause need not exceed that of conventional weapons, there are reasons for the special opposition to CBW.[8] The association of chemical weapons with "poison" and of biological weapons with "germs," concepts that evoke disgust in their everyday application, partly accounts for the opprobrium involved. Because these weapons could wreak indiscriminate destruction, the bulk of their victims are innocent civilians, making the weapons appear unfair as well as frightful. Finally, it has been pointed out that CBW are weapons of the weak, requiring less expertise and infrastructure to develop than nuclear, and even many types of conventional, weapons. This may also account for the taboo placed on them in a normative order developed mainly by the powerful.[9] An extensive regime of international law, revolving around the 1972 Biological and Toxin Weapons Convention and the 1993 Chemical Weapons Convention, has codified the international community's opposition to weapons of this sort.

Terrorism   While terrorism has a very long history, its scope has increased in recent decades, and the attacks of September 11, 2001, have been its most dramatic manifestation. However, terrorism has presented definitional challenges: one person's terrorist may be another's "freedom fighter," and the definitional ambiguity is compounded by terrorism's location midway between crime and war.[10] If a fairly widely accepted definition exists, it is provided by the U.S. government, according to which terrorism means "premeditated, politically motivated violence perpetrated against noncombatant targets by subnational groups or clandestine agents, usually intended to influence an audience."[11] The components of the definition are worth considering.

Although all military action involves premeditated and politically motivated violence, the remaining elements of this definition explain the special revulsion that terrorism evokes. Because it is directed against noncombatants, civilians are the victims of lethal harm (as with weapons of mass destruction), while they are neither responsible for the terrorists' grievances nor in a position to defend themselves, making their victimization intensely unjust by the terms of most ethical systems. Since the purpose is to break the opponent's will by random violence, it is almost impossible for victims to act in any way that would consistently ensure their safety. By contrast, even the repressive violence of the most unpalatable governments can generally be avoided by appropriate behaviors.[12] The purpose of terrorist violence being to impress a wide audience, it aims to be particularly dramatic, which, in many instances, implies massive and indiscriminate destruction of the sort condemned by the vast majority of cultures.[13] Further, because terrorists are subnational groups, their political claims are considered less legitimate than those of established political institutions. The classical Augustinian criteria for just war include, among the *Ad Bellum* principles, the rule that war must be pursued by the duly constituted authorities of the state, implying that terrorist war can never be a just war.[14] Where, as is usually the case, terrorists operate as "clandestine agents," a surreptitious, "sneaky" quality surrounds their acts, and special stigma often attaches to killers and destroyers who dare not reveal their names.

Aggression   While foreign conquest was once considered a legitimate prerogative of states, World War I, as well as the normative order established in the Covenant of the League of Nations and Woodrow Wilson's Fourteen Points, included explicit injunctions against aggression (though failing to provide the means of countering it). This prohibition was the foundation for condemnations of Italian action in Ethiopia, Hitler's attack on Poland, and the Soviet invasion of Finland. After World War II, the East–West rivalry often made it hard to disassociate the concept from self-serving Cold War calculations, as neither bloc was willing to apply it to the behavior of the bloc leaders or their followers. But communism's demise has removed the major ideological and strategic obstacles to international consensus on aggression.

Externally Consequential Repression   It is not enough that a regime's people should suffer from repression: if the regime is to be considered a renegade, there must also be harmful external consequences. There often are. Because boundaries are porous, because networks of international interdependence are dense, and because values and identities sometimes are shared, internal violence is apt to create painful ramifications abroad. In this way, massive domestic repression may produce effects directly harmful to other nations. Significant refugee flows resulting from massive domestic repression can perturb the economic and social structure of neighboring countries. Struggles within one nation involving an ethnic group whose members also have a substantial presence in other countries can galvanize ethnic minorities in these countries to secessionist rebellion. They may sometimes cause ethnic brethren to come to each other's succor across borders, thus transforming domestic into international conflicts. The Milošević regime produced an impact of this sort, as has the Bashir regime in Sudan. From Bosnia alone, 1.2 million people fled,[15] mostly to Germany, Austria, and Sweden. The war conducted against southerners in Sudan produced more than 4 million refugees — over half a million ended up in camps in Uganda, Kenya, Zaire, Ethiopia, and the Central African Republic.[16] More recently, mass violence by the Janjaweed militias, abetted by the Sudanese government, against African inhabitants of the Darfur region has caused (in addition to some 70,000 deaths) 1.5 million people to flee their homes, approximately 200,000 seeking safety in Chad (where Chadaian soldiers have clashed with Sudanese Arab militias). A country guilty of such repression qualifies as a renegade, and, as retreats from repression are often of a tactical nature, sufficient time must elapse since a renegade appears to have abandoned such practices[17] before it no longer qualifies on this score.

Although all four forms of renegade conduct may jeopardize the security of others, this is not their necessary defining feature. Externally consequential repression may produce only economic consequences for other countries. In any case, it is possible that behavior that one day will be deemed deviant (e.g., wanton and massive environmental destruction) would not have primarily security implications.

The Democratic Proviso   Most of the attributes defining renegades are behavioral: regimes are so considered because of what they *do*. But there is a sense in which they also are so defined by what they *are*: regimes considered renegades invariably are authoritarian or totalitarian. Not all nondemocracies are renegades, but all renegades are nondemocracies.

The rejection of democracy is, in a nontautological sense, both a defining feature of renegades and a necessary condition of their emergence. It is a defining attribute since renegades are labeled as such partly because of the perceptions they evoke, whereas democracies are less likely to stimulate apprehension even when they behave in a way that would cause trepidation in the case of nondemocracies. For example, we are far more concerned when nondemocracies acquire weapons of mass destruction than when democracies do. This is because the formers' domestic conduct indicates they partake of a different morality, making it harder to trust their intentions. Similarly, we are less worried that a government committed to domestic transparency would engage in military action involving such weapons. One of the defining attributes of a renegade regime, then, is that it is a non-democracy. It also is a necessary *condition* for deviant international behavior, since every regime exhibiting the behavioral attributes associated with deviant international behavior has, in fact, been a nondemocracy. We saw in chapter 2 that international deviance is both a social construction and an objective reality; if nondemocracy is a defining feature of renegades at the first level, it is a necessary condition at the second.

The question, given the above criteria, is which regimes, since the Cold War's end, have qualified as renegades? The time frame is important: while we view the Cold War as having ended in 1989, the year the Berlin Wall fell, this does not imply that the objectionable behavior could not have *originated* at an earlier time. But the practice must have been apparent since that date for a regime to be included in this study. This provides a common frame of temporal reference within which to ask which regimes have violated norms against terrorism, weapons of mass destruction, aggression,[18] or externally harmful domestic repression.

Culpable Regimes

Terrorism   An important source for determining who has supported terrorism is the U.S. Department of State's annual publication entitled *Patterns of Global Terrorism*. It contains two sets of pertinent information: (a) a section summarizing annual terrorist activity in various geopolitical areas, and, (b) a section giving an overview of *state*-sponsored terrorism. Both are necessary since the latter is intended to serve a political, as well as informational, purpose from the U.S. government's perspective. Publicly labeling certain states as supporters of terrorism is seen as a way of applying pressure on them and of mobilizing domestic and international support for punitive actions. As a check on the political agendas of that section, the first section provides explicit reports of instances of state-sponsored terrorism, even when they do not find their way into the section that deals with this expressly. On the basis of a parallel reference to both parts of the annual report, we may conclude that seven regimes have, in one way or another, supported international terrorism during the post–Cold War period.

According to the State Department, few regimes have been as guilty as

Iran. In addition to assassination campaigns against dissidents abroad — particularly against members of expatriate opposition groups, the Mojahedin-e Khalq and the Kurdish Democratic Party of Iran,[19] Tehran has provided arms, training, and funds to Lebanese Hezbollah, Hamas, and the Palestine Islamic Jihad. It has also provided safe haven to Turkish separatists of the Kurdistan Workers Party (PKK), likewise considered a terrorist group. With the election of President Khatami in 1997, the Tehran government sought to curb its support for terrorism, but opposition by the religious leadership, headed by Ayatollah Khamenei, has hampered such attempts.

Saddam Hussein's Iraq was considered a sponsor of international terrorism, though on a lesser scale than Iran. Baghdad's activities primarily targeted Iraqi dissidents living abroad but also encompassed terrorism of a wider scope. The most widely publicized action was the failed plot to assassinate President George H. Bush in 1993. Other activities included incursions by the Mojahedin-e Khalq into Iran from bases in Iraq. In addition, several foreign terrorist groups maintained offices in Iraq prior to the 2003 U.S.-led intervention — including Abu Abbas's Palestinian Liberation Front and the Abu Nidal organization.

Considered a pillar of international terrorism in the 1970s and early 1980s, Libya curtailed its involvement with such activities after the 1986 U.S. air raids, and especially since the 1990s. Nevertheless, the Libyan government was linked to the 1988 bombing of Pan Am flight 103 and continued to support terrorist groups opposed to the Middle East peace process. It may also have intimidated and assassinated dissidents abroad.[20] Policy only changed by the end of the decade. In 1999 Tripoli turned over the to the Netherlands tribunal two Libyans accused of masterminding the Pan Am bombing, while Qaddafi repeatedly asserted an antiterrorist stance. That same year, Libya expelled the Abu Nidal Organization and endorsed the Palestinian Authority as the only legitimate representative of the Palestinian cause. After the September 11 attacks on the United States, Qaddafi emerged as a vocal critic of terrorist activity.

Sudan's association with terrorism dates approximately from 1989, when General Omar Hassan Ahmad al-Bashir grabbed power in a military coup. Though nominally head of state, he contended for some years with the more powerful Hasan al-Turabi, Speaker of Sudan's Parliament and head of the extremist National Islamic Front — a tug-of-war that al-Turabi often won. By the early 1990s Khartoum provided refuge and training facilities for terrorist organizations that included the network headed by Osama bin Laden (expelled in 1996), the Abu Nidal organization, Hamas, and others. Policies toward terrorism changed with President al-Bashir's successful ouster of al-Turabi in December 1999. In 2000 Sudan signed all twelve international counterterrorist conventions, and it closed down the Popular Arab and Islamic Conference, a forum for terrorists.

There appears no evidence of direct Syrian involvement in terrorist activities since 1986. It has been praised by the State Department for seeking to moderate Hezbollah and Palestinian rejectionists, and for forcing many of the leaders of the Kurdistan People's Party (PKK) out of the country. Still, Syria remains accused of the somewhat lesser sin of providing safe haven to certain terrorist groups, including the Popular Front for the Liberation of Palestine-General Command and Hamas.

Although Afghanistan in the 1990s was left off the U.S. State Department's list of terrorist supporters, the Taliban had been the major backer of the world's largest and deadliest terrorist organization, Osama bin Laden's al-Qaeda, which trained tens of thousands of terrorists in its camps in that country and coordinated, from its headquarters, a network of terrorist groups with cells spanning some sixty countries.

Its key role in the anti-Taliban, anti–bin Laden coalition since 2001 notwithstanding, Pakistan had been guilty of terrorist sponsorship. Prior to 2001 it was the Taliban's only champion within the international community, it had backed terrorists involved in anti-Indian activity in Kashmir, and it provided hospitality to the Harakat ul-Mujahidin, a known terrorist organization associated with the hijacking of an Air India flight in 1999.

Cuba, despite its presence on the State Department's list of countries sponsoring terrorism, does not appear to have planned or executed terrorist attacks, or to have offered facilities to terrorist organizations. The U.S. government has claimed that Havana provides safe haven to a number of *former* terrorists, including U.S. fugitives accused of terrorism and Basque ETA terrorists. But providing sanctuary for retired terrorists does not signify support of terrorist activity any more than providing sanctuary to former Hitler officials necessarily links the host country to Nazi activity. The U.S. decision to place Cuba on the terrorist list appears more of a response to domestic political pressures than a reasonable description of the regime's policy.

In sum, seven countries have been implicated in international terrorism during this period, Iran and Afghanistan most actively. Two countries — Libya and Sudan — took significant steps to control terrorism, even before the events of 2001, and a third — Syria — scaled back its involvement with such activities and organizations. Thus, even within the set, meaningful variation can be found (and must be accounted for).

Weapons of Mass Destruction   Evidence can be ambiguous, especially where biological and chemical weapons are concerned; nevertheless, the nonpartisan Center for Defense Information (CDI) has provided a list of countries that, on the evidence available at the time of writing, are "known to possess or to be actively seeking some form of chemical-biological weapons capability." These are listed in the first column of table 3.1.[21]

Eleven countries are listed, including the United States, Russia, and China (which, as permanent members of the UN Security Council, are among the global community's norm-setters). Iran is known to have had a stockpile of chemical weapons in the past, which were employed in its war with Iraq. Although Tehran signed and ratified the 1993 Chemical Weapons Convention, the United States has shown evidence that Iran continues to possess a CW stockpile.[22] Iraq's chemical weapons program was considered one of the most ambitious in the developing world, and, on several occasions between 1983 and 1988, the regime used mustard gas and the nerve agents against Iran, as well as its own Kurdish population. Although, the UN Security Council established a special commission to oversee Iraq's destruction of WMDs, the latter's obstructionism led to the commission's departure in 1998, and subsequent U.S. and British bombing attacks did not induce Baghdad to reestablish verification. After 2003 the failure to find stockpiles of chemical weapons led to speculation that they had been destroyed sometime during the 1990s, although the capacity to produce them was retained during that period.

Libya appears to have had a chemical weapons stockpile (mustard gas), which may have been developed with Iranian help, while Sudan's program seems to have been assisted by Iraq.[23] Syria's chemical weapons program is thought to date from 1972 and to involve sarin and other chemical agents.[24]

TABLE 3.1   States Possessing or Seeking Chemical or
Biological Weapons Since 1989*

United States	Libya
Russia	Iran
China	Iraq
Taiwan	Syria
South Korea	North Korea
Israel	

* Source: Center for Defense Information

North Korea is not a Chemical Weapons Convention signatory, and its CW program dates back to at least 1981. South Korea, too, had worked on chemical weapons development, but, after signing the Convention it opened to inspection, and begun destroying, its stockpile. Israel is assumed to have a significant chemical weapons capability. Taiwan is also believed to be pursuing a chemical weapons program, initiated in 1983.

Syria is deemed technically capable of developing biological agents, but no significant program has been detected.[25] Iran, too, is thought to have pursued a biological weapons capability. It is likely that Israel has conducted research into such a capability, but there is no evidence of a stockpile.[26] Libya is reported to have undertaken research and development in this area. North Korea has pursued biological warfare capabilities since the 1960s and may have agents available for use.

Table 3.2 lists the nations possessing nuclear weapons, as well as those assumed to be seeking them (designated "high risk states"). Countries in column 1 include the major powers and norm-setters. Early acquirers of nuclear weapons all are members of the UN Security Council, and their nuclear position is acknowledged with no stigma. The column also includes Israel, India, and Pakistan. Although Israel has never publicly acknowledged the fact, few doubt that it possesses a significant nuclear arsenal containing, by some estimates, as many as one hundred weapons.[27] India tested a professedly "peaceful" nuclear device in 1974, but its program lay dormant for

TABLE 3.2 State of Nuclear Proliferation Since 1989

States Possessing Nuclear Weapons	High-Risk States During this Period
United States	Iraq
Russia	North Korea
United Kingdom	Iran
France	Libya
China	
India	
Pakistan	
Israel	

*Source: Based on Rodney W. Jones and Marc G. McDonough, *Tracking Nuclear Nonproliferation: Maps and Charts* (Washington, DC: Carnegie Endowment for International Peace, 1998), and BBC World News Service Online, "The World's Nuclear Arsenal," May 2, 2000.

a number of years. In 1998, however, it detonated a nuclear bomb, and Pakistan soon did the same. Both nations are now acknowledged, though unwelcome, members of the nuclear club.

In column 2, Iran, Iraq, Libya, and North Korea, at one time or another, sought the ability to produce nuclear arms. North Korea's program, widely publicized in the 1990s, was especially advanced. In 1994, by the Agreed Framework signed with the United States, it agreed to forgo further development in exchange for U.S. help in developing its civilian nuclear power program. As President Bush appeared to be retreating from the agreement, however, Pyongyang threatened to reactivate its program.[28] In October 2002 North Korea admitted that it had been pursuing an illicit uranium enrichment program for nuclear weapons. It also restarted a mothballed nuclear power station (expelling International Atomic Energy Agency inspectors) and reprocessed thousands of spent nuclear rods at the Yongbyon facility. Iraq's nuclear facilities were largely destroyed by U.S. air attacks during the Gulf War and dismantled by UN inspectors. But when the inspectors were thrown out in 1998, speculation increased of a revived Iraqi nuclear effort. Although no nuclear weapons were found following the Invasion of Iraq, evidence of earlier programs appeared fairly conclusive. Apparent Iranian nuclear ambitions have caused international disquiet. Tehran agreed, in December 2003, to allow intrusive inspections of its nuclear facilities and declare the scope of its programs, but the IAEA accused it of failing to declare uranium enrichment facilities.[29] Soon thereafter, the regime announced plans to build a heavy-water reactor capable of producing weapons-grade plutonium. While Libya did explore nuclear options, its program was not far advanced.[30]

External Aggression   Not every decision by one country to hurl its armed forces against another need amount to "aggression": the circumstances are often too complex and shrouded in too much interpretational ambiguity. Apart from cases of self-defense — even "anticipatory" self-defense when the evidence of an impending attack is strong enough to justify preemption — one might hesitate to designate as aggression armed skirmishes along a genuinely contested border, military action to protect a minority threatened with genocide (or other considerable harm), or even intervention in a neighboring state that is meant to terminate fighting that could produce vast refugee flows into one's own. Also, peacekeeping operations do not constitute aggression.

Still, a core meaning makes it possible to designate, with little ambiguity, certain cases of military action as aggression. Just about every one of these involves significant armed incursion into a country presenting no credible threat to the attacker, undertaken against the wishes of its legitimate government, and with the purpose of appropriating territory or economic assets, or of establishing a servile government. Thus, for example, few would deny that Russia's 1939 invasion of Finland, the Soviet invasion of Czechoslovakia in 1968, or, say, Germany's 1914 invasion of Belgium constituted aggression.

The best strategy, for our purposes, is to establish a list of interstate conflicts since the end of the Cold War and ask whether they originated from acts that meet the standards of aggression. We are helped here by the fact that a variety of research programs have recorded armed conflicts over the past several decades, some of which involve interstate (as opposed to intrastate) clashes. The following is a list of those occurring since the end of the Cold War.[31]

Few of these cases could confidently be said to have involved "aggression." The fighting between Armenia and Azerbaijan in 1990 occurred when the former backed the rebellion by the majority Armenian populations of Nagorno Karabak, a region imbedded in the state of Azerbaijan and that sought unification with the mother country. It would stretch semantics to brand this aggression. The fighting between Peru and Ecuador was marked by skirmishes over a boundary contested since colonial times, but this included no meaningful incursions by the armed forces of either side into the other's territory. Although the Eritrean–Ethiopian conflict did, in addition to border incidents, include reciprocal air attacks; this, too, was a matter of settling a territorial dispute, and the issue was soon resolved.

In 1998 South Africa dispatched six hundred troops into Lesotho, but it is hard to think of this as aggression. Lesotho had been wracked by violent

TABLE 3.3 Interstate Conflicts Since 1989

Armenia-Azerbaijan	1990
Persian Gulf War	1991
Ecuador-Peru	1995
Eritrea-Ethiopia	1998
South Africa-Lesotho	1998
Congo-several parties	1998
Yugoslavia-NATO	1999
Afghanistan-U.S.–led Coalition	2001
U.S.-led Coalition against Iraq	2003

demonstrations surrounding charges of electoral fraud, and a military coup was threatened. South Africa had traditionally had a "big brother" relation vis-à-vis Lesotho and seems to have responded to an invitation by its king and prime minister to help restore order.[32] In any case, there was no apparent national gain, from Pretoria's perspective, from the intervention. NATO's action against Yugoslavia was intended to stop the ethnic cleansing of the Kosovar Albanians by Milošević's security forces.

The purpose of the 2001 U.S.-led operation against Iraq was to expel Saddam Hussein's forces from a country they had, illegally and brutally, occupied. The forcible removal of his regime in 2003, given the reasons that prompted it, does not easily qualify as aggression. The 2003 war, while not formally endorsed by the UN Security Council, was nevertheless fought in support of previous Security Council resolutions.

Many countries had armed forces on the territory of the Democratic Republic of Congo after Laurent Kabila ousted President Mobutu in 1997. Some of these (Uganda, Rwanda, and Burundi) had intervened to prevent cross-border raids (mainly by Hutus) against their own country and its Tutsi population, raids that Kabila did little to stop. Others (Namibia, Zimbabwe, and Angola) fought to bolster Kabila.[33] Even though many of the parties also sought access to Congo's mineral wealth, it is hard to qualify these as clear-cut instances of aggression, since the foreign troops were there with the incumbent government's blessing.

The only interstate conflict of this period that could unambiguously be qualified as aggression was Iraq's invasion of Kuwait in 1990. On August 2 three divisions of Iraqi forces, along with air support, were launched against this small but wealthy emirate. While Baghdad had economic grievances against Kuwait and maintained nebulous historical claims to its territory, the action satisfied any reasonable definition of aggression, one that the international community was virtually unanimous in denouncing.

Externally Harmful Domestic Repression   The fourth criterion defining renegades in the post–Cold War context is externally harmful internal repression, often directed against minority groups. Massive and brutal regime mistreatment of ethnic communities has produced international implications of two kinds. Fleeing abuse, large streams of refugees become a burden to their host countries because of their economic cost and the social resentments their presence sometimes causes. Beyond this, repression directed against ethnicities that are also minorities in *other* countries (the Kurds, for example) may produce a broader contagion of ethnic rebellion, as feelings of group identity become inflamed elsewhere, following mistreatment in a particular country. Accordingly, and in a spirit of collective self-preservation, members of the international community seem to have agreed to stigmatize as renegades regimes that mistreat portions of their own population, gravely affecting other countries in the process.

However, some threshold of consequence is required, and at least four instances of ethnic mistreatment during this period should be examined: the depredations of the Milošević regime in Yugoslavia, Saddam's Hussein's actions against Iraqi Kurds, the Sudanese government's war against the population of its southern regions and Darfur, and the 1994 massacres in Rwanda.

The global community expressed revulsion at the violence directed by Bosnian Serbs (and, initially, by Bosnian Croats) toward Bosnian Muslims in the early 1990s. The fact that Serb forces were supported by Belgrade and partly responsive to its guidance made the Milošević regime complicit in their crimes — as the International War Crimes Tribunal in the Hague subsequently concluded. Moreover, the suffering of the Bosnian Muslims created a large outflow of refugees to Italy, Austria, and other countries. Ultimately, NATO bombing of Bosnian-Serb positions, and the subsequent Dayton Accord, set Bosnia on the road to peace.

The killing and ethnic cleansing of Albanians (a large majority of the province's population) in Kosovo by Milošević's security forces provoked massive outcries abroad and a seventy-eight-day NATO air campaign against Yugoslavia. Refugees were part of the international consequences of the regime's actions,[34] but there were other issues. Neighboring Macedonia, with over 20 percent Albanian population, was particularly vulnerable to instability by contagion (as subsequent developments demonstrated). There was a risk that Turkey, a NATO member with cultural and historical links to the local Albanians, might take action in support of its brethren. Under the circumstances, and given Greek ties to Orthodox co-religionists, the possibility of a clash between two NATO members could not be excluded. Finally, Russia's historical links to Serbia could have created a fissure in Moscow's relations with the West, reversing the welcome rapprochement that followed the Cold War's termination.

The Kurds, numbering some twenty million, are the fourth largest ethnic group in the Middle East and the most numerous stateless people in the word. Within Iraq, they represent 15–20 percent of the population and, since 1931, have waged an intermittent separatist revolt against Baghdad. Their bloodiest repression at the hands of the government occurred during the Iran–Iraq war, when the Kurds sided with Iran. Saddam Hussein's forces razed Kurdish villages and, in one particularly appalling attack with chemical weapons, killed an estimated five thousand Kurds in the town of Halabja.

In March 1991, after Hussein's defeat in the Gulf War, and encouraged by expectations of U.S. support, the Shiite minority in southern Iraq rebelled against Baghdad. In the wake of this uprising, the Kurds of northern Iraq revolted as well. But the regime's forces rallied, crushing both rebellions, and the resulting refugee exodus encompassed 10 percent of Iraq's population. Iran received 1.4 million Iraqis, Turkey 450,000, Saudi and Kuwait together took in some 35,000; others escaped to Syria and Jordan.[35] Baghdad's treatment of the Kurds, and the international consequences produced, would, by the criteria adopted here, further qualify Iraq's as a renegade regime.

Sudan's civil war, waged intermittently since 1955 and with greater intensity since 1983, initially pitted the Arabic and Islamic North against the largely African South, which continues to adhere to tribal customs and religions. Each side bore some of the responsibility for the violence, but its level intensified after the military coup of 1989, ending three brief years of democracy and parliamentary rule. The new military ruler Omar al-Bashir, backed by Hasan al-Turabi's National Islamic Front, intensified efforts at forcing Islamic law on the country and, more significantly, escalated bombing of civilian targets in the south, withholding food aid from these regions as well. Altogether, the conflict has cost some two million lives; destruction and starvation have displaced over five million people, a significant fraction of whom became refugees in neighboring countries. The subsequent genocidal measures against the African population of Darfur were, in many ways, a continuation of the regime's policy. By the standard of internal repression with international consequences, the Bashir regime qualified as a renegade.[36]

The worst instance of genocide since World War II was witnessed in 1994 in Rwanda, where, over a hundred-day period beginning on April 6, at least 800,000 of the country's minority Tutsis and moderate Hutu politicians were killed, often with clubs and machetes, by rampaging Hutu extremists guided by the Presidential Guard and the Interhamwe youth militia. The global community's passivity scarred its collective conscience, and there certainly were international implications: initially, as persecuted Tutsis fled to neighboring countries, mainly Uganda and Burundi, and then, following the Hutu defeat, as many thousands escaped reprisals by crossing into Zaire (subsequently renamed the Democratic Republic of Congo) and contributing to the conflict that has engulfed that country since. That Rwandan Hutu leaders responsible for the massacres had engaged in horrendous behavior is beyond doubt: the issue is whether we can sensibly speak of a renegade *regime*.

Initial planning for the massacres was, by all accounts, closely linked to President Juvenal Habyarimana, who had ruled the country with dictatorial powers since 1975, and to a secret clique of Hutu extremist politicians, the Akazu, working with the president.[37] In 1993 international pressure led Habyarimana to accept the 1993 Arusha Accord, providing for a transitional government with participation by opposition parties and national elections. Leading figures in the transitional government, including Prime Minister Agathe Uwilingiyimana and Foreign Minister Anastase Gasani, were opposition leaders, and by no means part of a "Habyarimana regime." On April 6 the president was killed when his plane was shot down while returning from a visit to Tanzania. Almost immediately, the roundup and massacre of Tutsis and moderate Hutus began. The prime minister and other leading opposition figures were killed, and an extremist government of dubious legality controlled by the Presidential Guard was appointed. The massacres were conducted by the Guard and the Interhamwe, along with elements of the army and local police, and they continued until July, when the Rwandan Patriotic Army, the major Tutsi force (many of whose soldiers had been concentrated in neighboring countries), defeated the Hutu, ousted the interim government, and installed president Bizimunga, a moderate Hutu, as head of state.

The issue here is that it is hard to pinpoint a Rwandan regime. The transitional government does not qualify. The interim government had neither the independence nor the continuity to be considered as such. The genocide was the product of an extremist political clique linked to the dead president: it is hard to consider this an authentic "regime."

The Bottom Line   Having determined who has violated the core norms of international behavior since the end of the Cold War, we designate the culpable as renegades. Permanent members of the UN Security Council (by definition, norm-setters) do not qualify by the terms of this study, nor do authentic democracies. Two apparent renegades — Iran and Yugoslavia — came closer to democracy than the others, but not close enough: while both had multiparty systems and competitive elections, other political features disqualify them. In Yugoslavia's case, the attempts (not entirely successful) by the Milošević regime to muzzle the media and to rig elections, as well as the intimidation (and, in a few instances, assassination) of opposition figures,[38] make it difficult to think of this as a fully democratic regime. With regard to Iran, although a representative assembly does exist, a nonelected Islamic Guardian Council passes on all legislation to assure its conformity with Islamic principles, while a jurisprudent, the supreme religious leader appointed by the ulama, may dismiss the elected president, command the armed forces, control the Guardian Council, and appoint key members of the judiciary—hardly an institution compatible with normal conceptions of democracy.[39]

The regimes of nine countries, then, qualify as renegades by our criteria (see table 3.4).

A first observation is that many more renegades are associated with terrorism and weapons of mass destruction than with the other two forms of renegade conduct. This is perfectly natural. Support for terrorism or, say, the pursuit of biological weapons is determined by a potentially broad set of circumstances. External aggression and massive assaults on the rights of ethnic groups are rooted in very specific geopolitical conditions. Each instance of the latter two forms of behavior encountered external military responses, indicating that they are, if anything, of even greater concern to the international community and its norm-setters.

A second observation is that regimes exhibit renegade conduct in different amounts. Iraq rates by each of the four criteria; at the other end of the scale, Afghanistan qualified by just one. Still, number of categories does not nec-

TABLE 3.4 Renegade Regimes

Country	Initial Emergence as Renegade	Basis for Renegade Status	Evolving Status
Iraq	1980	1, 2, 3, 4	Compliant (2003)
Iran	1979–1980	1, 2	Unrepentant
Libya	early 1970s	1, 2	Compliant (2003)
Syria	1972	1, 2	Partially Compliant (1986)
North Korea	early 1960s	2	Unrepentant
Pakistan	1998	1, 2	Partially Compliant (2001)
Yugoslavia	1992	3	Compliant (2001)
Afghanistan	1996	1	Compliant (2002)
Sudan	1989	1, 3	Partially Compliant (1996)

Key: 1: Terrorism; 2: Weapons of Mass Destruction; 3: Repression with International Consequences; 4: Aggression

essarily establish degree of delinquency. Both Libya and Syria qualify by two criteria, but Libya's support of terrorism, and its WMD programs, was on a greater scale than Syria's. While Pakistan and Afghanistan sponsored terrorism, the latter's culpability appears, in retrospect, to have exceeded the former's scope. And so forth.

Finally, renegades follow very different trajectories. Three (Iraq, Afghanistan, and Yugoslavia) now have compliant regimes, but in each case the regime was forcibly ousted — it did not reform. Two (Iran and North Korea) remain substantially unrepentant. Only one regime reformed to the point of full compliance. The U.S. State Department found no instances of Libyan-sponsored terrorism since 1994, observing that Libya "appears to have curtailed its support for international terrorism."[40] In 1999 Libya delivered the Lockerbie bombing suspects for trial in the Hague (under Scottish law), and Qaddafi denounced the September 11 attacks, even sharing intelligence on al-Qaeda with the United States.[41] In December 2003 he announced his intention to abandon all WMD programs, inviting international inspection of the fact. Finally, three regimes (Sudan, Syria, and Pakistan) have partially reformed. Between 1995 and 1997 the Sudanese government curtailed the activities of Islamist terrorist organizations on its territory; expelling, in 1996, Osama bin Laden, and all apparent connection to terrorism was abandoned around 1999. But governmental human rights abuses and associated refugee problems were only partially mitigated by peace talks between government and rebels, and by the peace agreement signed in January 2004. Continued fighting and ethnic violence in the western province of Darfur have caused significant demographic displacements and a refugee exodus into Chad, keeping the regime among the ranks of partially compliant renegades. Although Syria has not been directly implicated in any terrorist operation since 1986, it continued, as late as 2004, to provide safe-haven to a number of active terrorist organizations,[42] and most indications continue to point to chemical weapons programs. After the September 11 terrorist attacks, in response to U.S. pressure and economic inducements, Pakistan abandoned its support for the Taliban (and thus for al-Qaeda) and curbed its support of Kashmiri terrorists fighting for independence from India.[43] It did, however, retain its nuclear weapons program.

The Comparative Imperative

We have assigned ourselves a dual task: (a) to explain the emergence of primary renegades, and (b) to account for the trajectory of secondary renegades. The two tasks involve different analytic challenges. One issue, with regard to the first, is that we cannot discern the genesis of renegades if only they are examined. This would amount to an extreme case of "selecting on the dependent variable," that is, of choosing cases in a way that prejudges the value of the outcome — as, for example, by basing an examination of the relationship between income and education on a scrutiny of those who are wealthy, or by studying the impact of national income disparities on government stability via an examination of unstable governments. That problem is not present when analyzing the trajectory of secondary renegades: since they follow different paths, our dependent variable does indeed vary.

The likely consequence of limiting variation in the value of a continuous dependent variable to one end of the continuum is a misestimate of causal effects,[44] and, especially in small-N studies, an underestimate of the importance of associated explanations.[45] However, when variables, as is here the case, are measured at the binary, rather than interval or ratio, level, the conundrum is starker still. One way to view the problem is via the distinction between the necessary and sufficient conditions for the occurrence of a phenomenon. A necessary condition (C) for some outcome (O) is one without which O cannot occur (a necessary condition for a figure to be a square is that it should have four sides). A sufficient condition ensures the occurrence of O (a sufficient condition for passing a class is to get an A in it). A necessary condition need not be a sufficient condition, and vice-versa (being a quadrilateral figure is a necessary, but not sufficient, condition for being a square; falling asleep at the wheel generally is a sufficient, but not a necessary, condition for an automobile accident).

The point of the distinction is that a study of binary variables involving only instances where the value does occur allows conclusions about necessary, but not about sufficient, conditions. Thus, in table 3.5, the study would

TABLE 3.5 The Structure of Causation

	Outcomes		
Antecedent Conditions	O	Non-O	
C	a	b	Row 1 (sufficiency)
Non-C	c	d	Row 2
	Column 1 (necessity)	Column 2	

examine only cases under column 1: if all (or, in a stochastic model, most) cases were in cell *a* (cell *c* being substantially empty), one might claim that C is a necessary condition for O. A claim of causal sufficiency, however, would require that whenever C occurs, O does also, and the needed information would appear in row 1, which includes cases of O's nonoccurrence (column 2). (For sufficiency to obtain, all or most entries in row 1 should be in cell *a*, cell *b* being entirely or mostly empty.) Establishing necessary conditions is a meaningful contribution to knowledge,[46] but any study that neglects sufficient conditions has limited explanatory reach.

John Stuart Mill proposed that tests of both sorts be performed. In a first step, the researcher assesses whether all cases displaying the outcome also exhibit the antecedent condition (is the condition of necessity met?); in a second stage, the researcher asks whether instances of the antecedent condition concur in displaying the consequent condition (is the condition of sufficiency met?).[47] In terms of table 3.5, this means that an examination of the distribution of cases between the two cells of column 1 (*a* and *c*) must be supplemented by an investigation of their distribution between the two cells of row 1 (*a* and *b*). The main point, for our purposes, is that no discussion of sufficiency is logically possible without reference to cases where O is absent (cell *b*).

Social science explanations rarely rely on a single antecedent condition. Usually, the occurrence of a phenomenon depends on some configuration of circumstances; at times a number of configurations are involved. Within the configuration, conditions may individually be necessary and/or sufficient. Sometimes, a set of necessary conditions may be jointly sufficient (as being a rectangle and equilateral are jointly sufficient for conditions for a square). However, whether we are dealing with simple or compound conditions, the logic displayed with regard to table 3.5 applies — any discussion of sufficiency requires consideration of cases of the outcome's nonoccurrence.

A question remains regarding the value of cell *d*'s information (non-C, non-O), since it affects neither necessity nor sufficiency. That information, however, is crucial for a credible discussion of *causality*. Although there exists no entirely satisfactory conception of causality in the philosophy of science literature, empirical scholarship generally equates the concept with our evidence for it — in other words, as David Hume argued, an antecedent condition can be considered the cause of an outcome only to the extent that the two occur jointly (and that the cause should naturally precede the outcome).[48] This means that there should be a fairly regular conjunction of C

and O, *as well as* of non-C and non-O. Thus, for smoking to be considered
a cause of cancer, it is not enough that smokers should tend to have cancer:
nonsmokers should tend not to. Similarly, it is not enough that regimes
fulfilling the conditions of our theoretical framework should become renegades; it also required that those who do not fulfill them should not. Information on the non-C, non-O conjunction involves the information provided
by cell *d*: it requires further instances of occasions where the outcome has
not occurred (in our case, further instances of nonrenegades).

Accordingly, a meaningful analysis of the genesis of renegades (O's) requires their comparison to a set of regimes that are not renegades (non-O's),
and rules for selecting the latter must complement those used in selecting
the former.

Comparison Set: Criteria for Selection

On what basis should the selection of nonrenegades proceed? We cannot
consider them all. Renegades are few and far between, and the circumstances making them a likely occurrence are much less numerous than those
that make them an unlikely occurrence, limiting the analytical value of
many possible comparisons. What useful insights, for example, could we
expect from comparing Afghanistan to Denmark, Syria to Canada? In any
case, a comparative analysis involving every regime is not feasible at the level
of specificity involved in this study. A random sample of nonrenegades is
practically feasible but not analytically desirable. As a representation of the
entire population of regimes, it has the same problems as those associated
with a study of that population as a whole. Moreover, in small-*n* research,
random selection can, in fact, cause serious biases.[49]

The most sensible approach starts from the premise that, if cases are
similar in important ways, then the fact that some exhibit an outcome while
others do not should be attributed to the remaining differences. The challenge, when comparison with the entire remaining population (or a probability sample thereof) makes no sense, is to decide which criteria of similarity
are most important. The notion of necessary conditions for an outcome
provides useful guidelines here. As Charles Ragin observes, "The constitution of positive cases provides the best clues for the constitution of negative
cases. The best guide for defining the set is provided by analysis of the
positive instances. Negative cases should resemble positive cases in as many

ways as possible, especially with regard to the commonalities exhibited by the positive cases."[50]

In turn, as we have seen, conditions that are common to all cases displaying the outcome may be considered necessary conditions for its occurrence.[51] So, one useful way of settling on a comparison-set of nonrenegades it to select regimes sharing one or more necessary conditions for the emergence of renegades. If this is done, we may assume that the reasons some regimes become renegades while others do not are rooted either in the conditions of sufficiency or in necessary conditions not included as selection criteria.

Asking what necessary conditions lie behind renegade behavior requires us to identify relevant conditions that all renegades share. We have already established that all are nondemocracies, and that there are reasons for thinking that such regimes are more likely to engage in behaviors that violate central international norms.[52] But there is another interesting circumstance that is proper to every one of our nine renegades: a need to establish new principles of regime legitimacy, a sharp discontinuity separating the new principles from those that preceded them. None of our renegades came to power via fully institutionalized means; none could convincingly claim a right to rule rooted in the legitimacy of the *process* that brought them to power. Each established its position by rejecting foundational political principles that applied before its accession to power.

It is not surprising that there should be a link between deviant international conduct and the lack of a securely established basis for legitimacy, since an inability to ground a right to rule in institutionalized political principles encourages other, occasionally extreme, methods of asserting it. Sometimes the regime benefits from stances antipodal to those of its rejected precursor — indicating new blood, vigor, and values. Thus, a campaign of ethnic cleansing may establish a contrast with a predecessor accused of laxness regarding the dominant ethnicity's interests; a program of nuclear weapons acquisition might contrast with a prior government's alleged inattentiveness to national security and prestige; and so forth.

Ayatollah Khomeini's desire to establish an Islamic Republic on the ruins of the secular and Westernizing rule of Shah Mohammad Reza Pahlavi represented a stark change in the basis whereby the right to govern was asserted in Iran. Similarly, the pillars on which the Taliban proposed to erect Afghanistan's political system had very little in common with those on which its predecessors, or any other modern nation, had attempted to found their rule. Muammar Qaddafi displaced a weak and seemingly rudderless monarchy with an ardently Arab and mildly socialist regime. The aggressively nationalist government of Slobodan Milošević based its right to rule on the claim that it was serving the interests of Serbs, not the communist ideology of the previous regime.

Some discontinuities are more subtle but nevertheless meaningful. Nimeiri's overthrow, in 1985, by Sadiq al-Mahdi removed some of Sudan's apparently democratic trappings, but it was the al-Bashir coup in 1989 that established a regime firmly based on the dual foundations of military coercion and Arab Islamism. Both Saddam Hussein and Hafez al-Assad emerged from unstable Baathist regimes that, several years previously, had displaced timidly Westernizing systems, yet both leaders based their rule on principles owing little to Baath ideology. In Assad's case, the radical Jadid regime was replaced by far more pragmatic military rule. In Hussein's case, the Baathist governing principles of Ahmad Hasan al-Bakr yielded (even before 1979) to a violently repressive dictatorship tethered to a personality cult.

In many ways, the most interesting case of a revised basis for regime legitimacy was North Korea's. At one level, it appears (and is often accepted) that Kim Il-Sung sought to establish an authentically Marxist system in a country whose politics had no such tradition. But a more complex and unique foundation for rulership evolved during the late 1950s and very early 1960s. Because, as late as the mid-1950s, the legitimacy of communist regimes seemed to require their endorsement by the Soviet Union, nations, like North Korea, that also looked to the People's Republic of China for ideological guidance faced a dilemma. As evidence grew of a schism between the two major communist powers, an important pillar of regime legitimacy became increasingly wobbly. However, even before the split became apparent, Kim Il-Sung, whose ideological worldview initially was grounded in rigid Stalinism, could not endorse Nikita Khrushchev's revisionist outlook and denouncement of Stalin's more ruthless practices. This further threatened the ideological premises on which his rule stood, and by the late 1950s a new foundation for ideological legitimacy appeared in the form of *Juche* (meaning "subject" or "subjectivity"), a doctrine that, more than Marxism, has guided Pyongyang. Intense nationalism and a call for extreme self-reliance replaced any concept of "proletarian internationalism" as a guide to the country's relationship with the outside world. Moving even further from orthodox Marxism, the regime abandoned the cornerstone belief that human and social relations are shaped by forces and relations of production (society's economic infrastructure). In the new perspective, the "brain" (*noesu*) of the sociopolitical organism, defined by its top leadership, determines the direction of social change, imparting a Hegelian, rather than Marxist, cast to the official ideology. This, coupled with a number of Confucian elements, represented a substantial revision of the previous basis of the legitimizing ideology.[53] To some extent, it may account for the need to chart a course in international relations guided by none of the prevailing normative systems.

Members of the Comparison Set

The regimes comprising our comparison set are the Suharto regime in Indonesia; the army-backed regime that emerged in Algeria following suspension of the 1992 elections; the 1983–1999 military regime (involving a succession of leaders) in Nigeria; the Aliyev regime in Azerbaijan; the post-Nasserite regime in Egypt; and the regime of Yemen following its reunification in 1990. Each satisfies what have, so far, emerged as necessary conditions for the emergence of renegades: (1) they strive for a foundation of legitimacy different from that characterizing regimes they displaced, and (2) they do not rise to the standards of democracy. In addition, and in a rough manner, the comparison set approximates the economic conditions and geographic distribution of the set of renegades, further improving the bases for comparison.

In the case of Indonesia, Sukarno's charismatic authority was replaced by rulership completely devoid of charisma, his left-leaning nationalism by a rightist mindset eschewing both nationalism and any semblance of ideological fervor. The Aliyev regime in Azerbaijan moved into the void left by the demise of communism and the end of Soviet authority in 1991 and by the instability initially following independence. The period of Nigerian military rule marked the abandonment of the quasi-democratic and electorally based regime of President Shagari in 1983, and the continuing search for postindependence principles of political rule. The Algerian case is a bit more complex. The regime that removed Chadli Benjedid replaced a regime based on a compromise between moderate Islam and a mild, statist socialism with one founded far more explicitly on coercion and a commitment to quelling, repressively if necessary, the power of radical Islamism. The Saleh regime in Yemen replaced the political systems of both parts of the previously divided country — nominally Marxist South Yemen and traditional but authoritarian North Yemen — by one formally committed to democracy, but really a hybrid of tribalism and pre-democratic forms.

Egypt saw a transition from the postindependence regime identified with Gamal Abdel Nasser to a less personalist and differently rooted regime. In Nasser's case, the bases for regime legitimacy were a fervent Arab nationalism, a commitment to socialism through land reforms and state direction of the economy, extensive military participation in government, and mobilization of society through a single political party, the Arab Socialist Union. During Anwar Sadat's presidency, reliance on Arab nationalism as a basis of regime legitimacy was abandoned, socialism was progressively replaced with far greater scope for private enterprise and foreign investment, the military was squeezed out of top political positions, and the Arab Socialist Union was disbanded and replaced by a three-party system, dominated by the regime's National Democratic Party.[54]

These regimes, therefore, satisfy at least two of the apparently necessary conditions for primary renegades. Why did they not become so? Why did neither Egypt nor Indonesia seek nuclear or biological weapons? Why didn't Algeria, Yemen, and Azerbaijan encourage international terrorism? Why didn't Nigeria, like Sudan or Yugoslavia, undertake a program of massive ethnic repression, qualifying it as a renegade? The answer must be that conditions beyond the two necessary ones were not met, and our theoretical framework guides the search for these unmet conditions.

To Summarize

Requiring a list of renegade regimes, we proceeded inductively. Starting with a general definition, we identified the specific forms of behavior that violate core international norms in a way threatening to others. Settling on a list of four behaviors, we further identified those regimes that, in terms of their conduct in these regards, objectively qualify as renegades. In contrast to the abstract character of the previous chapter, this one required immersion into empirical detail on currently dominant international norms, on the specific conduct of certain nations, and on the responses of others. From this largely descriptive welter of information, a mosaic of renegade conduct came into focus, reflecting the conditions of the post–Cold War world, as thus far they have developed.

Because very limited inferences could be drawn from an examination of renegades alone, we then selected a set of regimes with which the renegades could be compared, in an attempt to establish causal explanations of the emergence of deviant regimes. This was done by identifying a set of regimes sharing two apparently necessary conditions for renegade behavior: a nondemocratic government and a sharp discontinuity in the principles on which the regime seeks to establish its right to rule.

4   Primary Renegades and the Genesis of Deviance

Here we examine the conditions leading to the emergence of primary renegades, asking whether their genesis confirms the theoretical framework's expectations, and we direct the same question at our comparison set of nonrenegades. In terms of number of cases, we are awkwardly situated between two research traditions. Nine renegades and six regimes within the comparison set precludes, given our complex theoretical structure, the sophisticated statistical analyses employed for large-N studies (degrees of freedom simply are not there); at the same time, our N exceeds that generally associated with focused, comparative case studies. This, however, is the international reality; it cannot be molded to conventional research designs, and the analysis will adapt by proceeding in two stages: (1) a comparative study of renegade and nonrenegade regimes, with a focus more finely grained than compatible with statistical analysis, while falling short of that typically seen in comparative case studies; (2) a simple, different, and intuitively meaningful quantitative analysis of the sort appropriate to the material we are dealing with.

The Incentives of Primary Renegades

Our cornerstone expectation is that renegades emerge when deviant behavior is expected to benefit their domestic position, whereas behavior and benefits may be indirectly or directly linked.

Indirect Links

Links are indirect when the regime strives to solidify its domestic standing via politically rewarding behavior that, incidentally, violates core international norms. Here, ideational impulses may produce a stake in deviance, which, however, may be offset by a concern with the economic consequences of misconduct, and we ask whether, in the case of renegades, the former occurred whereas the latter did not. To begin with, have these regimes based their legitimacy on a strong ideational program implying grievous wrongs that the regime would right?

Ideational Drives and the Stake in Deviance   *Ethno-Nationalism.* There are two paths via which intense ethno-nationalism can produce renegade behavior. One starts from the conviction that hostile foreign forces have undermined the community's dignity and significance, and it leads to boldly redemptive policies — often melding, in the process, its parts into one coherent whole, to the regime's great merit. These acts of national self-affirmation (e.g., acquisition of nuclear weapons) may well breach international norms. The other path involves a regime in a multiethnic society that bolsters its position by promoting the interests of one ethnic group against those of others, generally claiming to right historical wrongs. In so doing, it may be guilty of violence, with consequences that reach beyond the country's borders.

The first path is exemplified by the defiant acts via which the North Korean regime has affirmed the nation's status and its own authority. Although an ethnically homogenous country, nationalism is a core element of North Korea's political ethos and an important component of the dominant ideology (*Juche*). Three circumstances best account for the form North Korean nationalism has assumed. The first is the Confucian legacy, as Kim Il-Sung built the official ideology on the notion of the household as elemental community, presenting the nation as a vast, organic family that emphasizes the role of the father (himself) to which filial piety is due.[1] Nationalism has also been shaped by contrasts drawn with South Korea, whose people are depicted as pitiful objects of foreign domination, lacking their northern neighbor's blissful independence. Most importantly, North Korean nationalism is a response to perceptions of past subjugation and humiliation at the hands of foreign powers. According to the regime's ideologues, "Korean history is one of exploitation by such foreign powers as the Chinese, Russians, Mongolians, Japanese, and Americans; in the process, the Korean people endured national humiliation, physical suffering, and the deprivation of human dignity."[2]

This subservience was in large part attributable to tepid nationalism, with the associated pathologies of military weakness, insufficient pride, and a lack of ideological unity. Something stronger was needed.[3] "It was a harsh nationalism that dwelt on past wrongs and promises of retribution for 'national traitors' and their foreign backers. [It] stressed the 'priority' of all things Korean against the 'contamination' of foreign ideas and inculcated in the population a sense of fear and animosity toward the outside world."[4]

Linked to this is the notion that North Koreans are a "chosen people,"[5] elevated to a higher plane of virtue and earning the envy and hostility of others. An aggressive quest for independence, national self-affirmation, and security against foreign belligerence was required, implying, in the North Korean case, an external paranoia encouraging renegade policies, particularly the pursuit of nuclear weapons.

Iraqi nationalism under Saddam Hussein also expressed a quest for national self-affirmation that would redound to the regime's credit. Unlike Korea, the country is ethnically fragmented: between Shiites (over 60 percent of the population) and the traditionally ruling Sunnis, as well as a number of smaller religious groups. The chasm between Arabs and ethnic Kurds (most of whom are Sunnis) further complicates the situation. In a quest for identity for a country with little natural basis for unity,[6] Saddam Hussein revived ancient symbols of national splendor and memories of the glory of Mesopotamia (with which Iraq's present borders are roughly coextensive), while his propaganda machine compared him to Nebuchadnezzar, Hamurabi, and Saladin. A heroic "Iraqi man" was heralded, transcending religious, ethnic, and class divisions, a bulwark against anti-Iraqi plots by the United States and Zionist forces.[7] The attempt to ground the regime in intense national awareness benefited from a perception of external enmity, as Hussein emphasized the importance of national dignity and Iraq's long struggle against "slavery" and "exploitation." As elsewhere, a sense of national purpose via a defiance of global norms dovetailed with claims of wrongs at foreign hands, including those of leading norm-setters. This history of victimization was to be transcended by future power and greatness worthy of the Mesopotamian heritage. As Saddam Hussein explained in 1980, "We draw a large picture of Iraq. We want Iraq to possess a weight like that of China, a weight like the Soviet Union, a weight like the United States, and that is indeed the factual basis of our actions."[8] Aggressive attempts at territorial expansion and acquisition of an arsenal of weapons of mass destruction can be understood in this light.

A regime-driven quest for national affirmation also fueled Pakistan's transgressive behavior. Three issues have threatened national unity: (1) the enduring quarrels between Shiites and Sunnis, (2) the difficulty of fully integrating into the nation the Pashtuns, the country's largest ethnic group, and (3) the desire to incorporate parts of Kashmir into the mother country. The need to forge a sense of national achievement by confronting these challenges explains many regime policies, especially when coupled with perceived wrongs at the hands of arch-rival India. The 1998 decision to test a nuclear weapon followed successful Indian tests, as domestic forces pressed for the bomb at a time when Prime Minister Sharif's standing was weak. The main Islamic fundamentalist party, Jamaat Islami, organized street demonstrations calling for nuclear status. Benazir Bhutto, Sharif's chief political rival, was in the streets with a similar demand. In Pakistan, a stack of thin gold bracelets is a sign of femininity; offering a bracelet to a man expresses contempt for his weakness. At a rally in Sharif's hometown, Bhutto ripped of her bracelets and cast them toward the crowd in a gesture that said, "Give these to Mr. Sharif—he doesn't have the guts to stand up to India."[9] When Sharif decided to proceed with the tests, widespread public adulation greeted the decision, and a poll by the Pakistan Institute for Public Opinion found 97 percent support for the testing.[10] The decision to go nuclear was largely driven by a need for national affirmation with regard to India.

Nationalism also prompted Pakistan's support for terrorism within Kashmir. Most Pakistanis believe that Kashmir should be part of Pakistan, and that the arrangements that deprived Pakistan of sovereignty over the province were deeply iniquitous. Islamic fundamentalists and elements of the military and security services most passionately hold the belief. Musharraf came to power on a hard-line platform on Kashmir, and Pakistan encouraged raids across the line of control into Indian-administered Kashmir, as well as proindependence terrorist acts within that region.[11] The struggle for Kashmiri independence is an integral part of the national purpose, and no leader indifferent to that cause could claim political legitimacy.

About half of Iran's population is Persian and a quarter is Azeri, with Kurds, Turkmens, and Bakhtiaris comprising most of the balance; thus the need to assert a national identity. But Iranian nationalism under the ayatollahs has influenced the country's international posture largely via its religious purpose. Spearheading a global Islamic Revolution,[12] Iranians were a chosen people, whereas the country's commitment to a revolutionary and "pure" form of Islam would inevitably place it in opposition to those whom this revolution was destined to engulf. These were enemies of the Faith, hence enemies of Iran, largely responsible for the odious secularism of the shah. Confrontation with the outside world was inevitable and, within the logic of the confrontation, ends justify means — a reality uniquely grasped by the theocratic regime.

A source of Libya's renegade behavior could also have been found in national self-affirmation, in this case encompassing the entire Arab Nation. Entranced with Gamal Abdel Nasser's pan-Arabism, his boldness (as reflected in the nationalization of the Suez Canal), and the reverence in which he was held within much of the Arab world, Qaddafi sought to fashion himself as his heir. The first phases of his political evolution centered on Arab nationalism as a primordial value.[13] With the humiliation of Arab defeat in the 1967 war, and as Anwar Saddat seemed to abandon Nasser's pan-Arabic cause, a sense of having inherited the mantel suffused Qaddafi's political identity. Again, the notion of a chosen people surfaced. "At the heart of this Arab nationalism was the feeling that the Arab people had special qualities, values, and distinctions which set them apart from outsiders and gave them the right and duty to manage their own resources and shape their own destiny."[14]

Whereas Qaddafi "saw Libya as the head, the vanguard and the hope of the Arab nation, and thus as a custodian of Arab nationalism,"[15] he probably also expected that a position as hero of the Arab nation would further bolster his domestic standing, and that a bold foreign policy might infuse Libya's disparate parts with a common identity. The country's fragmentation is linked to differences in historical experience among its three provinces (Tripolitania, Cyrenaica, and Fezzan) rather than to ethnic fissures, and, in addition to provincial identities, many Libyans identify as members of tribes and villages rather than with the nation.[16] Given the shaky national identity, Qaddafi probably viewed the pursuit of Arab nationalism as a way of blurring the divisions within Libyan society.[17] In any case, Arab problems and backwardness were blamed on centuries of subjugation by Western powers and on their current anti-Arab policies. Extreme measures seemed justified by the nobility of the cause and the perfidy of its opponents.

Some regimes followed the second path to renegade behavior. If five sought self-affirmation for a nation deemed a single collectivity, two became renegades because of policies directed against communities within the country. This was especially true in Yugoslavia, a country suffering exceptional fragmentation.[18] Bosnia encompasses a population of Bosnian Muslims, as well as Serbs and Croats. Croatia had, in its eastern regions, a sizable Serbian minority. Serbia's Vojvodina region is home to many ethnic Hungarians, while the Kosovo province has a majority of local Albanians, who also account for a portion of Macedonia' s population. Seeking in the grievances of the dominant Serbs a substitute for the foundation of legitimacy that communism previously provided, Milošević (himself a former party apparatchik) whipped up a frenzy of ethnic indignation. Many Serbs felt that postwar Yugoslavia had unjustly deprived Serbia of its dominant position within the federation, which had been cruelly truncated by placing numerous Serbs in other republics (mainly Bosnia and Croatia). Serbs also felt that the 1974 Constitution, granting Vojvodina and Kosovo independent votes within the federation, made theirs the only of the country's republics without sovereign rights. At the same time, Kosovo Serbs were increasingly threatened by pressures from the Albanian majority,[19] while those in Croatia and Bosnia sought unification with brethren in Serbia proper.

Milošević courted popular veneration by casting himself as protector of all Serbs, harping on myths of Serbian victimization by villains both in Yugoslavia and abroad, at a time when nationalism was replacing both pro- and anticommunist sentiment as a rallying cry within Serbia. He was helped by the political strategies of leaders in other parts of former Yugoslavia. As free elections brought anticommunist nationalists to power in Croatia (Franjo Tudjman) and Slovenia (Milan Kucan), a subtle symbiosis of interests developed between the three leaders: the nationalist extremism of one justifying "defensive" nationalism by the others, the political position of each benefiting in the process.[20] Milošević's excesses were worst, as apparent during the struggle on behalf of Croatia's Serbs, where indiscriminate destruction (especially in Vukovar) did much to fuel foreign disgust with his regime, whose subsequent complicity in the depredations against Bosnian Muslims firmly rooted it in the camp of renegades. But for Milošević, this was an opportunity to churn the tide of ethnic feeling that had carried him to power, claiming that Serbia's enemies also were to be found outside Yugoslavia's borders, among Western powers in particular.[21]

The Bashir and Turabi regime's repression of non-Arabs also made it a renegade, although, in Sudan's case, we encounter not dismemberment of a multinational state but a straightforward struggle for ethnic hegemony within a unitary state.[22] The conflict's rhetoric might characterize it as a religious clash, but, peeling away layers of surface appearance, the ethnic aspect emerges very clearly. As one Sudanese official, explained the situation:

> It is not primarily a religious war, but a racial-cultural war which the
> north presents as a religious war because the majority of Sudanese are

Muslim, while at the same time the majority are Arabian. The northern Arab elite uses African Muslims to fight African Christians or believers of traditional religions to maintain its position of power in
Khartoum.[23]

Predictably, Sudanese Muslims were portrayed as the victims of a history plagued by anti-Arab, anti-Islamic forces, the injustices being reflected in Sudan's political structure and in a distribution of natural wealth
(mainly oil) favoring southerners. At the same time, a broader Arab-Islamist
mission justified violence against southerners and the regime's hospitality to
terrorists.

Not all renegade behavior was connected to ethno-nationalist symbolism.
In Afghanistan and Syria no credible link could be found, despite some
degree of ethnic fragmentation. Afghanistan is a divided country; Pashtuns
dominated under the Taliban while other groups, the Shiite Hazaras in
particular, were cruelly repressed. But defiance of the international community and hospitality to al-Qaeda terrorists were not driven by nationalism.
Al-Qaeda fought alongside the Pashtun Talibans against remnants of domestic resistance to its rule, and, if these battles are considered an aspect of
ethnic struggles, then a link can be claimed. But al-Qaeda and Taliban were
bonded primarily by Islamist convictions, implying that religious themes,
rather than tribal politics, accounted for the regime's support of a major
terrorist organization.[24]

Syria's situation bears no clear relation to that of the other renegades.
Most Syrians are Arabic-speaking Sunnis, but with a fragile sense of nationhood.[25] The country's borders scarcely correspond to those historically meaningful to many Syrians,[26] and the dominant Sunni culture masks sectarian
and religious friction.[27] The absence of national identity within truncated
borders was initially managed by identifying with the wider cause of pan-
Arabism; but the disappointing experience of union with Egypt (1958–1961)
dampened pan-Arabic ardor. Being Alawi, the regime was led to prove its
Syrian credentials by a policy implacably hostile to Israel and staunchly pro-
Palestinian, but Arabism and Islam have not determined Syria's foreign pol-
icy: its decades-long feud with Iraq eventually led it to side with non-Arab
Iran in the Iran-Iraq War, and its 1976 intervention in Lebanon supported
Maronite Christians against their Muslim opponents.

If attempts to build regime legitimacy on ethno-nationalist foundations
are not coincident with renegade behavior in all cases, they are in seven of
the nine, indicating that internationally censured conduct is more likely by

regimes grounded in nationalist fervor. The same applies to religious extremism.

The Impact of Religion. Where religious beliefs are extreme and implacable, where they assign absolute virtue to believers and absolute iniquity to those who are not, and where regime support rests on its position as champion of the Faith, that regime may place itself in unbounded opposition to the rest of the international community, an opposition that becomes a pillar of its domestic legitimacy. Here, renegades rarely claim to address a specific injury to the Faith, but rather injustices deeply embedded in the stream of history, claiming that they will boldly promote the religion in the face of its adversaries.

Fundamentalist Iran exemplified all of this, especially during the years immediately following Khomeini's Islamic revolution. The idea that government is in God's hands undermined any justification for a secular state, vesting absolute authority in the Prophet Mohammed, the infallible Imams, and the *faqih* (clerical guardians) entrusted with temporal and spiritual authority while awaiting the appearance of the Twelfth Imam — expected eventually to appear as *Mahdi* (Messiah), to rule the affairs of humanity. The faqihs' job, while awaiting the Mahdi, is to prepare for the establishment of an "Islamic World Government."[28] Here, the country has a special role to play, since, in the regime's view, "government of God" had thus far been established in a single "redeemer nation," making Iran the "only true Islamic independent country and the only depository of the essence and message of God,"[29] thus investing it with a duty to spearhead a global revolution, spreading its message and building a coalition of the socioeconomically and religiously oppressed. Much of this activism was targeted against Islam's enemies: Zionism, secular Arab governments, godless communism, and, especially, the United States (the Great Satan).

If the Sudanese government's war against its southern regions was rooted in race, its rationale was mainly religious. The war's intensity coincided with the initial burst of Islamism under Nimeiri, intensifying with the 1989 coup. Inasmuch as part of the regime's initial renegade status flowed from its treatment of southerners, a jihad on behalf of the Faith was one of its foundations. In addition, Sudan's Islamists promised to extend Islam beyond the Arabic cultural area, regarding Sudan as a "springboard for Islamist penetration of black Africa."[30] They saw themselves as a people with an exceptional mission, laboring alongside Iran to unify the international Muslim Nation, with Sudan as its nucleus. The regime's early support of Islamic terrorist groups was justified by that mission, which could also rationalize mistreatment of unbelievers.

Although clearly fundamentalists, the Taliban did not offer a developed statement of doctrine. Representing an extreme Deobandism developed by semieducated mulahs in rural *madrassas*, their beliefs were neither integrated into the main currents of Islamic thought nor systematically codified.[31] The credo nonetheless demanded implacable opposition to modernity and inflexible commitment to certain social rituals and protocols of conduct.[32] While current scholarship on the Taliban provides little evidence that defiance of the outside world was steeped in neo-Deobandi beliefs, their narrowness and the ferocity with which they were forced on Afghans suggested little tolerance for dissidents at home or abroad and few qualms about the manner in which they could be treated, and it implied a commitment to a broader Islamist mission pursued by any means required. From this perspective, the Taliban's embrace of al-Qaeda and terrorism is understandable.

Even secular regimes with no aspirations to leading a holy war sometimes trumpet their religious credentials in a search for expanded popular support. In so doing, they may benefit from policies placing them on the side of the zealots and in opposition to core international values. Although emphatically a secularist, Saddam Hussein exhibited surges of Islamic fervor when politically opportune. Following the Iranian Revolution, he became aware of Baathism's feeble emotional appeal, especially compared with the enormous zeal commanded by Shiite Islam. To ensure backing from the nation's religious majority, he renovated Shiite shrines and rebuilt their towns, encouraging Shiite participation in government and the military.[33] During the war with Iran, he professed a deep religiosity, which he stressed even more after the invasion of Kuwait, ordering that the Islamic battle cry, *Allahu Akbar* (God is great) be added to the country's flag, and beginning every speech with *basmati* (in the name of God).[34] Subsequently, construction was begun on the Saddam Mosque, destined to be the largest in the world with space for 45,000 worshippers, and intended "to help him drum up political support in the Muslim world."[35] Its religious face made the regime's legitimacy harder to challenge, making it also desirable that international influence should match the country's exalted stature, and explaining a desire for the power and prestige provided by weapons of mass destruction.

Similarly, the religious foundations of renegade behavior in Pakistan reflected needed domestic support for a secular regime. Zia-ul Haq, and especially Nawaz Sharif, made substantial gestures toward the country's Islamists to enlist their backing for the government and for Mujahedins fighting the Soviets in Afghanistan. In the process, Pakistan became home to a number Jihadi groups, many of which, after the Soviet withdrawal, became agents of Pakistan's foreign policy, especially of its efforts to force India out of Kashmir.[36] A symbiosis of interest developed between the foreign Jihadists, Pakistan's own fundamentalist-Islamic community, and the state's military and intelligence service (ISI). Under Musharraf, their interlinked agendas became a source of support for, and a constraint on, regime policy: ensuring backing for the Taliban in Afghanistan and for a vigorous anti-Indian policy that included occasional resorts to terrorism.[37] The need to maintain the goodwill of those on whom the regime's position hinged, and whose ideational programs reflected intense religious beliefs, accounts for key aspects of Pakistan's renegade behavior.

Religion is not part of the legitimizing myth of all primary renegades. Although Libyan culture is thoroughly Islamic[38] and Qaddafi is a devout Muslim, the regime has been unbendingly secular, ruthlessly discouraging religious authorities from becoming a countervailing source of power. For Qaddafi, Islamic and Arabic identity were inextricably linked, making Islam a natural part of his pan-Arabist policies,[39] but defiance of the international community did not rest on hostility toward things non-Islamic, and it was not meant to buttress his position with diehard Islamists. Religion has not guided those Syrian policies qualifying it as a renegade, nor any significant aspect of Assad's policies. The regime's Baathist roots made it firmly secular, and the rulers' Alawi faith, with which not very many Syrians identified, could not have driven national policy. As Syria backed Shiite Iran it its war with Sunni-ruled Iraq, and since it intervened in support of Christian Maronites against Lebanese Muslims, the justifications for major policy could not involve religion.

The behavior of two further renegades also was not grounded in religious fervor or government ploys to secure the support of religious groups. For North Korea, this was precluded by the regime's ideological foundations, in which religion played no part. Pretty much the same applied to Yugoslavia, where Milošević and his lieutenants rose to power from positions within the post-Tito communist hierarchy, and whose Socialist Party was the renamed successor to the League of Communists.[40] At the grass roots, the surge of Serbian nationalism was entwined with a revival of the Orthodox faith, and this benefited the regime by inflaming the nationalism on which its legitimacy rested, fueling, in turn, hostility to Muslims and often to things Western. Still, the regime did not invoke religious symbols to justify assaults on other ethnic groups nor court the support of the Orthodox religious establishment.[41]

The conclusion is that the Manichaeism of radical religious beliefs may encourage policy excesses by regimes dependent on the endorsement of religious communities. This can even apply to secular rulers seeking in pious professions a source of domestic legitimacy. Religion may play its role independently or as a component of nationalist identity, where it amplifies the feelings associated with ethno-nationalist self-affirmation and elevates the community's sense of grievance against others to a transcendental, metaphysical plane. Nevertheless, since its impact was evident only in five of our nine cases, religious mobilization is not a necessary foundation of renegade behavior.

The Ideological Imperative. Just as nationalism and religion cannot always be disentangled, so they are often fused with political ideology. Ideology's impact is strongest where grounded in religious beliefs with widespread temporal applications and requiring a struggle against the values of those whose natural nemesis the regime claims to be. Ideological crusades are sometimes intended to remedy specific injustices but more often meant to assert the nation's and regime's position as champion of sociopolitical virtue.

Thus, Islamist ideology has drawn a parallel between struggles pitting oppressors and oppressed at the intrasocietal and international levels, claiming that the Western world is deeply hostile to Islam. In every instance considered here — Iran, Sudan, and Afghanistan — the ideology justified support for those struggling on behalf of the Islamist creed and implied endorsement of their methods. In the process, Islamist ideology produced renegade behavior.

From Khomeini's perspective, the world is divided into two camps — the arrogant exploitive powers (*Mustakberin*) and the downtrodden (*Mustazefin*) — a distinction separating those who adhere to the path of Satan and disbelief from those who stick to God's path. From this follows the partition into *Dar-ul-Islam* (the realm of Islam, of peace and enlightenment) and *Dar-ul-Harb* (the realm of nonbelief, war, and corruption).[42] The political and the spiritual are tightly interwoven, as political action blends with divine duty. Alien normative assumptions must be rejected; in any case, foreign norm-setters are *Mustakberin*, who must be challenged and defeated. According to Khomeini, "We must settle our accounts with great [powers] and superpowers, and show them that we can take on the whole world ideologically, despite all the painful problems that face us."[43] Iran's stance against the international normative order follows these beliefs, and support of international terrorism could be justified in their terms.

Similar beliefs with similar policy implications guided the Sudanese regime. Ideology did not address international issues with the focus devoted to narrower social issues,[44] but the sense of Muslim exceptionalism and antipathy toward non-Muslims produced, as with Khomeini, a political assumption of victimization at foreign hands. As Turabi explained it:

> [Muslim minorities] are facing real challenges in non-Muslim countries; some of their most sacred territories are under occupation; and their role in the world is negligible. Freedom, democracy, and pluralism are mere slogans raised to suppress the Muslims. . . . We are under the military control of our enemies who, if not occupying our land, are busy creating conflict among us and arming all the warring parties. We are not allowed to develop our own industrial base, while their ambassadors, journalists, and their media penetrate our societies and recruit agents, individuals, and political parties to serve their interests.[45]

The outside world having declared its hostility to an ideology steeped in Turabi's conception of Islam, an alien normative order could not be a moral constraint on regime policies.

The fusion of ideology and religion was even more pronounced within Taliban Afghanistan, where it was almost impossible to distinguish political doctrine from theological premises mandating a unity of religious and secular authority, strict protocols of social conduct, and rigid constraints on some segments of society, particularly women and children. Antipathy to anything other than their own narrow beliefs followed from the primordial character these were assigned, placing the regime at loggerheads with the values of most other countries, a clash that became a pillar of regime legitimacy, as the fact of confrontation was assumed and advertised by the regime.[46]

In three other instances (Korea, Libya, and Yugoslavia), ideology was tailored to legitimacy needs, justifying the regime's special mission while setting it apart from the international order, but it had no religious roots. In the early 1950s North Korea's Kim Il-Sung decreed the philosophy of *Juche*, stressing national consciousness and autonomy, and exempting the country, by an ideal of extreme self-reliance, from expectations that would flow from a broad identification with the international community.[47] *Juche* provided an ideological rationale for harsh measures against Kim's opponents and for resisting the de-Stalinization encouraged by Khrushchev. It provided grounds for dismissing foreign normative premises, and it furnished reasons why the outside world, the "imperialists" especially, should be hostile to a nation standing for such elevated (and, to them, threatening) principles. It also embodied a sense of bitter historical grievance for foreign powers, ranging from China, to Japan, to the Soviet Union, to the United States.

Self-reliance, in *Juche*, has been connected to a militant nationalism that assumed that individual life gains its meaning via incorporation into the collectivity, where the ultimate collectivity is the nation. Defense of the nation, in turn, calls for a foundation of basic (i.e., heavy) industries, and, above all, for a powerful and self-sufficient military. Strength alone wins the respect of those who would challenge the nation's autonomy. In this regard, some have claimed that the government would have been illegitimate in the context of *Juche* had it *not* sought to acquire a nuclear weapons capability.[48] Bearing *Juche*'s torch, North Korea was conceived as having special international responsibilities, and parallels with Khomeini's Iran cannot be avoided. The best scholarly treatment of this ideology explains this:

> As the only genuine socialist system left, according to Juche theoreticians, North Korea has a historical mission to save humanity from capitalist materialism, consumerism, decadent culture, and moral decay. North Koreans are told that they have a sacred mission that must be fulfilled, or human history will end. The world will be hostile toward them out of fear of being overwhelmed by the virtuous ideology of *Juche*.[49]

Libya, too, produced a secular and egalitarian ideology, grandly titled the Third Universal Theory, that assumed Libyan ideological exceptionalism and international leadership.[50] Proclaimed in 1973, and later codified in Qaddafi's *Green Book*, the theory rejected both communism and capitalism in favor of direct democracy based on "popular congresses," where authority would be delivered to the people. Justice implies freedom from want and oppression, both domestic *and* international, requiring that all Arab nations, ultimately all Third World countries, form a united front against their exploiters. As in other renegade ideologies, a stark "we–they" sentiment, including feelings of past victimization and exploitation, permeated political doctrine. This, again, was an ideology claiming a unique grasp of the human condition and positioning Libya at the head of the struggle to change an unjust world order.

While lacking the sweeping pretension of *Juche* and the Third Universal Theory, the Milošević regime cobbled together an ideological rationale for a strong state and externally directed resentment. With communism's collapse, the regime sought to replace the previous ideological edifice with "a synthesis of state socialism and Serbianism."[51] What evolved was a doctrine placing collectivism over individual freedom and the institutions of civil society, and urging struggle against external foes. Here, "a conception of the national enemy or enemies — that is any ethnic group in Serbia or in any other republic viewed as opposing Serb interests — became the regime's central focus, and also served as a surrogate for the class enemy or retrograde economic and bureaucratic forces previously identified in communist doctrine."[52] This soon included bitterness toward an international community that rejected Serbia's nationalist claims. Textbooks at the time of the war in Bosnia were "brimming with xenophobia, contempt and hatred for neighboring countries, the European and world community," while "such texts fit well into the propaganda system which has made the war psychologically possible."[53] This was the same propaganda system on which the regime's claim to legitimacy rested, and it provided a rationale for defying internationally accepted principles of behavior, especially toward other ethnicities.

Ideology's connection to renegade behavior notwithstanding, it played no significant role in Iraq, Syria, or Pakistan. In the Iraqi and Syrian cases, the political creed rested on Baathist ideology, established in Syria in the 1940s and encouraging pan-Arabism, secularism, a vague socialism, and opposition to colonialism and its vestiges.[54] While Baathism furnished the institutional structure for regime rule, it did not make deep inroads into Iraqi society (a main reason for Saddam's turn to religion),[55] and its grip on the Syrian imagination always was weak.[56] In any case, the activities that made these regimes renegades — territorial aggression and pursuit of weapons of mass destruction in the Iraqi case, support for terrorism in both cases — were not rationalized, directly or indirectly, by Baathist themes. Nor has ideology played much of a role in Pakistan. Musharraf offered no organized statement of political principles upon coming to power (beyond nationalism, Islam, and a censure of corruption). When the regime changed course following September 11, it emphasized its commitment to secularism and modernization, and to the proper relation between government and Islamic hierarchy, but this did not amount to an ideology, and it did not overlap with Pakistan's primary renegade stage.

Still, an ideological basis for renegade behavior can be found in six of our nine cases. Where it had an impact, the ideology claimed unique regime insight into core social and political problems; it encompassed a theme of national exceptionalism and of the country's victimization at the hands of foreign powers, and it professed the conviction that the regime is uniquely called to conduct the struggle against the nation's oppressors and the world's ills.

Examination of the various ideational sources of renegade behavior yields three general conclusions. Most importantly, their impact is powerful and pervasive, and any ideational category (ethno-nationalist, religious, or ideological) can produce such behavior, although more than one category usually is involved. Their common denominator is a belief that the community has been deeply wronged, a Manichean vision pitting absolute virtue against its opposite, and a claim the regime and the country are called to a unique mission. Under the circumstances, hostility from the less virtuous and enlightened must be expected, while the stakes in the struggle justify extreme means.

Economic Objectives   Ideational drives behind renegade behavior should be balanced by economic concerns, sanctions being the common response to breaches of core international norms. But none of our nine renegades was deterred by the prospect of economic punishment, and this must be accounted for. Clues flow from (a) the place in the hierarchy of values to which the pursuit of wealth is relegated, and (b) the way in which national income is distributed. In the first case, material achievement may be subordinated to loftier goals — if economics must be sacrificed to higher ideals, no right-thinking person should object, while the regime should be rewarded for keeping values in proper perspective. In the second case, the domestic political costs of sanctions can be controlled by channeling existing national income to those whose backing the regime most needs, so that vested interests in supporting the government may thrive even during hard times. The two approaches can go hand in hand, and while neither is sustainable if the overall pie shrinks too much, they mitigate the political hazards of economic punishment. Both approaches can even help manage the consequences of noneconomic retaliation, including some level of military reprisal, since, here too, many of the consequences are economic.

Downplaying Economic Performance   North Korea illustrates this method of maintaining regime legitimacy in the face of bleak economic prospects. The assumption (imbedded in *Juche* ideology) that spiritual incentives are the only effective incitement to societal achievement degraded economic measures of regime performance: self-reliance, a sense of national collectivity, and a vigorous commitment to Korean reunification were the only standards by which the regime should be judged.[57] As Kim Il-Sung explained: "[If we only] foster individual selfishness among the people, and try to move the people merely with money, we cannot arouse their collective heroism and creative initiative."[58] Swamped by propaganda, without appeal to crass materialism, North Koreans were to be exhorted to prodigious levels of performance. Thus the "Chongsanri method and spirit,"[59] introduced in 1960 as a method of agricultural management, relied on work incentives that were spiritual and ideological, not material, to galvanize agricultural workers to improved production. A similar philosophy of incentives, the Taean method,[60] was ushered into the industrial sector the following year: party cell leaders inspiring workers, via ideological fervor, to achieve production goals.

Because fundamentalists like Khomeini have argued that society's spiritual core atrophies if in thrall to material preoccupations,[61] renegades immersed in radical Islam have good reasons for subordinating the quest for wealth to the concerns of a just, Islamic, society. The most important achievements of government here are the spiritual fulfillment of its people, while religious and economic precepts rarely attach much value to growth per se. The manner in which wealth is distributed, and the purpose to which it is put, matter far more than the amount amassed. Since authentically Islamic patterns of distribution and expenditure are inimical to most foreign values, one must expect international ill-will, while appreciating that an economy guided by justice is less vulnerable to external pressure than one devoted to growth. Government should be evaluated by the extent to which it promotes virtue, not affluence, and only economic policies grounded in Islamic ideals can serve this goal. As Hasan al-Turabi observed,

> Islamic movements alone are able to put into action economic programmes that cater for the religious and temporal needs of society, linking this life to the life to come and striking the magic balance between development and equity, man and the environment, material prosperity and moral values, science and beauty, and between other divergent aspects of life.[62]

The Taliban, too, were disturbed by the "amoral character of the entire growth industry"[63] steeped in the crass ethos of Western culture and secular liberalism. The economy should foster an Islamic vision of social harmony and justice — a proper relation between public and private sphere, a sense of mutual responsibility among economic actors, and a guaranteed minimal level of welfare — mere growth being neither here nor there. Even Qaddafi's economic vision developed in his Green Book, although based as much on secular as Islamic virtues, emphasized basic needs and egalitarianism rather than the accrual of wealth.[64]

Though not all renegade regimes explicitly downplay the value of economic growth, some insulation from the political consequences of material hardship comes from even an implicit assumption that something more valuable than wealth is being promoted and that, if foreign sanctions are the price, then it is worth paying. Thus, the nationalist aspirations of Yugoslavia and Pakistan have, for many citizens, outweighed the importance of income, even though these two regimes, as well as those of Syria and Iraq, did not make a doctrinal point of minimizing the value of prosperity.

Encouraging Vested Economic Interests in Supporting the Regime   Primary renegades have also sought to give crucial segments of society a stake in the regime even under difficult conditions. The main purpose of preferential treatment may not be to manage the domestic political risks of external economic punishment — often it just follows from the regime's ideological premises — but this benefit cannot be ignored, particularly where the influence of favored groups is considerable.

The North Korean regime, especially since the early 1960s, neglected popular standards of living while indulging the national security establishment. By the second year of the 1961–1967 Seven Year Plan, it promoted a full-fledged war economy, focusing on heavy industry and military production.[65] Although the regime's efforts to downplay the importance of personal income, along with prevailing egalitarianism, helped mute popular frustration with dismal living standards, those within the privileged sectors of the economy must have perceived the silver lining.

Few renegades directed as much of the country's income toward the national security establishment as North Korea, but many favored these sectors at the expense of others. Saddam Hussein spent considerably on advanced weaponry, raising the salaries of military personnel, and ensuring their preferential access to housing and consumer goods. He also solicited the goodwill of other pivotal groups. Large sums were directed toward conciliating the country's Shiite majority, renovating shrines and rebuilding their towns. A new highway was built between the holy cities of Najaf and Karbala, with housing and tourist facilities along the way. Illustrating the significance of government largess, communities closer to Baghdad, or considered a greater threat, received more economic favors than those further away.[66]

Slobodan Milošević also promoted the economic fortunes of narrow segments of Serbian society, forging potent vested interests in his regime. Stalled privatization and some renationalizations allowed him to create an economic elite on whose support he could count,[67] and he invested considerably in the police establishment's loyalty. Internal security forces were given missions and weapons (including anti-aircraft and heavy artillery) not normally associated with police functions, as well as salaries and other perquisites superior to those of the military and other state employees. The gap between the standards of living of the police and other public employees increased along with the country's economic difficulties, as a symbiosis of interests ensured the former's interest in supporting the regime no matter how badly the rest of the country was faring.

While treating the national security sector well, the Syrian regime also sought to muster other support via its redistributive policies. Conservative Muslim opposition was anticipated, and Hafez al-Assad encouraged a countervailing coalition of both modernizing and traditionally disposed interests. Economic liberalization was promoted to please the urban middle class while landless peasants were wooed with a program of land redistribution coupled with extensive irrigation projects. Family allowances were increased and health insurance was improved, as were pensions and social security. It is not certain that any of this was intended to ensure loyalty in the face of possible economic sanctions, but that may have been an incidental benefit that made renegade foreign policy less perilous politically.

Sudan's Bashir-Turabi regime did its best to favor actual or potential allies. Ever since it was in a position to do so, the National Islamic Front (NIF) entrenched its backers in the most dynamic sectors of the economy. The NIF began by acquiring leading positions in the Bank of Sudan; then, to boost its support in the countryside, BoS required that all banks devote 40 percent of local currency to fund agriculture. In addition, the regime's privatization program aimed to place firms that were wholly or partially state-owned in the hands of NIF sympathizers. For example, the White Nile Tannery and Sudan textiles were sold cheaply to members or supporters of the NIF.[68]

Some renegades' redistributive policies reflected their ideological programs. Khomeini's Iran, striving to transcend the struggle between exploiters and exploited, channeled money from the state, national security establishment, and economic elites to the nation's dispossessed — creating, temporarily at least, a stratum of society whose economic betterment was owed to the fundamentalist regime. Although the Islamic Revolution devastated the national economy, one of its first moves was to raise the minimum daily wage by 167 percent.[69] Nationalization of banks, insurance companies, and, later, a number of manufacturing facilities provided the government with the means to pursue redistributive policies, as did the creation of the Mustazafin Foundation, financed by the assets of the Shah, of Iranians who fled the country, and of executed regime opponents.

Qaddafi's regime also offered a radical view of economic justice. An early measure was to increase the wages of all Libyan workers, and to provide an array of social, educational, and health care services. It launched housing projects and ambitious programs of land redistribution. In 1973 the regime mandated that all firms with more than ten employees give a quarter of their profits to their workers. While many of these initiatives were financed by a prospering rentier economy almost wholly dependent on oil revenues, the effect was to identify some sectors of society as ideologically and economically favored.[70]

If the Iranian and Libyan regimes showed real concern for the dispossessed, the Taliban, its religious roots notwithstanding, was startlingly indifferent to the destitute and to the impact of its policies on their predicament. The regime was most attentive to the interests of warlords and regional potentates, whose economic fortunes rested on the opium trade and smuggling from Pakistan and the Gulf states. The Taliban tolerated an opium economy and provided the rural security in which it could flourish, while a further collusion of interests between political authorities and economic profiteers was ensured with high government positions for smugglers and truck traders.[71] Whatever hardships the rest of the population endured, powerful vested interests were created in the Taliban's continued incumbency.

Except for Musharraf's Pakistan, all of our renegades attempted to bind the economic interests of key segments of society to the regime's survival, while several sought, simultaneously, to downplay the importance of economic achievement. Such strategies diminish concerns with foreign economic retaliation, allowing the regimes to act on incentives associated with their ideational goals, implying that regimes with a stake in deviance may not be deterred by an economically rooted stake in conformity.

Direct Links

The political benefits to the regime from its delinquent behavior generally spring from broad national sympathies with its objectives; the link is thus indirect. But collision with the international community may also directly shape domestic political rewards, so that the very assumption of external enmity boosts the regime's position, allowing opponents to be portrayed as associates of external enemies and, sometimes, generating a rally-round-the-flag effect.

With primary renegades direct benefits do not flow from the *responses* of others (they have not yet reacted to renegade behavior), but from the assumed incompatibility between national objectives and external norms, implying that foreign nations harbor malevolent intentions. Domestic opponents can then be linked to the country's natural foes, often justifying repressive measures against them, while the regime reaps the political rewards of its readiness to stand up to international pressure. Direct links are more apparent with secondary renegades, who can point to concrete instances of external pressure and hostility, but they may also exist at the primary stage, as long as the policy objectives are naturally antithetical to those of leading foreign nations.

The early period of Iran's Islamic Revolution was marked by rifts even among Islamists who disagreed on such issues as the role of the state in secular matters, the place of democratic procedure within a theocratic regime, and foreign policy priorities. Khomeini's closest followers often accused their detractors of treasonous foreign sympathies. After the shah's ouster, although Khomeini retained ultimate authority, state power was divided between Mahdi Bazargan, as head of government, and the Islamic Revolutionary Council (IRC). Differences between Khomeini and Bazargan surfaced when the latter urged moderation on matters of revolutionary justice, and, in particular, on the issue of the U.S. hostages captured by pro-Khomeini militants. But the hostage crisis benefited the regime's domestic position: "By concentrating Iranian attention on the past and present misdeeds of the U.S. in Iran, the American hostage crisis united the nation, and strengthened the radicals within the regime at the expense of the moderates."[72]

The press, at the IRC's behest, insinuated that Bazargan had sinister links to Zbigniew Brzezinsky, President Carter's national security adviser,[73] eventually forcing him to resign while Khomeini transferred much of his authority to the IRC. Abol Hassan Bani-Sadr, elected president in 1980, soon emerged as symbol of a liberal Islam pitted against the rigid Islamic Republican Party (IRP), preferred by Khomeini. Accused by the IRP of being in cahoots with the Central Intelligence Agency, Bani-Sadr was ousted in June by the Majlis. The new prime minister, Muhammad Reza Bonahar, declared that the government "is resolved to stand against the factionalists and not allow society to become a haven for the factions attached to imperialism and international Zionism."[74] Thus, charges of an American affiliation helped the regime undermine its opponents and cement its own position.

Though Qaddafi, during this early period, did not systematically charge putative opponents with disloyal foreign sympathies, the theme of nefarious foreign influences was floated in tandem with warnings against reactionary and bureaucratic forces, and against internal enemies such as communism, the Muslim Brotherhood, and Baathism. Thus, the Zwara Declaration of 1973, adumbrating Qaddafi's political doctrine, called for the elimination of ideological strands described as "political illnesses," an administrative revolution to bring power to the people, and a cultural revolution to eliminate "foreign cultural influences."[75] Going even further, he urged the "burning of books that contain imperialist, capitalist, reactionary, Jewish or Communist thought,"[76] much of which was associated with alien perspectives. The opposition of things Libyan to things foreign served to curb opposition to the regime.

Two weeks after assuming power, in July 1979, Saddam Hussein announced the discovery of a plot to overthrow the regime. Unsurprisingly, the "conspirators" were found to be part of a design led by U.S. imperialism in the interests of Israel. Such charges, while widening the chasm between Iraq and other countries, presented some benefits: "By fueling the xenophobic sentiments of his subjects against the 'evil forces of imperialism and Zionism,' he managed to rally the masses behind his leadership." [77] The assumption that those opposing Saddam acted at the behest of foreign enemies made a rift with part of the international community politically useful, casting suspicion on anyone displaying less than wholehearted support of his regime.

Milošević also portrayed the international community, the West in particular, as the enemy of Serbian aspirations. He explained the breakup of Yugoslavia to a Russian journalist:

> I will tell you bluntly, it is German policy that lies behind all of these events. It is the German-Catholic alliance's interest to destroy not just our country but yours too. . . . It all began with the unification of Germany. As soon as that happened, Germany began punishing the victors in the Second World War. . . . Yugoslavia was the first casualty of revanchism.[78]

Having defined the West as the foe, the regime's opponents were charged with seditious foreign sympathies. Prime Minister Milan Panić, who became critical of Milošević's policies, was accused of letting "foreign powers dominate the government's policy," thus endangering "the very survival of the Serbian people."[79] The regime described Yugoslav politics as a struggle between "patriots" (Milošević's supporters) and "traitors" (the opposition), implying that the fidelity to Serbian interests of those seeking accommodation with the international community should be questioned. When Panić challenged Milošević in the Serbian presidential election, he was forced to defend himself from claims of treasonous U.S. connections. Increasingly, reasons were found why the West and those sympathetic to its positions were enemies of the Serbian people. "Within such a world-view international isolation became a state of virtue rather than a national disaster."[80]

Thus, even primary renegades may find that a clash between domestically resonant goals and international values primes the domestic political reward structure, so that the regime's opponents can be vilified as foreign sympathizers or agents and support drawn toward itself. The symbiosis between the assumption of international enmity and society's mobilization around the regime may become so firm that explicit accusations of that sort become redundant. While Kim Il-Sung's purges of the late 1950s required that his detractors be branded foreign stooges, such charges eventually became superfluous. He rammed the assumption of external threat so deeply into the nation's political psyche that any political opposition was assumed to imperil the nation's security. In this manner, the purges of 1966 could be undertaken with no need for elaborate justification.

Accordingly, the prospect of political benefits from assumed international hostility can prompt deviance even before the international system has stigmatized the regime and responded accordingly, but this is not required for the genesis of primary renegades, as long as the delinquent policy itself can bolster the regime's position. Thus, not all primary renegades seek to structure domestic politics around an assumption of unholy alliance between their rivals and foreign foes. Such assumptions were unnecessary to Assad's regime during its early years. They were not a meaningful part of the politics of Musharraf's Pakistan. There is little evidence that, as primary renegades, the Taliban or the Bashir regime relied on imputed foreign sympathies to discredit their opponents. In each of these cases, it appears that the strength of its objectives was considered sufficient to legitimize the regime and discredit its opponents.

Our cases so far suggest a link between, on the one hand, certain ideational pursuits, political-economic conditions, and domestic political strategies, and, on the other hand, the genesis of primary renegades. But, as argued in chapter 3, only limited inferences about the causes of an outcome can be drawn from an exclusive examination of cases where it has occurred. Accordingly, we now compare the renegades to the regimes in our comparison set and within the terms of our theoretical framework

A Comparative Perspective

If we seek information about sufficient rather than necessary causes, or about the covariation of outcomes and antecedent conditions, we must also examine regimes that, on the basis of antecedent evidence could have been *expected* to become renegades, and ask why they did not. In chapter 3, we settled on six cases of regimes displaying two apparently necessary conditions for renegade status: (1) a lack of authentic democracy, and (2) a quest for a new basis of regime legitimacy. These were the Algerian regime following suspension of the 1992 election, the Aliyev regime in Azerbaijan, the post-Nasserite regime in Egypt, the regime of the Nigerian generals, the Suharto regime in Indonesia, and the regime of Yemen following its reunification in 1990. We begin, as before, by considering indirect links between regime position and transgressive international behavior.

Indirect Links

Ideational Sources   Not one of the six regimes sought to build its legitimacy on grand ideational professions or on fears of external threats to the country's ethnic integrity, faith, or ideological programs. Given a nondemocracy seeking a new basis for legitimacy, the manner in which ideational themes are exploited is a powerful predictor of renegade conduct.

If nationalist drives have not led regimes within the comparison set to violate basic international norms, this is not because they have been spared ethnic and other forms of internal fragmentation. Indonesia's largest ethnicity is the Javanese, but even they account for less than half the population, while Sundanese, Madurese, Coastal Malays, and other groups make this one of the more heterogeneous countries in the world. Azerbaijanis face the presence of minority Armenians striving, within Nagorno-Karabakh, for union with Armenia. Nigeria is fractured among more than 250 ethnic groups, the Hausa, Yoruba, and Igbo being the most numerous. Although 80 percent of Algeria's population is Arabic, Berbers are a vocal minority. Moreover, internal fissures are not the only threat to a sense of national identity, since the 130-year history of French colonialism has imprinted layers of French culture competing with the dominant Arabism. Only Yemen and Egypt have a largely homogenous population.

Despite national fragmentation, none of these regimes built their legitimacy on ethnic grievances or by seeking national self-affirmation in the face of external enemies. This does not mean that concerns about national cohesion have not marred Nigerian or Indonesian politics, or that resentment against Armenian separatists and the Armenian state have not affected Aliyev's regime in Azerbaijan. But in none of these cases has the regime's right to rule rested on the claim that it would address an ethnic or nationalist imperative. Post-Nasser Egypt also saw a gradual abandonment of pan-Arab nationalism as its leitmotif. Some enduring distrust between North and South aside, nationalism has played no great role in the politics of Saleh's Yemen. The Algerian regime undertook a program of Arabization — directed against Berber identity and the lingering influence of French culture — and only here do we find a meaningful element of nationalism at the base of regime legitimacy; but in this case a very mild nationalism. By eschewing radical nationalism, the regimes within the comparison set are similar to those of Syria and Afghanistan under the Taliban. Why then did the latter, but not the former, become renegades? One possibility, preserving the role of ideational influences, is that religion exerted a different impact in the two sets of countries.

Religious foundations of regime legitimacy permit excesses not easily justifiable by anything less than the imperatives of the True Faith, but there are no such foundations within the comparison set. Nigerian society is intensely religious, roughly equally divided between Muslims and Christians, and its military rulers are associated with the Muslim North, but the regime did not base its rule on religion. Even plans to join the Organization of the Islamic Conference were dropped in the face of Christian opposition, and while a number of Nigerian states adopted the Shariah, this was not encouraged by federal authorities. Algeria, though mostly Muslim, has always had secular governments opposed to a political role for the clergy. For much of postindependence history, Imams had to be appointed by the state, which sought to co-opt moderate clerics into its structure of power. The regime cracked down on the FIS after its electoral victories in 1992, ultimately causing it to disband. In Azerbaijan, Aliyev, a former Communist Party boss, had no more grounds for building legitimacy on a religious foundation than did Milošević. In any case, Azerbaijan Muslims (who account for over 90 percent of the population) appear to have stronger ties to family, clan, and ethnic group than to religious groups.[81] Indonesia (88 percent of whose population is Muslim), has had secular governments. The Suharto regime was deeply averse to any form of ideational mobilization, and by the mid-1980s traces of previously influential Muslim parties had been obliterated. Although Suharto engaged in a light amount of religious symbolism (most notably, a pilgrimage to Mecca in 1991), there had been no movement toward a Muslim polity and very little attempt to shroud the regime's pragmatically modernizing policies in religious garb.[82] The post-Nasser regime (like Nasser's own) claimed Islamic credentials, but within a secular context — earning the regime the enmity of Egypt's religious fundamentalists. Yemen has its Islamic hardliners (the Islah Party) but they are not a meaningful part of the ruling General Popular Congress (GPC) and have exerted little influence on President Ali Abdulah Saleh. In sum, religion, like nationalism, has not provided a major fount of legitimacy for the regimes in our comparison set. What about ideology?

Several renegades developed a unique ideology implying political exceptionalism and placing the regime at loggerheads with less "enlightened" beliefs. Within the comparison set, however, one searches in vain for evidence of ideological ardor. Generally, the absence is understandable. A former communist like Aliyev could not easily package his pragmatism as ideological doctrine; nor could the Nigerian military dictators plausibly have couched their raw pursuit of power and wealth in ideological terms. Algerian leaders from Ahmed Ben Bella to Chadli Benjedid espoused a mild form of socialism, but the post-1992 regime was more concerned with curbing Islamic fundamentalism than with articulating an abstract political creed. The Suharto regime, which seized power on an anticommunist platform, was suspicious of anything suggesting ideological enthusiasm. In what has been termed a "deliberate disavowal of politics,"[83] it was guided by an authoritarian, modernizing pragmatism. The regime came to adopt an essentially corporatist notion of how interests should be aggregated, and the closest it came to an articulation of political principles was a vague reference to Pancasila, an amorphous concept developed at independence and claiming to incorporate the five general principles embraced by all Indonesians.[84] Nasser made much of Egyptian socialism — a "scientific socialism" suited to national conditions and at variance with "godless" Marxism — but his successors spurned ideological fervor. Economic renewal with greater respect for market principles (the regime's Infitah) came to dominate Egyptian political-economic beliefs. Although socialism has not officially been abandoned, pragmatism is indubitably the key to national policy.[85] With the Saleh regime in Yemen, there is no evidence of explicit ideology, beyond a general commitment to eventual democracy.

We assumed that ideational forces might provide a stake in deviance while economic needs create a stake in conformity, but we found no evidence of ideational drives within our comparison set. Since, however, economic policies are shaped by core beliefs, the absence of a pronounced ideational foundation of regime legitimacy has also boosted the deterrent effect of potential economic sanctions.

Economic Concerns   For the renegades, economic concerns failed to create a decisive stake in compliance because the regimes downplayed the importance of economic growth and/or because they created a core of vested economic interests more dependent on the regime than on the international economy. The contrast with the comparison set is stark: here, no regime dismissed the importance of prosperity in favor of loftier ideals. Unapologetic materialism may, in part, reflect weak ideological or religious pillars of regime legitimacy. The Nigerian and Indonesian leadership's brazen pursuit of personal enrichment, and the massive corruption they encouraged, would, in any case, have made it difficult for them to argue lucre's subordination to grand ideals. Less unabashed venality marked Azerbaijan, and especially Algeria, but these regimes have based their legitimacy on pragmatic improvements in their countries' political and economic conditions, not exceptional ideational missions. The main themes of Azerbaijani politics revolve around stability, Nagorno-Karabakh, and improved living standards. Algerian politics, although marked by the chasm separating fundamentalist and secular Islam and to a lesser extent by Arabization, has touted stability and economic betterment. Egypt's Infitah was an explicit doctrine of economic growth on market principles, and it has become the guiding theme of the country's politics. Once one of the poorest countries in the world, Yemen discovered oil in the early 1980s, which launched its economic growth, and there is no evidence that wealth is not considered very desirable. The difference between renegades and the comparison set is conspicuous.

Were they to invite economic sanctions, could regimes within the latter have expected that, as a result of preferential access to national wealth, a powerful segment of the population — one whose welfare was shielded from international retaliation — would defend them? The point obviously is moot, but the political risks would have been substantial, since structures of power and privilege may not have provided the regime with sufficient buffer against the resentment of those bearing the full brunt of the hardships.

While Algerian governments, from independence until 1992, professed a partiality for the urban and rural working class, not much of this survived the change of regime. In addition, as a result of economic stagnation, social investment in housing, welfare, and infrastructure declined, while scarce resources have been deflected toward the importation of basic goods.[86] At the same time, and despite the role of the security forces in a country torn by internecine conflict, no rich clique appears to have benefited from improper government favors. Like Azerbaijan, Yemen is pervaded with microcorruption; like Algeria, there are no major economic elites benefiting from an illicit connection to government. Egypt's Infitah leaves little room for policies favoring the poor, but it would be hard to identify a powerful group of rich beneficiaries of corrupt regime connections.

The Azerbaijani, Nigerian, and Indonesian cases differ from the above. While microcorruption pervades Azerbaijan's social fabric, there have also been malodorous practices at the pinnacle of political authority — including nepotism (Aliyev's son was made head of the State Oil Company and eventually succeeded his father in October 2003) and economic favors for regime supporters[87] — creating vested economic interest in the regime's survival. The Indonesian situation is straightforward. Suharto made himself a billionaire, and also members of his family, by grabbing control of state monopolies and exploiting the opportunity that *yayasans* (purportedly charitable foundations) provided for shielding wealth from public scrutiny.[88] Suharto cronies (largely from the military establishment) benefited from state economic concessions, special access to government permits and monopolies, soft loans, and so forth, creating vested interests in supporting the regime. Of the three, only the Nigerian case is ambiguous. Nigeria's was an exceptionally corrupt and incompetent government,[89] the leadership's practice of skimming off oil profits reaching "astronomical proportions,"[90] but virtually all the proceeds went into the pockets of the leaders themselves, rather than of groups on whose support they may have been forced to rely.

If the comparison regimes had considered behaving in an internationally delinquent way, the domestic risks of sanctions would, in most cases, have exceeded those faced by the actual renegades.

Direct Links

Primary renegades sometimes use the presumption of international enmity to link their rivals to nefarious foreign forces and rally increased support for themselves, but we find little evidence of such tactics within the comparison set. These regimes often are internally beleaguered, and they deal roughly with their opponents, but they have not often accused them of acting in the interests of foreign enemies. Egypt and Algeria have treated their Islamist elements as domestically rooted threats. One encounters few pronouncements by the Nigerian generals or the Azerbaijani government linking those who would oppose them to external foes. Even during the brief 1994 civil conflict in Yemen, no charges of treasonous loyalties were leveled.

The only regime that sought to boost its legitimacy by accusing its opponents of unsavory foreign ties was the Suharto regime in Indonesia, which, during the massive killing and imprisonment of real and suspected communists, occasionally linked its victims to foreign communist powers.[91] Still, this is our single example of an attempt to derive a domestic political benefit from the assumed hostility of some part of the international community.

A Quantitative View

At this juncture, it may be useful to express our findings in numerical form. Let us begin with two observations from a "truth table" summarizing our findings in binary terms (table 4.1).

The first is that primary renegades and nonrenegades differ starkly on the causal variables: the former generally score positively; the latter rarely do (sums of predictor categories scored as 1 are displayed in the last column). Therefore, much in our theoretical framework and associated analysis helps discriminate one group from the other, confirming the value of the chosen approach. The second observation addresses *configurations* of circumstances that best predict the genesis of renegades. Although indirect (ideational and economic) links do better than direct links, several configurations are possible. Renegades may score positively on one, two, or three of the ideational categories and on one or two of the economic ones, and sometimes also on direct links. The lack of a characteristic pattern extends to ideational predictors: when renegades score positively on some subset of ideational categories, no specific subset (e.g., nationalism and religion) is unambiguously favored. Thus, for example, two of our renegades score positively on both religion and nationalism, three score positively on nationalism and ideology, one scores positively on religion and ideology, two score positively on all three ideational dimensions, and only one (Syria) scores on none. Predictive power rests in the ideational basis of regime legitimacy, not in the specific

TABLE 4.1 Truth Table for the Genesis of Renegades

Country	Renegade	Indirect Links					Direct Links	Σ
		Ideational		Ideology	Material			
		Nationalism	Religion		Downplay Economic	Insulating Supporters		
Afghanistan	1	0	1	1	1	1	0	4
Pakistan	1	1	1	0	0	0	0	2
Iran	1	1	1	1	1	1	1	6
Iraq	1	1	1	0	0	1	1	4
Libya	1	1	0	1	1	1	1	5
Sudan	1	1	1	1	1	1	1	5
Syria	1	0	0	0	0	1	0	1
N. Korea	1	1	0	1	1	1	1	5
Yugoslavia	1	1	0	1	0	1	1	4
Algeria	0	0	0	0	0	0	0	0
Indonesia	0	0	0	0	0	1	1	2
Azerbaijan	0	0	0	0	0	1	0	1
Egypt	0	0	0	0	0	0	0	0
Yemen	0	0	0	0	0	0	0	0
Nigeria	0	0	0	0	0	0	0	0

TABLE 4.2 Primary Renegades and Ideational Drives

	Renegade	Non-Renegade
Ideational Drive	Afg, Pak, Iran, Iraq, Libya, Sudan, N. Korea, Yugoslavia (8)	(0)
No *Ideational Drive*	Syria (1)	Indon, Azerb, Algeria, Egypt, Yemen, Nigeria (6)

configurations of its categories. At the same time, all of our renegades (with the exception of Pakistan) scored positively in at least one of the variables that indicate an ability to weather foreign economic punishment. As expected, direct links do not predict the genesis of renegade regimes as well as indirect links.

We may pin some further numbers on our findings. Though our N is larger than in many comparative case studies, the statistical techniques generally used for binary dependent variables are pretty much precluded by minimal degrees of freedom. Instead, the analysis will be cast in terms that I believe to be (a) suited to the amount and nature of the information involved here, and (b) meaningful in terms of the way in which our minds generally conceive of causality. The method has the added advantage that, should the reader be unhappy with my interpretation of some case, he or she can introduce the modification into the analysis and assess the implications for the final conclusions.

Let us consider the odds of encountering a renegade given the presence or absence of the antecedent conditions, comparing this to the relative odds of encountering a nonrenegade, given the presence or absence of the antecedent condition. The resulting quantity, the *odds-ratio*, is frequently encountered in the statistical literature for the analysis of cross-tabulated data (though not often seen in political science). [92] The logic is that, given an antecedent (C) and consequent condition (O), both of which measured in binary terms, we can express the likelihood of experiencing the outcome, given the antecedent factor, as:

$$\Omega_c = P(O|C)/P(\sim O|C),$$

where $P(O|C) = P(O \cap C)/P(C)$, and identically for other conditional probabilities.

$$\Omega_{\sim c} = P(O|\sim C)/P(\sim O|\sim C)$$

Ω_c captures the *odds* that O would be present given the presence of C; $\Omega_{\sim c}$ depicts the odds that O would be present in the case of $\sim$C. The two odds can be contrasted by examining their ratio:

$$\omega = \Omega_c /\Omega_{\sim c}$$

Beginning with indirect links, and asking whether the regime relied on one or more of the ideational bases of legitimacy (if so $I = 1$; if not $I = 0$) and whether it became a renegade ($R = 1$) or not ($R = 0$).

$$\Omega_{R,I = 1} = P(R = 1|I = 1)/P(R = 0|I = 1),$$

and

$$\Omega_{R,I = 0} = P(R = 1|I = 0)/P(R = 0/I = 0),$$

$$\omega = \Omega_{R,I = 1} /\Omega_{R,I = 0} = 74,$$

indicating a very much greater likelihood that a renegade would emerge when its legitimacy rested on a radical ideational base than when it did not

Moving to the economic variable, and inquiring whether at least one of the two economic strategies coincides with renegade behavior, we obtain table 4.3.

Here, going directly to the final odds-ratio, $\omega = 16$.

Although the ratio is not quite as high as in the previous case, it is nevertheless substantial, indicating that the odds of becoming a renegade assuming the appropriate economic strategies is 16 times greater than without them.

Finally, we ask if renegade behavior goes hand-in-hand with a direct link (see table 4.4).

In this case, $\omega = 10$: the odds that a regime would become a renegade are ten times greater when such conduct provides a direct political benefit

TABLE 4.3 Primary Renegades and Economic Strategies

	Renegade	Non-Renegade
Renegade Economic Strategy	Iran, Iraq, Libya, Sudan, Afg, Syria N. Korea, Yugo (8)	Indonesia, Azerbaijan (2)
No Renegade Economic Strategy	Pakistan (1)	Algeria, Egypt Yemen, Nigeria (4)

TABLE 4.4 Primary Renegades and Direct Links

	Renegade	Nonrenegade
Direct Link	Iran, Iraq, Libya, Sudan, N. Korea, Yugo (6)	Indonesia (1)
No Direct Link	Afg, Pak, Syria (3)	Alg, Azerb, Egypt, Yemen, Nigeria (5)

than when it does not. Taken together, the results coincide strongly with expectations. Ideational bases for regime legitimacy are, by far, the most powerful predictor. Not every individual ideational category is this potent; separately, each has a ω close to that of the economic and direct-political variables. Taken together, however, the effect is powerful, and it says much about the circumstances that drive primary renegades.

Another way to consider these relationships is through the distinction between necessary and sufficient conditions. Although we usually say that a condition is or is not necessary, is or is not sufficient, we also can conceive of a continuum of certainty — saying, for example, that a cause *tends* to be sufficient or necessary — the strength of that tendency expressed as some number between 0 and 1. Since a necessary condition is one without which the outcome cannot occur, it involves only the first column of tables 4.2–4.4. The extent to which the cause tends to be necessary is expressed as the

TABLE 4.5 Primary Renegades: Necessary and Sufficient Conditions

	Necessary	Sufficient
Ideational	$P(R=1|I=1) - P(R=1|I=0)$ $= 0.85$	$P(R=1|I=1) - P(R=0|I=1)$ $= 1.0$
Economic	$P(R=1|E=1) - P(R=1|E=0)$ $= 0.59$	$P(R=1|E=1) - P(R=0|E=1)$ $= 0.60$
Direct	$P(R=1|D=1) - P(R=1|D=0)$ $= 0.38$	$P(R=1|D=1) - P(R=0|D=1)$ $= 0.65$

difference between the conditional probability of the outcome when the assumed cause is present and the comparable conditional probability when it is absent — a number that will vary between 0 and 1 (if the outcome is always present given the condition, and always absent without the condition, the conditional probability would be 1). Since sufficiency assumes the outcome, it involves only the first row of the tables. Here extent of sufficiency can be expressed as the difference between the conditional probability of getting the outcome with the antecedent condition and the probability of not getting it with the antecedent condition. Table 4.5 displays the results.

The results confirm what we have seen so far. The strongest set of both necessary and sufficient conditions is that of an ideational nature. Neither necessity nor sufficiency is quite as pronounced for the economic variable, although here the condition of necessity fares better than in the case of direct links. The theoretical frameworks expectations are thus substantially vindicated by both the qualitative and the comparative analyses.

The pattern of causation behind the genesis of primary renegades is summarized in figure 4.1.

To Summarize

The comparative analysis yields three general conclusions. The first is that transgressive behavior is usually driven by attempts to bolster regime position via a zealous pursuit of radical ideational goals, exempting the regime from common normative expectations of other nations. The second is that renegade behavior is more likely where regimes feel able to weather international retaliation — because material hardship may not affect their

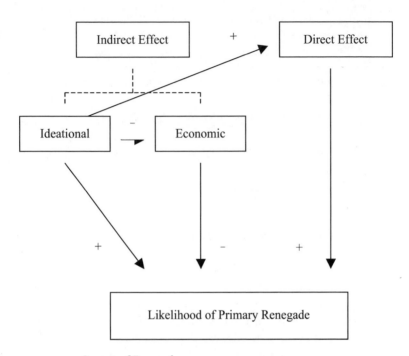

FIGURE 4.1 Genesis of Renegades

legitimacy or because economically favored groups would defend them.
Both conclusions establish an indirect link between delinquent conduct and
regime position. Our third conclusion concerns direct links, finding that,
even at the primary stage, they sometimes encourage renegade behavior.
This is most probable where the ideational premises are deemed necessarily
incompatible with those pursued elsewhere.

5 Secondary Renegades and Nonmilitary Responses

Other nations, norm-setters most notably, have now responded to the regimes, and different assumptions apply. While both indirect and direct links mattered for primary renegades, more weight was attributed to the former. For secondary renegades, objects of international reprisals, the opposite applies. Although, before, ideational aspirations dominated economic concerns, the situation is reversed at the secondary stage: on the one hand, with the passage of time economic needs weigh more heavily than lofty ideals; on the other hand, external retaliation typically targets the country's economy. Consequently, economic considerations loom large in the thinking of secondary renegades.

Economic sanctions are the preferred method of dealing with those who violate major international norms. They are a tangible expression of displeasure, and they rarely imply excessive costs for the nation imposing the sanction.[1] Their main purpose is to create such hardship within the target country that anger is directed toward the responsible regime, impelling it to abandon or mitigate its transgressions. Their popularity notwithstanding, the literature has concluded that sanctions are not particularly effective.[2] Does this judgment apply as well when the targets are renegade regimes?

The Impact of Sanctions

In response to sanctions, renegades can move toward compliance, or not. Syria, Pakistan, and Sudan have partially reformed, five renegades did not reform at all (three were forcibly ousted), and Libya alone is now a fully compliant regime. As far as the effectiveness of sanctions for behavior modification is concerned, then, we encounter four cases of potential (partial or complete) success (Libya, Sudan, Syria, Pakistan), and five instances of apparent failure (Iran, Iraq, Yugoslavia, Afghanistan, North Korea). Since every renegade suffered economic reprisal, and since the course of their behavior has varied, let us ask how effective sanctions are at modifying renegade behavior. Two models might guide our examination.

Two Models of Sanctions Effectiveness

The Incentive-Offsetting (IO) Model   It is often assumed that sanctions enter the regime's calculations as an independent consideration, one that, through the hardship caused, offsets whatever stakes in delinquency had driven its behavior. Here, sanctions do not alter existing drives, they counteract them — adding a stake in compliance to the existing stake in deviance: the relative weight of the two determining the course of regime behavior. This perspective suggests that the effectiveness of sanctions depends on the thoroughness with which they are applied: the heavier the sanctions, the more likely compliance.

To establish whether this has, indeed, been the case, we need a credible measure of the weightiness of sanctions, whereas a simple and meaningful distinction separates comprehensive from partial sanctions. Some sanctions involve a general ban on imports and exports from the target country, as well as on aid and financial transactions, often including a freeze on that government's assets abroad. Others are more limited, focusing on a specific type of transaction or restricted set of transactions. Thus, for example, economic sanctions on Syria involved a ban on U.S. military sales (1980) and economic aid (1986) but did not prohibit trade or private investment. The 2003 Syrian Accountability Act allows the president considerable latitude in implementing its provisions, which after considerable congressional pressure led him (in May 2004) to impose a ban on exports to, but not imports from, Syria. By contrast, sanctions against Iraq were comprehensive and inflexible, including a full UN trade embargo (1990) and a curb on multilateral assistance, plus, on the U.S. side, a freeze of Iraqi government assets (1990). We may thus distinguish two groups of renegades: those subjected to comprehensive sanctions by the United States and/or the United Nations, and those punished by restricted limitations on economic relations. By this standard, six of the renegades endured comprehensive sanctions, while three faced partial ones.

Have comprehensive sanctions, as the IO model predicts, been more effective than partial sanctions at inducing improved behavior? Table 5.2 organizes our renegades according to whether they have reformed (wholly or partly) or not, and whether they were subjected to comprehensive or partial sanctions. The IO model suggests that most reformed renegades should have suffered comprehensive sanctions; most unreformed renegades, partial sanctions.

TABLE 5.1 Targets of Comprehensive and Partial Sanctions

Comprehensive	Partial
Iran[a]	Pakistan[g]
Iraq[b]	Sudan[h]
Libya[c]	Syria[i]
Afghanistan[d]	
Yugoslavia[e]	
North Korea[f]	

a. Comprehensive U.S. trade and financial sanctions (1984, amplified in 1987, 1995 and 1996)

b. Full UN trade embargo (1990, modified 1991); U.S. blocked Iraqi assets (1990).

c. U.S. ban on military sales (1978), expanded to a ban on trade in 1982, with further amplification in 1986, and 1996. UN embargo on flights and arms transfers (1992); UN freezes Libyan funds (1993). U.S. sanctions lifted (2004).

d. U.S. ban on trade with Taliban, freeze of Taliban assets and ban on financial transactions (1999). UN flight ban (1999). UN freeze on Taliban assets and ban on military transactions (2000).

e. UN ban on military transfers (1991). Full UN trade embargo and flight ban (1992). U.S. trade embargo and blocking of assets (1992). UN sanctions suspended (1996).U.S. sanctions suspended (1996). UN ban on military transfers (1998). U.S. trade restrictions (1998). UN sanctions lifted 2001. U.S. sanctions lifted 2001.

f. U.S. ban on trade, financial transactions, travel, blocking of North Korean property (1950). Ends ban on exports and on travel (2000).

g. Denial of U.S. support for multilateral aid (1998). Relaxed two months later, and again seven months later. Suspension of Japanese aid (1998). U.S. and Japanese sanctions lifted (2001).

i. Ban on U.S. military transfers (1980), foreign aid (1986); partial European community sanctions (1986). , Syria Accountability Act (presidential flexibility) (2003).

TABLE 5.2 The Effectiveness of Comprehensive and Partial Sanctions

	Reformed	Unreformed
Comprehensive	Libya (1)	Iran, Iraq, N. Korea, Afghanistan, Yugoslavia (5)
Partial	Pakistan, Syria, Sudan (3)	(0)

In fact, calculation reveals that the odds of encountering a reformed renegade with comprehensive sanctions is less that twenty times the odds of encountering one with partial sanctions ($\omega = 0.04$). The weight of sanctions seems to produce an effect *opposite* to that intended. At this juncture, one might argue that what matters is the duration of the sanctions, not their scope; but this is not what the evidence indicates. Libya was subjected to sanctions lasting more than twenty years before becoming fully compliant, but Iran's sanctions have lasted almost as long, and North Korea's much longer, yet they remain noncompliant. Pakistan's and Sudan's sanctions were of short duration, whereas both are partly compliant. One could also suggest that our finding expresses a "selection effect," in the sense that the worst reprobates are not only most likely to be heavily sanctioned but also least likely to reform. This, however, is a dubious line of argument, since there is no reason why Iran or Libya, for instance, should have been considered more stubbornly evil than, say, Sudan or Syria. In any case, as we have seen, "contingencies" unrelated to the target's behavior often influence the extent of its punishment. The conclusion seems inescapable: as far as renegades go, light sanctions are more likely to induce the desired changes than are heavy sanctions. This is dramatically contrary to the IO model's expectation. We need a better model of sanctions effectiveness.

The Incentives-Restructuring (IR) Model   The more sophisticated IR model assumes that sanctions-induced hardships not only offset regime incentives to engage in transgressive behavior but may actually reconfigure those incentives, making it *less* likely that behavior would improve. This counterproductive outcome can stem from three consequences of external economic punishment for the regime's political standing. The first concerns commitment to the ideational agenda on which the regime seeks to establish its right to rule. The second involves the economic interests that stand to support the regime. The third bears on domestic perceptions of the regime and its opponents.

Commitment to the Regime's Ideational Agenda. Almost invariably, renegade regimes base their domestic authority on apparently elevated ideational goals — of an ethno-nationalist kind (as with the Milošević regime), of a religious sort (the Tehran regime, for example), or of political-ideological nature (e.g., the Korean regime in its *Juche* phase). Because policies that weaken support for these objectives invariably undermine the regime's position, we ask how support might respond to sanctions, assuming that regime policies would adjust accordingly. The IO model suggests that ideational goals should lose their luster for people enduring sanctions-induced privations, encouraging renegades to abandon the policies that brought the sanctions. But this is not what the IR model predicts: by its logic, sanctions actually could *increase* commitment to the regime's ideational objectives.

Most people place a higher value on what they stand to lose than on what they stand to gain, whereas international retaliation would be perceived as threatening the regime's professed ideals and their attainment. Prior to the international retaliation, the values pursued are, as a rule, considered unattained; they are something to be aimed for; once sanctions are applied, whatever had been achieved with regard to ethno-nationalist, religious, or ideological values is now threatened from the outside. The implications follow from the assumptions of *prospect theory*,[3] a body of theory challenging core assumptions of expected utility theory and whose predictions enjoy substantial confirmation. One of its core tenets is that people are risk-averse with regard to gains but risk-acceptant where losses are concerned, and that the value functions of individuals are considerably steeper with respect to losses than to gains, implying that people also tend to be *loss-averse*, so that the prospect of a loss of a certain magnitude is not balanced by the prospect of a comparable gain.[4] Thus, where values that have at least partially been attained are threatened from outside, they may appear more valuable than when they were merely an unattained objective, but this implies a credibly severe threat.

Domestic Economic Interests (Rent-Seeking Elites). No regime can neglect the consequences of economic hardship on its domestic position. We observed that renegade behavior was more likely at the primary stage where regime backers could be shielded from the consequences of sanctions, and the reasoning carries over to the secondary stages — but other mechanisms also now operate. As with ideational values, domestic economic interests may now be pushed in one of two directions. Those segments of society that had supported the regime may, following economic privations, withdraw that support, impelling the regime to abandon its delinquent behavior. But *new* clusters of interest, tied to the persistence of renegade behavior, could also emerge, as sanctions frequently open new opportunities for gain for those who can profit from shortages and dislocations. Black and gray markets thrive, as powerful players carve out near-monopoly positions in the provision of scarce goods, and as smugglers realize large profits on scarce but price-inelastic goods. Even those who engage in legitimate production, but who previously suffered from foreign competition, might find their position enhanced, as long as the domestic market does not wholly collapse. Such rent-seekers need political allies to maintain their profitable situation, encouraging association of newly enriched groups with organs of state power, giving the regime an additional source of support. The interests of rent-seeking elites may then strengthen, not weaken, the regime's stake in deviance.

Perceptions of the Regime and Its Opponents. The IO model implies that sanctions should undermine support for the regime, discouraging renegade behavior, but the opposite can occur if they produce a rally-round-the-flag and if the opposition can be linked to hostile foreigners. If regime objectives are widely esteemed, then increased opprobrium should attach both to the foreigners hostile to these objectives and to their domestic allies. But if support for these aims is withdrawn (because they seem inimical to other, more immediate, needs), then regime opponents may appear in a more benevolent light. Other things being equal, severe external punishment is more likely to generate a rally effect and to cast those associated with foreign goals in an unattractive light. Plainly, sanctions that bolster the regime's position give it little incentive to alter its course.

Sanctions and the Incentives-Restructuring Model

The IR model thus allows that sanctions, especially when severe, can be counterproductive. We will begin with a comparative examination of the extent to which the model's predictions are borne out, comparing the impact of comprehensive and partial sanctions. This will be followed by a simple quantitative test of the IR hypotheses.

Commitment to Regime Values   *Comprehensive Sanctions.* Ethno-nationalist sentiment in Yugoslavia was amplified during much of the 1990s by

Serbian feelings of victimization at foreign hands, strengthening Milošević's support. By implying a "cultural identity of guilt, [sanctions] were bound to be counterproductive, reinforcing the very loyalties and political appeals they were aiming to deny."[5] As a dissident Yugoslav journalist explained: "With the help of sanctions and the growing power of the patriarchal conservative Serbian villages, [Slobodan Milošević] is slowly becoming the embodiment of the national identity in many Serbs' minds."[6] Opinion surveys indicated that feelings of nationalism and xenophobia increased during the first half of the decade as the sanctions bit harder and harder.[7] Foreign hostility reinforced "we–they" feelings and, by appearing to threaten Serbia's nationalist aspirations, heightened the regard in which they were held.

It also appears that sanctions and other retaliation against Afghanistan's Taliban regime encouraged radicalization of its worldview and aggravated its sociopolitical implications. According to a close student of the Taliban:

Events since 1998 in Afghanistan have demonstrated that what are perceived as hostile acts by the USA, acting alone or through the umbrella of the UN Security Council, have the effect of further radicalizing the political environment. Such radicalism has manifested itself both in actions that may be regarded as anti-Western and anti-Christian and those that could be characterized as representing an ultra-conservative perspective, such as the destruction of the rock-face Buddhas in Bamyan in February 2001.[8]

The North Korean case is a difficult one. There is a problem of timelines, since comprehensive U.S. sanctions, steeped in Cold War reasoning, dated from the early 1950s, while the regime became a renegade, by our criteria, some years later. At the same time, North Korea's international environment, far more than that of most countries, was disjointedly multidimensional. Relations with the United States existed on a plane that did not always intersect with that on which relations with the Soviet Union appeared, which in turn seemed independent of the dimensions within which relations were Japan were conducted, and so forth. Thus, being cut of economically from the Soviet Union in the 1960s had little relation to the fact of U.S. sanctions, or to Japan's willingness or unwillingness to maintain commercial relations. Still, we may ask whether times of greater economic isolation and compulsion coincided with increased stress on *Juche* doctrine. The coincidence was indeed there. The first major wave of ideological development was felt in the late 1950s and early 1960s, when Pyongyang faced not only U.S. hostility, but estrangement from the Soviet bloc. A second wave was, likewise, related to a combination of continuing U.S. economic retribution coupled with the termination of economic and military aid from the former Soviet Union, as well as increasingly frosty political and economic relations with Japan. Hardening ideological positions were reflected in writings of Kim Jong-Il, where the premise that all foreign powers are exploitative and imperialistic was forcefully reiterated, as was a demand for unswerving commitment to the ideology.[9] The Korean leader warned that "One-step concession and retreat from socialist principles has resulted in ten- and hundred-concessions and retreat, and finally invited the grave consequence of ruining the working parties themselves."[10]

An interesting twist appears in the Iraqi case. Before international sanctions, an eclectic but moderate combination of Iraqi nationalism and Baathist ideology constituted what ideational program the regime had. With external sanctions and hostility, the regime turned to Islam for its legitimacy, claiming that support for itself implied support for the Faith. In 2003 religious leaders reckoned that more than a hundred new mosques had been constructed in Baghdad.[11] Hussein began lacing his speeches with religious rhetoric, hinting that he was a descendant of the Prophet Mohammed, and lavishing patronage on Shiite shrines. The salience of religious motifs stemmed not only from an Iraqi perception that Islam was threatened by the West, but also from economic misery and insecurity of daily existence, exacerbated by international sanctions and causing people to seek solace in faith. As one pilgrim to the shrine of Imam al-Kadhim explained: "Most people feel that life is difficult. They come here to make it easier. They wish for God to provide for better conditions, for their families, for their houses and for their way of life."[12] Thus, an ideational impact was produced via a circuitous route. Sermons were often imbued with anti-American and anti-Israeli rhetoric, clerics frequently defining the struggle with such enemies as noble Jihad, implying that to fight for Saddam was to fight for God.[13]

Not all comprehensively sanctioned renegades saw a surge in ideational commitment. With Iran, external pressure did not increase religious zeal. Islamic passion peaked with the Islamic Revolution; international condemnation and U.S. sanctions did not increase popular or elite commitment to the Islamist agenda. Partly, the extreme pitch of Islamist ardor at the time of the revolution left much more room for subsequent decline than further accretion.[14] As disenchantment with social strictures, political repression, and, especially, economic privations set in, the clergy and Islamic ideologues increasingly were held accountable.[15] By the 1997 elections that swept reformist Khatami to the presidency, economics was the major determinant of electoral choice.[16] It appears that external economic and diplomatic pressure did not bolster ideationally based support for the regime.

Similarly, in the Libyan case, no discernible increase in ideological fervor was recorded by observers in response to the 1982 U.S. trade embargo, the severance of diplomatic relations with the United States two years later, or the multilateral, UN-mandated sanctions of 1992. If the sanctions, along with flaccid oil prices during much of that period, had an impact on ideational commitments, it was of a different sort. The regime responded to economic stagnation with progressive economic liberalization, accompanied by growing income gaps in what had been an exceptionally egalitarian society. But the official egalitarian ideology became rather meaningless in the new social context, creating an ideational vacuum that, by most reports, was increasingly filled by Islamism.[17] However one looks at it, it cannot be claimed that the regime's ideationally-rooted legitimacy benefited from international responses to its misconduct.

The Iranian and Libyan cases aside, the bulk of evidence indicates that severe sanctions bolster the position of renegade regimes as they benefit from the protective reaction to these domestic values provoked by a perception that they are being assaulted by hostile foreign forces How do comprehensive sanctions compare with those of a partial nature?

Partial Sanctions. In the Syrian case, ideational professions were not a significant element of regime legitimacy: Arab nationalism was not one of its pillars, Alawi identity could not form a religious rallying cry (since the ruling Alawis were a rather small minority), and little enthusiasm surrounded Baathist ideology. Predictably, sanctions yielded no political boon to the regime via their effect on the values it stood for. Nor did they bolster the ideational foundation of Musharraf's regime in Pakistan, which, unlike its predecessor, did not seek to build its support on Islamist goals or to develop special ideological themes. The sanctions could, conceivably, have created a nationalist reaction but did not: they were of brief duration. In any case, the regime sought to establish its position on pragmatic, especially economic, achievements, as Musharraf condemned hard-line Islamists and argued that religious fanaticism interfered with economic recovery and harmed the country's image abroad.[18] Thus, the sanctions that followed the 1998 nuclear tests did not influence the ideational basis, such as it was, of regime support. Finally, nothing indicates that international pressure affected the intensity of Sudan's political Islam, where a progressive erosion of religious and ideological enthusiasm became evident by the late 1990s.

In 1996 the country's foreign minister observed that "Ideology now, I think is clear, is part of history."[19] A few years later, Prime Minister Meles Zinawi of Ethiopia concluded, with respect to Sudan, that, "the virulent, export-oriented Islamism has dwindled in significance and has become inward looking."[20] The rather mild international response did not stimulate a defensive rally around Islamist values. Perhaps more importantly, as will be argued in the following section, light sanctions did not undermine a budding bourgeoisie whose fortunes grew in tandem with the nation's oil industry, and whose primary interests were economic rather than spiritual or ideological.

The evidence so far is compelling: light sanctions rarely stimulate ideational commitment, while severely penalized regimes often benefit from a temporary strengthening of the ideational foundations of their support — implying that sanctions do not merely serve to offset the initial drives behind renegade behavior but may also stimulate counterproductive incentives.

Rent-Seeking Interests   Another explanation for the counterproductive consequences of heavy sanctions is that they may generate economic interests dependent on their maintenance: thorough economic isolation can undermine the power of the (often incipient) middle class while creating a symbiosis of interests between regime and elites that benefit from the attendant shortages. Those who are best served by cross-border economic transactions cease to be politically effective, while those who profit from isolation become a pillar of regime support. The likelihood of improved conduct dwindles correspondingly. We will explore this possibility, inquiring whether it is affected by the severity of sanctions.

Comprehensive Sanctions. The 1979 revolution seems to have joined Iran's hardliners and economic elites embedded in the statist economy. This bond probably was further reinforced by the external pressure placed on the regime, mainly by the United States.

The Islamic constitution created a three-sector economy: the state sector (encompassing major industries and services, as well as foreign trade), the cooperative sector (concerned with production and distribution according to "Islamic criteria"), and a private sector, limited to small-scale agricultural and manufacturing activities. The state sector was dominant; state monopolies covered basic industries and services, and these were protected from foreign competition by the rule prohibiting the import of goods that could be produced domestically in sufficient amounts. In addition, merchant associations with close ties to conservative factions were encouraged. When

President Rafsanjani stepped into office in 1989, five-year development plans were instituted to guide the economy, and, with President Khatami's election in 1997, modest privatization was attempted, though the basic structure of the economy remained unchanged.[21] But the position of both men, and their ability to pursue their desired reforms, was undermined by continuing external hostility, including extensive U.S. sanctions, perpetuating the interests of the state sector whose position depended on the avoidance of meaningful political and economic reforms. At the same time, a flourishing underground economy took root, eventually accounting for 25–40 percent of all economic activity.[22] Wedded to the Islamic state, it came to be referred to as the Trade Mafia: "U.S. trade sanctions against Iran have been extremely beneficial to the Trade Mafia," by creating a political and economic situation allowing it "to effectively eliminate healthy and vibrant competition while maintaining their monopolies."[23]

The association of interests dependent on sanctions-induced scarcities with renegade regimes was even more apparent in Yugoslavia. As Lenard Cohen observed:

> The private or para-state elite grew substantially larger after the imposition of United Nations sanctions against Yugoslavia (May 1992 to December 1995) as a result of the war in Bosnia, when goods became extremely scarce. Owners and managers of enterprises importing oil, strategic raw materials, spare parts, etc., or exporting goods that could raise foreign currency, were able to make huge profits. Extra-legal wartime trade in arms and war materials, and stolen humanitarian aid, also proved enormously lucrative.[24]

Black-market operators established firm connections with the country's political rulers, creating a new political-economic class. The collapse of normal commerce "put most of the weak in Yugoslavia in the hands of the Milošević's cronies. In return for loyalty to the regime, [the cronies] are given access to exclusive opportunities for currency manipulation, smuggling, black market operations and trade monopolies."[25]

Although sanctions were relaxed after the 1995 Dayton Accords, those who wrested control of the state monopolies and black-market operations did not loosen their grip on their sources of profit, a grip that their connections to the Milošević regime helped them retain. There were reports of a police general who headed a car-theft ring, of a close associate of Milošević's receiving a monopoly over oil imports, and so forth.[26] Thus, along with the destruction of the country's middle class, an elite linked to the sanctions and fused at the hip to the regime and its security forces was created, becoming a bulwark of regime support.[27]

Hussein Iraq's black-market activities went, if anything, beyond those witnessed in Yugoslavia. The fortunes of the professional middle class lay in tatters, but favored supporters joined regime insiders to reap the spoils of smuggling and various forms of government-sponsored corruption. Saddam's relatives administered an array of sanctions-busting enterprises, while politically important segments of society were allowed to share the benefits. Oil smuggling, principally via Syria and Turkey, guaranteed the regime and chosen supporters significant illicit revenue,[28] which "provide[s] a powerful line of patronage through which the regime can build loyalty within the crucial, higher echelons of the Sunni elite and afford them a stake in the maintenance of the current political order."[29] Illicit gains also surrounded contracts within the Oil for Food program. Various Iraqi (and foreign) companies furnishing equipment necessary to oil production under that program were required to provide the Oil Ministry (and thus the regime) with a 10 percent kickback. However, trading companies allied with Hussein's family and the security agencies were exempted, and favored companies were far more likely to get contracts.[30] In addition, food and medicines purchased under that program often were resold on the black market by operators closely connected to the regime.[31] Those allowed to share in the illicit activities included Tikritis, Baath Party officials, and senior members of the military and security services. While the vast majority of the population suffered painful privation, an elite whose wealth depended on sanctions-related shortages became a pillar of regime support.

The situation in Taliban-ruled Afghanistan was not very different. The country's history did not leave it with much of a middle class to be destroyed, but economic isolation produced a number of characteristic outcomes. It encouraged extensive smuggling, involving largely electronics and consumer goods, brought into Afghanistan and then smuggled into Pakistan, where they sold for less than legally imported goods. Levies on these (as well as on opium production) furnished one of the few sources of revenue available to the authorities.[32] Since economic relations with the outside world could have provided revenues of another sort (e.g., import duties, taxes on foreigners doing business in Afghanistan), the regime may have been less willing to countenance illicit activities without the sanctions. At the same time, the smugglers, and the warlords whose protection they enjoyed, came to benefit from the country's economic closure, providing added support to the regime.[33]

The record of the remaining two, comprehensively sanctioned, renegades bears scant resemblance to the previous four cases. There is little evidence that sanctions on Libya created a structure of economic interests encouraging continued deviant behavior. The middle class, never decimated, maintained a politically significant position, whereas the regime's unwillingness to countenance illicit black markets, or any major form of corruption, meant that the nexus between sanctions-profiteers and political authorities did not develop.[34] Probably, a lack of support from rent-seeking elites (and Qaddafi's unwillingness to turn to Islamists) eventually impelled the regime to strengthen the commercial middle class. This coincided with economic and political reforms favoring a portion of the bourgeoisie with a vested interest in Libya's reintegration into the international community. Economic liberalization included expanded privatization of enterprises, the lifting of injunctions against retail trade, and curtailing subsidies that many companies had enjoyed.[35] Through the 1990s, economic reformers competed for influence with hardliners "who saw Libya's past radicalism as the basis of the regime's legitimacy."[36] By the late 1990s the former prevailed. As Qaddafi proclaimed in 1998: "We cannot stand in the way of progress. No more obstacles between human beings are accepted. The fashion now is the free market and investments."[37]

Not everyone benefited equally from the relaxed economic conditions: the state's reduced commercial role and the limited number of merchants with currency and contacts with foreign companies put those thus favored in a semimonopolistic position.[38] In this manner, however, economic liberalization generated an elite with little dependence on the state for its fortunes, and whose interests were incompatible with economic isolation. When U.S. sanctions were supplemented with comprehensive UN sanctions in 1991 (a result of the Lockerbie incident), it is possible that these interests lobbied hard for gestures by Qaddafi that would appease the international community. The Libyan case illustrates the importance of a viable middle class and an absence of powerful black-market interests — both of which comprehensive sanctions undermine.

Nor did sanctions create vested interests supporting the North Korean regime. Although there are indications that the government itself may have engaged in narcotics trafficking to raise money for basic government operations,[39] it is hardly conceivable that, in an economy so regimented and society so controlled, entrepreneurs would arise to profit from domestic scarcities, or that a regime so firmly in control of the tools of coercion needed support from such sources. The national security establishment — the military in particular — has always enjoyed a privileged position in North Korea, but this position is deeply rooted in the regime's governing doctrine. It would be hard to attribute it to economic sanctions.

Nevertheless, evidence of economic interests linked to the persistence of sanctions, and thus to continued renegade behavior, is found in four of the six regimes subjected to comprehensive sanctions, suggesting that this is the usual consequence of thorough economic isolation. The comparison with partial sanctions is instructive.

Partial Sanctions. If particularly onerous sanctions often undermine a country's middle class, and thus a likely advocate of regime moderation, while linking other group interests to continued renegade status, then lighter sanctions should encourage improved compliance with major international norms. Such, indeed, has been the case with the compliant renegades, where the relative lightness of the sanctions ensured the survival of a vigorous middle class whose interests resided not in artificial scarcities but in vigorous and internationally connected commercial activity, and whose political influence was directed accordingly.

In the Syrian case, a commercial bourgeoisie emerged with the incremental economic liberalization begun in the early 1980s and extending, through several stages, into the 1990s.[40] Economic transformations included a relaxation of the foreign exchange regime, deregulated foreign trade, the introduction of joint-stock companies, and a considerably widened scope for private (including foreign) investment. The result was a remarkable growth of the private sector and the associated development of a commercial bourgeoisie and political elite sharing a stake in the liberalized economy.[41] As a consequence, a foreign policy that had always been responsive to domestic needs[42] became increasingly alert to the interests of a bourgeoisie that was rivaling the Baath Party as a pillar of regime support. The need to satisfy this bourgeoisie and to service patronage networks became an important determinant of Syrian foreign policy.[43] Had crushing economic sanctions destroyed that bourgeoisie, there probably would have been less pressure for accommodation with other nations.

Syria's decision to back the U.S.-led coalition against Iraq in 1991 was met with appropriate rewards. Not only were diplomatic relations with Britain (suspended in 1986) restored, but the European Community's sanctions (dating also from 1986) were lifted. In addition, Syria received some two billion dollars from the Gulf states for its help in the war.[44] Following September 11, Bashar Assad's government condemned the terrorist acts, shared relevant intelligence with the United States, and acted to limit Hezbollah attacks from Lebanon against Israel. While few tangible rewards followed immediately, President Bush lobbied effectively against congressional efforts (the Syria Accountability Act) to ban military and dual-use technologies to Syria and to curtail U.S. investment in that country.[45] When this was passed anyway, the president showed little inclination to use the discretion it gave him to tighten sanctions, yielding only partially to congressional pressure in May 2004.

Syria did not abandon all ties to terrorism or its programs related to weapons of mass destruction. Interests linked to the international economy are not all that drive the regime's policies, but they have had an impact, and it is unlikely that they would have flourished in conditions of total economic isolation.

Sudan, too, did not suffer a great burden of sanctions. The multilateral measures were purely diplomatic, while the U.S. sanctions, imposed in 1997, involved restrictions on economic relations that were, in any case, trivial.[46] From the late 1970s, the National Islamic Front adopted a strategy of securing key positions within the nation's budding financial sector, initially via the Faisal Islamic Bank — the first Islamic bank in the Middle East. President Nimeiri gave NIF cadres significant shares in this enterprise and employed them in its various branches.[47] Using their positions in the financial sector, they acquired a large portion of national economic assets (including the oil industry) and its trading activities. Thus, an elite, linked to the political leadership and with a direct stake in international economic relations, was created. Although Chinese, Malaysian, and Canadian companies have made major investments in the oil sector, the benefits of U.S. investment have been apparent. Still, Sudan's oil revenues made it less dependent on private Islamists for financing, allowing it to sever its links to such sponsors of terrorism as Osama bin Laden.

Sanctions against Pakistan were so brief, and the Musharraf regime's opposition to corruption so firm, that significant black-market interests had no chance to develop, while the commercial bourgeoisie never was destroyed. Sanctions were imposed in 1998, but the following year a waiver exempted U.S. grain sales from the sanctions, which, by the fall of 2001, were lifted as a reward for Pakistani support of U.S. war aims in Afghanistan. As a result of that collaboration, the United States pledged over one billion dollars in aid, Paris Club creditors restructured much of the country's debt, and an International Monetary Fund poverty-reduction program was offered. Whatever corruption may have existed was not primarily the product of international isolation.

In the short to medium term, then, renegades are more likely to be *strengthened* than weakened by particularly harsh sanctions. Partly, this is because sanctions spawn monopolies and black markets committed to the regime whose behavior produces the profitable scarcities. By contrast, a relatively light sanctions regime allows the survival of a domestic bourgeoisie with a vested interests in expanded contact with abroad and motivated to support regime moderation.

Regime Political Positioning   Does punitive international pressure, via the hardships and censure it implies, strengthen those who would oppose the guilty regime? Or does it, by the "we–they" feelings engendered, help renegade regimes discredit domestic opponents and rally support? In the long term, the former may be the case; in the shorter term, the latter appears more likely, but this may depend on the force of the international response.

Comprehensive Sanctions. Most observers agree that diplomatic and economic sanctions targeted at Yugoslavia at the time of the war in Bosnia allowed Milošević to whip up moods of national defiance in the face of foreign bullying. Support for the regime benefited in three ways.[48] First, the decimation of the middle class and the accompanying breakdown of civil society weakened forces that might have opposed the regime. As one observer described it: "It is all they can do to cope with the business of daily survival — finding gas, medicine, even food and clothing for their children. They have less and less energy available for opposition policies."[49] Moreover, in response to the hardships, some 200,000 professionals and intellectuals left the country, further reducing the pool of potential opponents.[50] Second, sanctions helped the regime shift blame for hardships to foreign opponents. When asked "Who is most responsible for Serbia's predicament: Milošević or the Western Powers?" most respondents initially pointed to Milošević, but as sanctions began hurting, opinion shifted, implicating the West and absolving the regime.[51] Finally, such perceptions made it much easier for the regime to deal with its opponents by linking them to hostile foreign forces.

It also seems that sanctions contributed to the unwelcome outcome of the Serbian presidential elections of December 1992. Milan Panić, the pro-Western businessman opposed to the regime's excesses, ran against Milošević in a moderate campaign that urged accommodation with the international community. Though polls indicated he could win a fair election,[52] he ultimately lost — a loss attributed, in part, to the fact that on November 17 the United Nations strengthened its sanctions, undermining Panić's position and vindicating Milosević's claim that the outside world was ganging up on Serbia.[53]

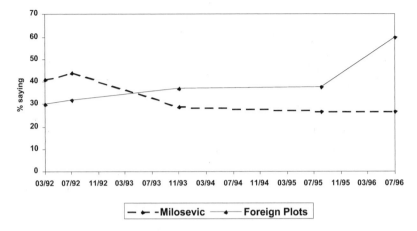

FIGURE 5.1 Who Is Most Responsible for Serbia's Predicament?

It appears that international, especially U.S., pressure against Iran boosted hardliners at the expense of more conciliatory reformers, perpetuating the behavior that it was designed to discourage. The year 1989 saw the election of moderate Hashemi Rafsanjani to the presidency, while Ayatollah Ali Khamenei, an Islamic conservative, ascended to the position of supreme leader. The former sought economic reforms and a more moderate foreign policy,[54] encountering staunch opposition from supporters of the latter. One of Rafsanjani's initiatives was to offer the U.S. firm Conoco a contract to develop Iran's offshore oil fields — a project rapidly vetoed by the Clinton administration, putting an end to Rafsanjani's conciliatory moves. The 1997 elections, largely driven by voters' economic concerns,[55] brought Moham-mad Khatami, an even firmer reformist, to the presidency, and disagree-ments with Khamenei's hardliners sharpened. One of Khatami's early acts was to call for "a dialogue of civilizations" with the United States. Washing-ton demurred, causing Khatami to reject further movement toward accom-modation. Khamenei and the hardliners were the beneficiaries.

The Bush administration adopted a particularly uncompromising atti-tude, including Iran in its "Axis of Evil" and inviting domestic opposition to the regime. By most accounts, this devastated Iran's moderate elements.[56] Having established itself as an implacably hostile force, the U.S. administra-tion lost the ability not only to hurt the Iranian hardliners with its pressure, but also to help reformists with its support: it simply forced the latter to close the distance between themselves and conservative forces.[57] And, when President Bush appealed directly to Iranians to support reform, Khatami urged his supporters in parliament to abandon their quest for improved relations with the United States because of what he deemed growing U.S. belligerence toward Iran.[58] A leading Iranian journalist lamented, "Unfortunately, the government of the United States usually chooses action that benefits the conservatives."[59] Similarly, U.S. pressure on Iran following revelations of its uranium enrichment program strengthened the position of those Iranian officials encouraging this program, by generating a public rally behind the leadership. As the director of a Tehran research institute explained, "Iranians are united not because of activities by the Iranian regime, but because of the U.S. position . . . now all Iranians believe we must promote our activities as a sign of independence."[60]

North Korea offers further evidence that external punishment can favor groups most inclined to defy key international norms. While the political system seems perfectly monolithic, fissures have appeared there as well. By the 1980s some within the leadership sought to address the country's economic predicament by a controlled reintegration into the international economic community. A joint venture law was passed in the mid-1980s, with the hope of enticing some foreign investment, and, in 1986, foreign companies were allowed to retain 20–50 percent of any earnings beyond their required contribution to the Korean government.[61]

In 1991 a special free-trade and investment zone was established in the Rajin-Songbong area, testifying to a desire, by at least some within the regime, for an end to the country's isolation. As it became apparent that the nuclear issue was the principle impediment to normalized external relations, reformers forced a successful showdown within the Workers Party Central Committee securing approval, despite hardliner opposition, for International Atomic Energy Agency (IAEA) inspection of North Korea's nuclear facilities.[62] There is evidence, too, that ultimate adherence to the 1994 Agreed Framework, theoretically ending the regime's nuclear weapons programs in exchange for Western concessions, including a U.S. pledge to terminate economic sanctions, also involved a clash with regime conservatives.[63]

The late 1990s portended a significantly reformed North Korea, while highlighting the regime's somewhat schizophrenic nature. The missile program, intended to yield a missile with intercontinental capabilities (the Taepodong 2), was frozen. North Korea signed the UN Convention for the Suppression of the Financing of Terrorism and according to the U.S. State Department, "reiterated its public policy of opposing terrorism and any support for terrorism."[64] A tentative rapprochement between the two Koreas was underway, the Clinton administration eased sanctions, and Madeleine Albright became the first senior U.S. official to visit Pyongyang. But the 2000 U.S. election altered the situation, as one of George W. Bush's early moves was to suspend movement toward normalized relations. His State of the Union address in January 2002, including North Korea in his "Axis of Evil," provoked a vociferous reaction. In October the regime indicated that it may have had a secret uranium program and in December it demanded the removal of IAEA monitoring devices on its nuclear facilities. Soon after, North Korea announced its withdrawal from the Nuclear Non-Proliferation Treaty (NPT). In February it resumed missile testing. If North Korean policy is determined by the balance of forces within the regime, then U.S. belligerence was counterproductive. Modest economic reforms were undertaken in 2002, but their effects and context remain shrouded in some mystery.[65]

The situation with regard to Iraq is interesting, in that members of the political elite may have perceived international pressure as a threat to national unity, one that would inspire resistance to the central government by Iraqi Kurds and Shiites. This allowed the regime to play to fears by Sunnis, especially within the office corps, that Shiites would dominate any post-Saddam regime.[66] In addition, the humiliation imposed by international sanctions, including the need to accept the UN Oil for Food Program, may explain some of the more assertive actions taken by the regime in the mid to late 1990s.[67]

An unrepentant renegade whose domestic position appeared unaffected by its collision with the international community was the Kabul regime. Although Taliban rhetoric incorporated reference to the struggle against Zionism and denounced the opposition Northern Alliance as a "Shiite–Communist confederation backed up by Iran, Russia, India, Turkey and others,"[68] there is little indication that such rhetorically shallow statements enhanced the movement's power, or that they were connected to sanctions. Most importantly, the rhetoric significantly preceded the sanctions (which dated essentially from 1999) and, in fact, coincided with the final consolidation of the Taliban's control over most of the country. Nor is there evidence that, by the late 1980s, Qaddafi managed to derive much political support from his continued external pugnacity. During the regime's initial years, defiant attitudes had generated some domestic support,[69] but this was no longer the case by the late 1980s, certainly not by the 1990s. "In all instances, local opinion confirmed that mobilization in the face of real or imagined foreign intervention had ground to a halt."[70]

Exceptions aside, four of the six renegades subjected to comprehensive sanctions demonstrate how renegade regimes can derive some domestic political benefits from foreign pressures and hostility. This can be contrasted to the situation with partial sanctions.

Partial Sanctions. Diplomatic sanctions conveyed international unhappiness with the Sudanese regime's behavior, but unilateral U.S. economic measures barely affected the economy. Symbolically laden but with slight practical impact, the foreign response provided no tangible resentments around which to rally support or stigmatize opponents. In this case, unlike some others, "The challenge constituted by sanctions could not be met by mobilizing national outrage at, and international sympathy over, the suffering caused by sanctions, because it was clear that the suffering did not stem from diplomatic sanctions."[71]

While sanctions did not prompt rally effects or the stigmatization of opponents in Pakistan, this was so for different reasons. Musharraf's potential detractors were, in addition to Benazir Bhutto and Nawaz Sharif, the country's religious hardliners — none of whom could, by any stretch of the imagination, be linked to foreign, especially Western, forces. It is as hard to see how the Syrian regime could have associated its domestic opponents with its external adversaries, since its major internal threat has come from Islamist sources, especially the Muslim Brotherhood, a force that could not plausibly be connected to Western powers. In any case, relations with Europe had, for the most part, been good, and, despite its economic sanctions, the United States maintained diplomatic relations with Syria, regarding it as a vital party to the Middle East peace process. Although Bashar al-Assad's political liberalization was temporarily halted two years after he came to power, this was not justified by threats from foreign foes.

Accordingly, regime position was more likely to benefit from external confrontation when sanctions were heavy than when they were light. Less severe foreign punishment generally diminished the rally effect and the payoff from branding the opposition as foreign stooges (effects that, at times, also resulted from the logical difficulty of linking opponents to foreign foes).

A Quantitative View

The evidence suggests that the IR model does a good job of explaining why severe sanctions are less likely than moderate sanctions to improve renegade conduct. Our grasp of this fact should further profit from the sort of simple, quantitative analysis conducted in the previous chapter, expressing the credibility of our observations in intuitively meaningful numbers. This provides the further benefit that a reader dissatisfied with any of my coding decisions can test the implications of desired changes.

The truth-table shown in table 5.3 summarizes our observations on whether a renegade reformed (wholly or partly), sanctions were comprehensive or partial, the regime benefited from a boost to ideationally based authority, sanctions generated support from rent-seeking elites, and sanctions improved the regime's domestic political position via a rally-effect and/or the chance to discredit opponents.

Based on table 5.4, we begin by examining the coincidence of renegade reform with the presence or absence of an ideational boost (I). Thinking

TABLE 5.3 A Profile of Secondary Renegades

Renegade	Reformed	Comprehensive Sanctions	Ideationally- Based Boost	Rent- Seekers	Improved Political Position
Iran	0	1	0	1	1
Iraq	0	1	1	1	1
Afghanistan	0	1	1	1	0
Yugoslavia	0	1	1	1	1
North Korea	0	1	1	0	1
Libya	1	1	0	0	0
Sudan	1	0	0	0	0
Syria	1	0	0	0	0
Pakistan	1	0	0	0	0

TABLE 5.4 The Impact of Ideational Boosts

	Reformed	Unreformed
Ideational Boost	(0)	Iraq, Afghanistan, North Korea, Yugoslavia (4)
No Ideational Boost	Libya, Syria, Pakistan, Sudan (4)	Iran (1)

again in terms of conditional probabilities and odds-ratios, we calculated for table 5.4 that $\omega = 0.04$. The odds that a reformed regime would have enjoyed an ideational boost are a small fraction of the odds that it would not have, indicating that such boosts are entirely counterproductive.

We also saw that sanctions may benefit a renegade's domestic position via the support of rent-seeking elites. This, too, is confirmed by the quantitative exercise (table 5.5). In this case, again, $\omega = 0.04$. The odds of having a reformed renegade assuming a rent-seeking elite are roughly one-twentieth the odds of one without such an elite — not a formula for sanctions success.

What about the ability of the regime to improve its domestic position, via its ability to discredit its opposition while redirecting support toward itself (table 5.6)? Once more, $\omega = 0.04$. It is *much* less likely (and by the same amount as in the previous case) that a reformed renegade would result from improved political positioning than from its absence.

A striking observation (apart from the identical odds-ratios) is that the upper left-hand cells are empty in all three tables: the presence of the IR

TABLE 5.5 The Impact of Rent-Seeking Interests

	Reformed	Unreformed
Rent-Seekers	(0)	Yugoslavia, Iraq, Iran, Afghanistan (4)
No Rent-Seekers	Libya, Syria, Pakistan, Sudan (4)	North Korea

TABLE 5.6 The Impact of Political Positioning

	Reformed	Unreformed
Improved Positioning	(0)	Yugoslavia, Iran, North Korea, Iraq (4)
No Improved Positioning	Libya, Syria, Pakistan, Sudan (4)	Afghanistan

impact is *never* encountered with reformed renegades: the absence of these effects seems a necessary condition for a regime to abandon at least some of its renegade ways. Membership in the other cells is similar across tables, with the exception of the lower right-hand cell.

The next question concerns the other half of the causal chain: how is the likelihood of witnessing the three incentives-reprogramming effects affected by the *severity* of the sanctions (table 5.7)? The answer is that, counterproductively to their purpose but in line with what the case studies revealed, these effects are much more probable where sanctions are heavy than where they are light. Here, $\omega = 12.6$. The odds of an ideational boost with comprehensive sanctions are more than twelve times the odds of such a boost with partial sanctions.

Does this relationship between IR effect and sanctions severity apply also to the emergence of rent-seeking elites (table 5.8)? Once more, $\omega = 12.6$: an effect identical to that involving an ideational boost. The odds of getting a rent-seeking elite are much larger with comprehensive than with partial sanctions.

What of the domestic political benefits (table 5.9)? $\omega = 12.6$. Yet again,

TABLE 5.7 Ideational Boosts and Severity of Sanctions

	Ideational Boost	*No Ideational Boost*
Comprehensive Sanctions	Yugoslavia, Iraq, Afghanistan, North Korea (4)	Iran, Libya (2)
Partial Sanctions	(0)	Syria, Pakistan, Sudan (3)

TABLE 5.8 Rent-Seeking Interests and Severity of Sanctions

	Rent-Seekers	*No Rent-Seekers*
Comprehensive Sanctions	Yugoslavia, Iraq, Iran, Afghanistan (4)	Libya, North Korea (2)
Partial Sanctions	(0)	Syria, Pakistan, Sudan (3)

TABLE 5.9 Political Positioning and Severity of Sanctions

	Improved Positioning	No Improved Positioning
Comprehensive Sanctions	Yugoslavia, Iraq, Iran, North Korea (4)	Afghanistan, Libya (2)
Partial Sanctions	(0)	Syria, Pakistan, Sudan (3)

the odds of getting a beneficial political effect with comprehensive sanctions are more than twelve times greater than with partial sanctions.

The similarities in our results are due to the similar distribution of cases across the two-by-two tables. The lower left-hand corner is empty in all three cases. What difference there is involves the upper right-hand cell. No regime subjected to partial sanctions experienced any of the IR effects associated with unreformed status — although some regimes enduring comprehensive sanctions also did not. This suggests that heavy sanctions are a necessary, though not sufficient, condition for such effects, and that partial sanctions anticipate their absence better than comprehensive sanctions do their presence. Still, strength of sanctions predicts the occurrence of IR effects, which, in turn, predicts the incidence of noncompliant and compliant renegades. The bottom line is quite contrary to what the IO model suggests and the opposite of the intended policy consequences. This is an interesting finding, one that may or may not apply to sanctions against regimes that are not renegades (ideational missions may be less of an issue for those that are not, rent-seeking may be less prevalent, etc.).

To Summarize

This chapter sought to explain the apparently paradoxical fact that heavy sanctions are less effective than light ones. The IO model dominates conventional thinking on sanctions, but the IR model emerges as a much better predictor of renegade behavior. It indicates that three counterproductive effects may follow the imposition of comprehensive sanctions by modifying the structure of regime incentives especially: (1) the commitment to the regime's ideational program may be strengthened by foreign pressure, (2) rent-

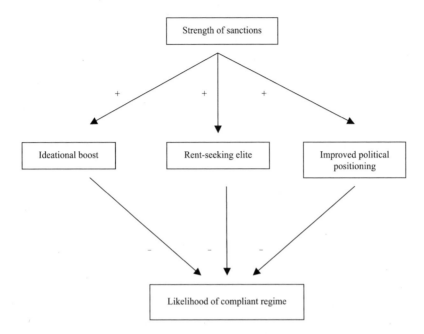

FIGURE 5.2 Economic Retribution and the Likelihood of Compliant Renegades

seeking interests supporting the regime and its policies may result from international isolation, and (3) the regime may benefit from sanctions-induced rallies, while the position of its opponents may be undermined. Each of these effects undermines the purpose of sanctions. Figure 5.2 illustrates the structure of this chapter's reasoning.

A Note on Libya

When Qaddafi, having abandoned support of terrorism, announced his readiness also to give up WMD programs, inviting verification by international inspectors, the regime became the only one of our renegades to reform to the point of full compliance, without the need for military intervention. Moreover, this happened despite comprehensive sanctions. How can this be accounted for? In the view of many U.S. neoconservatives, Qaddafi's WMD decision was a reaction to the U.S. military intervention in Iraq and his fear that Libya might be next unless it repented.[72] But this is doubtful, since the severing of Qaddafi's links to terrorism, and the abandonment of active

WMD programs, predated the U.S.-led invasion and even the 9/11 terrorist attacks. Ultimately, the main reasons for the decision to seek reintegration into the international community should be sought in two, probably related, developments. The first is a realization that the country's economic difficulties could seriously undermine the regime's position; the second is a shift in Qaddafi's own ideological convictions. The state of the Libyan economy had obviously deteriorated, a joint consequence of its isolation (which deepened after the Soviet Union's collapse) and its leader's disastrous economic experiments, whose political consequences included domestic unrest by Islamic militants and unhappiness within the military.[73] At Al Fateh University, for example, an underground movement waged a graffiti campaign denouncing the dilapidated condition of the institution.[74] The arrival of satellite television and the Internet in the late 1990s reportedly produced an "electronic perestroika," shocking Libyans by a realization of how badly their own country was doing.[75] In 2003 a new prime minister, Shokri Ghanem, was appointed with an explicit mandate to improve the economy, beginning with a thorough privatization of industry, and to join the World Trade Organization.[76] Two years before that, reforms had begun with a liberalization of foreign exchange, and the new prime minister sought joint ventures with foreign investors in such industries as cement and chemicals.

Simultaneously, Qaddafi seemed to undergo an ideological conversion — moving away from his pan-Arabism, Messianism, and the doctrines of the Third Universal Theory. In a September 2000 speech commemorating the Libyan revolution, he proclaimed that "Now is the era of economy, consumption, markets and investments. This is what unites people irrespective of language, religion and national identities."[77] To some extent, this conversion probably was linked to an appreciation that his doctrines had been counterproductive. It may also have reflected the influence of his reform-minded son and heir-apparent, Saif el-Islam. It is likely that Qaddafi, wishing his son to inherit a politically stable country,[78] proved receptive to the appropriate advice, adjusting his ideological convictions accordingly.

Although Libya had endured comprehensive sanctions, the regime remained intolerant of large-scale corruption or any hint of collusion between rent-seeking elites and the country's security forces. Had the regime been propped up by such a political configuration, and had the latter sought to protect the benefits isolation made possible, the Libyan developments would have been less likely. The regime's own rules prevented the pathologies associated with comprehensive sanctions from occurring, and, importantly, Libya was the only comprehensively sanctioned renegade not to have experienced any of the effects associated with the IR model.

6   The Value of Military Coercion

Recent decades, and the post–Cold War period in particular, have seen considerable reliance on military force to confront threats to world order, with one of the following objectives: (1) to induce the refractory regime to alter its objectionable policies, or (2) to ensure its removal. Both objectives imply either threatened intervention or the actual use of force, but they involve very different assumptions.

The Objectives of Force

Policy Change

If military force is to alter the regime's policies, it must reshape its *incentives*, decreasing stakes in deviance relative to stakes in compliance, or it must impair the regime's *capacity* to act on these incentives. In the former case, threats may suffice; in the latter, operational military activity is required.

Incentives   To meaningfully alter incentives, force must target the regime's dominant goal of maintaining its grip on power. The destruction and hardships associated with armed intervention could jeopardize the regime's relation with its power base or support by the general public. Intervention also could threaten the regime's instruments of coercion and control. Still, it

never is certain that threats or direct coercion would shape regime motivations in the manner desired.

As with economic sanctions, the hardships imposed may offset the drives
behind the delinquency, causing it to be mitigated or abandoned (the IO
model). But the structure of regime motivations could also be reconfigured
(the IR model), rendering the impact on its policy unpredictable. Economic
sanctions can reinforce the regime's position in three ways: by increasing
commitment to ideational goals, by creating rent-seeking elites, and by improving the regime's political position. The first and third consequences are
also apt to follow military threats: they may trigger a protective reflex within
the nation, increasing the attractiveness of regime goals and values, and they
may make it easier to demonize regime opponents (associating them with
foreign aggressors) while whipping up a rally-effect. And, as one of the best
studies of coercion points out, regime defiance of a coercer may enhance
its stature.[1] Thus, military threats can produce several, sometimes inconsistent, consequences for regime incentives, and their ultimate impact is poorly
understood.

Capacity   Actual intervention can impair a regime's capacity to act on objectionable incentives by destroying the economic foundations of its power
and its tools of coercion. Unlike efforts to affect incentives alone, this requires the operational use of military force.[2] Destruction often is directed at
the renegade's military and police establishment. Thus, many of NATO's
bombing sorties against Yugoslavia targeted security forces implicated in ethnic cleansing in Kosovo. Military action also may aim at the economic basis
of the regime's rule, to deprive it of the material foundations of its capacity
to do ill. The 1998 attacks on purported terrorist facilities in Sudan were
meant to damage the capacity of those responsible for bombing the U.S.
embassies in Kenya and Tanzania. While capacity alone can be targeted, its
degradation usually goes hand in hand with efforts to reshape incentives.
This was true of the NATO bombing of Yugoslavia in 1999, of U.S. air strikes
against Libya in 1986, and of operations Desert Shield and Desert Storm
against Iraq in 1991.

Regime Change

If a regime's incentives can be altered by spurring opposition by core
support groups or the mass public, its actual ouster might follow from that

opposition: military punishment causes domestic hardship, the regime nevertheless persists in its conduct, more pain is imposed by the interveners, and, ultimately, domestic forces topple the regime responsible for their predicament. Concurrently, a military pressure against which the regime cannot defend may humiliate, and thus delegitimize, it in the eyes of its supporters, also endangering its authority, particularly as its capacity to coerce is destroyed. If the regime is not removed internally, the direct purpose of force may switch to its ouster: the aim now is to destroy the regime's ability to defend itself and then to dislodge it — requiring the most intrusive form of intervention, a willingness to contemplate a long-term military presence, and an acceptance of associated costs and sacrifices. Although here we slip outside the terms of theoretical reference that have guided the rest of this study and that provided a framework for anticipating the renegade's choices, several of our assumptions have a bearing on the transition from a militarily removed renegade to a stable and internationally legitimate regime.

Table 6.1 displays the possible aims of military intervention as recorded for our renegades. Unsurprisingly, there are considerably more instances of threats (designed to alter incentives) than there are instances of actual recourse to force. The sequence of progression generally follows the above pattern: force seeking policy change and targeted at incentives and capacity (II) generally was preceded by threats aimed mainly at incentives (I). A direct attempt at regime change in Iraq (III) was preceded by action under column

TABLE 6.1 Primary Objectives of Military Coercion

I Policy Change (threats)	II Policy Change (operational use of force)	III Regime Change (operational use of force)
Libya 1981	Libya 1986	Afghanistan 2001
Libya 1985	Iraq 1991	Iraq 2003
Iraq 1991	Iraq 1998	
Iraq 1994	Yugoslavia 1999 (March)	
Iraq 2003		
Yugoslavia 1998 (June)		
Yugoslavia 1998 (October)		
Yugoslavia 1999 (March)		
Afghanistan 2001		

II. Only in the case of the intervention designed to secure the removal of the Taliban and the destruction of al-Qaeda was there a move directly from I to III.

Affecting Incentives: Threat and the Prospect of Policy Change

Where incentives alone are targeted, threats aim to make stakes in compliance exceed stakes in deviance. The hope, in a straightforward IO logic, is that expected damage to the regime's position from intervention-related hardships would outweigh the benefits from the objectionable policy. Success hinges on (a) how the regime estimates the likelihood that the threat would be implemented, and (b) how it reckons the anticipated consequences. The weightiest consequences anticipated by the target might well be those desired by the intervener: rifts within the regime, alienation of the population, a strengthening of the opposition. Nevertheless, the IR model suggests that expected consequences are not always unwelcome to the regime since the foreign menace can generate a rally-round-the-flag effect and allow it to accuse political opponents of providing comfort to the enemy. Defiance also means that the regime need not abandon transgressive policies that had brought it some political benefits. In any event, the record indicates that being in the cross hairs of major norm-setters has rarely altered the behavior of renegades.

Yugoslavia, 1998 and 1999

NATO military threats in the late 1990s were meant to compel the regime to abandon its repressive policies in Kosovo. The province had, for some time, been a regional powder keg, its grip on Serbian emotions stemming from its place in its history, as the cult of Kosovo stood at the heart of the national myth and cultural iconography.[3] In the eighteenth century a growing number of Albanians settled in the province, where, within a hundred years, they became the ethnic majority. After World War II Kosovo became a nominally autonomous region within Serbia, and the demographic balance shifted ever more decisively in favor of its Albanian population. The 1974 Yugoslav constitution, to the dismay of many Serbs, gave the region virtually all of the prerogatives of a republic, further fueling regional tensions and Kosovo-Albanian desire for full independence. By the early 1980s, violent protests erupted, and Serbian resentment reached its highest pitch. Slobodan Milošević launched a campaign for the rights of Kosovo Serbs, resulting, as he became head of the Yugoslav Communist Party, in the rescinding of Kosovo's autonomy in 1989. His nationalism propelled him to the presidency of Serbia, and the 1990s saw an intensifying cycle of Albanian rebellion and regime repression.

Morally bruised by its inability to stop the massacres and ethnic cleansing in Rwanda and Bosnia, the international community, NATO in particular, decided to act more forcefully on Kosovo. Through the 1990s, the Kosovo Liberation Army (KLA), initially considered a terrorist organization, expanded its activities, spearheading an anti-Serbian insurgency. The momentum of KLA activities increased in 1998, prompting Serb security forces to launch a major offensive that drove thousands of Albanians from their homes. The Contact Group[4] warned Milošević of possible military retaliation.

On June 15, 1998, NATO launched Operation Determined Falcon, intended to intimidate Milošević with military overflights of nearby Macedonia and Albania. By any standard, the operation was unsuccessful: Milošević refused to pull his forces out of Kosovo, and vicious fighting within the region continued. The first Kosovo-related threat failed, by most accounts, because it was taken for what it was: a symbolic act carrying no serious threat to the regime. General Klaus Naumann, chair of the NATO military committee, subsequently concluded that the Yugoslav leader "rightly concluded that the NATO threat was a bluff."[5]

In early October Belgrade ignored a UN resolution calling for withdrawal of its troops from Kosovo. Shelling of Kosovo-Albanian villages intensified, as did the displacement of thousands of Albanian families. By the middle of the month, Richard Holbrooke was dispatched to Belgrade, in the wake of an "activation order" authorizing NATO to undertake air strikes upon ninety-six hours of determining that Belgrade had not complied with its demands. Holbrooke threatened that attacks would begin almost immediately if Milošević remained obdurate. The threat was perfectly credible, and an agreement was reached providing for the withdrawal of significant Serb forces and the deployment of international (OSCE) observers in the region, but the effect did not last. The agreement implied no restraints on KLA forces, fighting soon resumed, and Serbian forces reentered Kosovo. In one incident, forty-five Albanian civilians were killed in the village of Račak in retaliation for the murder of four Serbian policemen by the KLA. The October threats cannot, therefore, be considered very successful. The Clinton administration summoned the parties to a meeting in Rambouillet (near Paris), demanding acceptance of an agreement significantly increasing Kosovo's autonomy while maintaining, temporarily at least, Yugoslav sovereignty over the province. Yugoslav and Serbian security forces were to be withdrawn and replaced by Albanian police, while NATO troops (which might be deployed through Serbia) would enforce the arrangement. Under intense U.S. pressure, the Albanian side signed, but Milošević refused to do so, marking the third ineffective threat of military action against him. On March 24 NATO planes undertook what was to be a seventy-eight-day bombing campaign of Yugoslavia.

Why did Milošević not heed, in October and again in March, credible threats of NATO bombardment? Three reasons suggest themselves. First, apparently assuming the strikes would be modeled after Operation Desert Fox in Iraq, he did not expect heavy bombing. During the October 1998 talks, Milošević's response to Holbrooke's threat of air strikes was, "I'm sure the bombing will be very polite." When General Michael Short disagreed, the Yugoslav leader repeated, "Yes, I understand, but I'm sure the Americans will bomb with great politeness."[6]

Beyond an expectation of modest damage, Milošević could not be seen to cave in to NATO threats without significant domestic political risks. Most Serbs cared deeply about Kosovo, according to a survey conducted by the Belgrade weekly *NIN*, which reported that 69.5 percent of the respondents were willing to fight, or have a member of their family fight, if need be to retain the province.[7] In any case, his reckless policies had already caused the ethnic cleansing, by Croatian forces, of the Serbs in Krajina and the simultaneous crumbling of hopes for a union with Bosnian Serbs. By 1998 Kosovo was all that Milošević had to show for his nationalist policies; retreat on that front would have left nothing. Also, at the time of the October crisis, he was facing a new opposition coalition, the Alliance for Change, whereas "one of Milošević's top priorities was to ensure that as little attention as possible would be directed at his willingness to bargain with the international community over the province, and ultimately to make concessions to foreign negotiators."[8] Finally, the NATO threat provided an excuse to tighten the reins of domestic control, to convert what had previously been a "soft" dictatorship into one more harshly repressive. The independent media was squelched, universities were brought to heel, some vocal dissidents were assassinated, and those apparatchiks of suspect loyalty were purged. Undoubtedly, Milošević understood that he could consolidate his dictatorship under the cover of foreign bombing.

As modest military punishment was expected, as the domestic political risks of compliance seemed considerable, and as some political benefits from defiance were apparent, it is not surprising, from both an IO and IR perspective, that the threat failed to budge Milošević. Because NATO pressure actually strengthened his domestic position, an IR logic further discouraged compliance.

Iraq, 1991, 1994, and 2003

When, on August 2 1990, 140,000 Iraqi troops and 1,800 tanks, spearheaded by two Republican Guard divisions, swept into neighboring Kuwait, the international community was galvanized into action. This was exceptionally brazen aggression, and it placed Iraqi forces in a position to occupy northeastern Saudi Arabia, making Saddam master of nearly half the world's oil. That same day, the UN Security Council, with a vote of 14–0, called for Iraqi withdrawal; four days later, it authorized an economic embargo of Iraq. Saudi Arabia requested deployment of U.S. troops to prevent an Iraqi attack against itself, and Operation Desert Shield was launched. Between August and mid-November a formidable array of U.S. forces (240,000 troops and 1,600 aircraft) was dispatched to the region, and an international coalition, with substantial participation from the Arab League, was assembled to confront Iraq. Although the initial purpose was to prevent aggression against Saudi Arabia, by early October U.S. war planners began considering steps to dislodge Iraq from Kuwait. President Bush decided to boost U.S. troop strength in the region to over 400,000, and on November 29 the UN Security Council authorized the organization's members "to use all means necessary" to secure the liberation of Kuwait.

Many expected that threat of war would lead Saddam to withdraw from the occupied land: since the disparity of forces pretty much guaranteed his defeat. Yet the Iraqi leader remained defiant, and it was only a major air and land campaign that dislodged him several months later. As in the case of Yugoslavia, the threat's ineffectiveness rested on the modest damage expected from foreign military action and in the immensity of what Iraq would have to give up to meet foreign demands.

Three phases in Saddam's reasoning can be inferred from his actions and utterances at the time. Phase 1, covering the initial weeks after the invasion, reflected disbelief that the United States and its allies considered their interests deeply enough engaged to warrant an invasion. Perhaps the ambiguous statements about U.S. commitment to Kuwait by U.S. Ambassador

April Glaspie, shortly before the invasion, made Saddam doubt that Washington's threats were earnest[9] and believe that relations with the United States would normalize after a brief period of U.S. posturing.[10] On August 12 he offered to pull out of Kuwait only if terms that he must have known were unacceptable to the United States were met, including the withdrawal of all Israeli troops from Arab lands and U.S. military departure from Saudi Arabia. Their nature makes it unlikely that the demands were meant as more than rhetorical flourish or that the consequences of their rejection were much feared. Coupled with Saddam's estimate that retaliation was unlikely, the benefits of successful defiance were great: there was the immense economic value associated with control of Kuwait's oil wealth, and there was the inestimable gratification of being within reach of hegemony in the Arab world, consistent with images of Iraq's past glory and future destiny. Both would have served to bolster his domestic legitimacy to a level commensurate with such grandiose achievements.

By late September Iraqi thinking seems to have entered its second phase: U.S. anger came to be taken seriously, along with uncertainty that it would be acted on. The regime doubted there was sufficient support within the United States for massive military action, expecting that the Bush administration eventually would compromise with Iraq.[11] Also, Saddam reckoned that the Arab coalition arrayed against him would not hold. To that end, he did his best to present himself as the champion of the have-not against the oil-rich Arab countries, hoping for support from Jordan, Yemen, Sudan, Libya, Morocco, and Algeria.[12] His sudden concern with Palestinian rights, and the point made in his August 12 initiative of demanding Israeli withdrawal from occupied lands, was meant to ingratiate him with those committed to the Palestinian cause, and he expected that a groundswell of public sympathy within Saudi Arabia, Syria, and Egypt would pry them from the American embrace. As the coalition fragmented, the United States would be willing to strike a bargain, one that might secure Iraqi "rights" with regard to the contested Bubiyan and Warba islands and the Rumaila oilfield. An agreement might include some of the August 12 demands, further bolstering Iraq's stature in the Arab world and, by extension, Saddam's domestic position. The important thing was not to flinch in the meantime, an apparent inflexibility demonstrated by a September 21 announcement rejecting any possibility of retreat from Kuwait.[13] The expected benefits of intransigence were considerable, the expected costs manageable.

Phase 3 was entered around mid-November, when any doubts about U.S. resolve were removed. By deciding to double the U.S. deployment by January, President Bush signaled an irrevocable intent — given the difficulties of maintaining so large a force in the Middle East for long and the loss of face implied by withdrawing while leaving Saddam in Kuwait. Assuming he stayed there, a military offensive became virtually inevitable,[14] especially since the UN Security Council had given Iraq only until January 15 to pull out of Kuwait. Yet, some of the phase 2 logic was extended to this period. If ground combat was initiated, Saddam seemed to reason, U.S. casualties would cause Washington to cut short the invasion,[15] and still he expected that Arab discomfort at backing the United States against another Arab country would devastate the coalition, but that this would only happen once fighting began, especially if Israel were drawn into the fighting.[16] As long as his power base remained intact, the fact of having stood up to the United States would strengthen his position in the Arab world even if Kuwait were lost. Thus, even during phase 3, the decision to stand firm may have been rational in light of the regime's expectations.

There is a parallel between the failure of armed threats in Yugoslavia and Iraq. In both cases, the expected costs of foreign military action were moderate: not so much because intervention was considered unlikely, but because of its modest anticipated scope. Milošević thought bombing would be "polite," meant more to make a point than to inflict damage. Saddam moved from considering a U.S.-led invasion unlikely to believing it would be short-lived, once opposition burgeoned in the Arab world and as the United States took its first casualties. In both cases, too, the political payoffs from successful defiance were substantial: in the final analysis, expected benefits exceeded expected costs.

Following the terrorist attacks of September 11, 2001, and the successful military action against al-Qaeda and its Taliban supporters, the mood in the United States favored decisive action against other objectionable regimes, a determination focusing mostly on Iraq. A sense of unfinished business was coupled with a claim that Saddam possessed weapons of mass destruction, a claim supported by Iraq's ambiguous record of compliance with the UN arms inspectors (culminating in its 1998 decision to cease all cooperation).

A campaign demanding that Iraq come clean about its weapons of mass destruction was buttressed by congressional support for war if it did not. Under the pressure, Saddam agreed to allow the UN arms inspectors back into Iraq, with free access to suspect facilities; but even as they resumed their activities, Washington continued to affirm that Iraq retained its WMD programs, warning of a last chance to avert war.[17] UN inspectors could not corroborate U.S. claims, and France, Germany, and Russia urged giving them more time to assess the facts, but the administration dismissed the UN reports. Early in 2003 the U.S. troop buildup reached its target strength. Toward the end of January, Hans Blix, the chief UN weapons inspector, reported that he had seen nothing to justify a war;[18] still, Washington pressed for a UN Security Council resolution authorizing military action. Given the lack of evidence on WMDs and the insistence of several Security Council members on continued inspections, no resolution was offered. The thrust of the U.S. campaign shifted to dismissing the validity of the UN weapons inspectors' work on Iraq,[19] proclaiming that "we don't need anybody's permission" to react.[20] Determined to do what it had set out to do, the United States attacked Iraq on March 20, providing another apparent example of a failed threat: Saddam's incentives were not, it seems, altered to the point of acceding to U.S. demands.

In fact, however, this case sheds no light at all on the ability of threats to induce policy change, since this can be assessed only where two conditions are met: (1) The threatener does in fact seek a policy change (rather than, say, the regime's ouster), and (2) the threatenee is materially capable of complying with the former's demands. Neither appears to have been the case here. Even assuming that the Bush administration really believed its own claims about Iraqi WMDs, there was not at the time nor has there been since credible evidence of their existence prior to the invasion. The inability of the UN inspectors to find a smoking gun, and the far more important inability of the U.S.-led occupying force to unearth any such evidence, suggests that there were no significant WMDs to own up to or dismantle. Even if thoroughly intimidated, Saddam could not very well have done what was demanded of him. In any event, subsequent evidence indicated that he attempted to strike a deal with the United States — offering, through back channels, to allow U.S. troops and experts unfettered searches for such weapons on Iraqi territory.[21] The offer was rebuffed, indicating that an invasion of Iraq and removal of Saddam were the ultimate objectives, and that putative weapons of mass destruction served to legitimize, not account for, the decision to go to war.

The year 1994 provided the only instance of an effective threat against Iraq. Late September saw a renewal of aggressive Iraqi rhetoric and, by early October, U.S. intelligence detected the deployment of two armored Republican Guard divisions near Kuwait's border. The United States responded by dispatching the aircraft carrier *George Washington*, as well as a Marine Expeditionary Unit and Army Mechanized Task Force, to the region. France followed, deploying a destroyer; Britain sent both a destroyer and a frigate.

The United States and Britain declared they would use force, if necessary, to deal with the Iraqi buildup, and the UN Security Council demanded that Iraq recall its forces. Saddam responded, pulling back the two divisions and recognizing Kuwaiti sovereignty and the border between the two countries. He engaged in no similarly provocative moves since the Western show of force.

By most standards, the threat effectively modified the renegade's incentives. Its success probably stemmed from the virtual certainty that the U.S.-led coalition would repel and punish the contemplated aggression, with consequences potentially more serious for the regime than those following Operation Desert Storm. But regime incentives may also have been different in 1994: while Iraqi aggression probably would have proceeded in the absence of a U.S. response,[22] Saddam's major purpose may have been to show his core supporters that he could defy the United States.[23] To the extent that the latter incentive dominated, the stakes in defiance were probably offset by the likely costs. In any event, this must be considered a case of successful IO-type deterrence.

Libya, 1985 and 1981

In the case of Libya, again threats were ineffective. Libya's sponsorship of international terrorism, especially via its support of the Abu Nidal organization, had been widely condemned by the international community. On December 27, 1985, virtually simultaneous terrorist attacks against the Rome and Vienna airports left 20 killed and at least 110 wounded, and credible intelligence pointed to Abu Nidal. On January 24 two U.S. aircraft carrier groups steamed into the Mediterranean, north of Libya. Although their stated purpose was to defend the freedom of navigation in international waters, the main goal, according to an administration official, "was to make [Qaddafi] understand what he would face if he promoted more terrorism."[24] In a continuation of this operation, on March 23, an armada of 3 U.S. aircraft carriers, 27 accompanying vessels, submarines, and over 200 planes undertook naval maneuvers near Libyan waters, venturing into the Gulf of Sidra, which Libya claimed as its territorial waters. A modest amount of fire was actually exchanged before the maneuvers came to a close.

Was this show of force a success? As the primary purpose was to stop future acts of Libya-sponsored terrorism, and since the bombing of the Berlin discotheque on April 4, which killed several Americans, was not deterred, success cannot be claimed. In some views, the short-term effects were opposite to what Washington desired.[25] It is hard to know what Qaddafi thought of the probability of further U.S. action, but his apparent surprise at the subsequent April 1986 bombing raid suggests that he did not anticipate significant retaliation. Most important, the very basis for his legitimacy was, in Qaddafi's view, his revolutionary symbolism and charisma, whereas terrorist sponsorship was the source of his claim to being a world-class revolutionary. No increased domestic commitment to his ideational goals was witnessed, nor was improved positioning relative to a (virtually nonexistent) domestic opposition. Nevertheless, the stakes in defiance were substantial, and there is little evidence that Qaddafi expected the U.S. show of force to yield meaningful offensive military action. His unsavory incentives were not offset.

To some extent, the 1985 threats mirrored those attempted five years earlier. In August 1981, on President Reagan's orders, the U.S. Navy undertook maneuvers in the Gulf of Sidra, an action leading to the downing of two Libyan jets. Although the professed purpose of the maneuvers was to make a point of defending freedom of navigation in waters that few nations other than Libya considered Libyan, the real intent was almost certainly broader: to impress Qaddafi with a demonstration of U.S. military power. It was part of a strategy "meant to heap considerable pressure on Qaddafi and induce a change in his behavior regarding terrorism."[26]

By no means was that objective achieved. Several well-publicized Libyan plans to assassinate foreign leaders (including senior U.S. officials) in 1981 and 1982, Libya's apparent support of Hezbollah's 1983 attack on the U.S. embassy in Beirut, and the rash of terrorist activities attributed to Qaddafi in 1985, necessitating that year's U.S. intimidation attempts in the Gulf of Sidra, testified to the failure of the 1981 show of force.

Afghanistan, 2001

Our final instance of a threat — one that, yet again, failed to force the desired policy change — involved the Taliban regime. Following the September 11 terrorist attacks, the Bush administration demanded that Osama bin Laden and his top associates be turned over to the United States. In a September 20 speech to Congress, the president's demands included the closing of all terrorist camps on Afghanistan's territory, giving the United States full access to the camps to verify compliance, and the delivery of all terrorists and members of their support structure. He required that "The Taliban must act and act immediately or they will share in [the terrorists'] fate."[27] Despite the forceful threats, the Taliban temporized during the weeks of the U.S. military buildup, seeking irrefutable proof of al-Qaeda's culpability, and finally refused to turn Osama bin Laden over. On October 8 air attacks were launched.

It is hard to doubt that Washington's threats were taken seriously, although the Taliban probably hoped that U.S. resolve would not survive a ground war with significant American casualties. What weighed more heavily, it seems, was the impossibility of complying with U.S. demands while maintaining the basis for the regime's legitimacy. A decision to deliver a fellow fundamentalist, one whose life purpose was to battle the same "infidel" that the Taliban had vowed to oppose, would have subverted the ideational basis for the regime's claim to rule. Mullah Omar himself explained that they could not deliver Osama: "If we did, it means we are not Muslims . . . that Islam is finished."[28] There is no evidence that the threats actually altered the domestic incentive structure in a way favorable to the Taliban, but it seems that a combination of low anticipated costs once a ground war was initiated and very high ideational stakes in defiance precluded policy change.

Military threats have rarely altered renegade policies. Only one of our nine threat episodes (Iraq 1994) was unambiguously successful. Failures are more closely connected to a low perceived probability of military action, or to a low estimate of its likely costs, than to such things as rally-round-the-flag effects or a reconfiguring of domestic politics beneficial to the regime. Unlike the situation with economic sanctions, then, the IO model does a better job of explaining the outcome than does the IR model.

This observation may be translated into the sort of quantitative expression on which we have so far relied (table 6.2). Beginning with the following truth table, we list the instances of threat examined here, asking whether they were successful (success = 1) or not (success = 0). We also ask if they were accompanied by a perception of high expected cost (probability of action as well as its likely destructiveness): if so, IO = 1; if not IO = 0. Finally, we examine whether they were coupled with invigorated political incentives to renegade behavior as a result of the threat (if so, IR = 1; if not, IR = 0).

This yields the information shown in table 6.3.[29] Here, $\omega = 13$, implying

TABLE 6.2 The Correlates of Military Threats

Threat	Success	IO	IR
Libya 1981	0	0	0
Libya 1985	0	0	0
Iraq 1991	0	0	1
Iraq 1994	1	1	0
Iraq 2003	na	na	na
Yugoslavia 6/98	0	0	0
Yugoslavia 10/98	0	0	0
Yugoslavia 3/99	0	1	1
Afghanistan 2001	0	0	0

TABLE 6.3 Military Threats and the IO Model

	Success	Failure
IO Effect	Iraq 1994 (1)	Yugoslavia 3/99 (1)
No IO Effect	(0)	Libya 1981, Libya 1985, Iraq 1991, Yugoslavia 6/98, Yugoslavia 10/98, Afghanistan 2001 (6)

that the odds of success with an IO effect are thirteen times greater than absent such an effect.

In table 6.4, $\omega = 0.82$, demonstrating that the odds of success are approximately the same with or without an IR effect. The difference between the two numbers indicates that the relative power of IO and IR effects are *opposite* to what we observed with economic sanctions. A possible explanation for the difference is that, with sanctions, rent-seeking behavior creates interests not produced by military threats. Moreover, when faced with something as momentous as military threat, opposition often makes common cause with the regime. For example, in the Yugoslav case, most of Milošević's opponents decided to face down the threat with the regime, making it hard to portray them as foreign lackeys.

TABLE 6.4 Military Threats and the IR Model

	Success	Failure
No IR Effect	Iraq 1994 (1)	Libya 1981, Libya 1985, Yugoslavia 6/98, Yugoslavia 10/98, Afghanistan 2001 (5)
IR Effect	(0)	Iraq 1991, Yugoslavia 3/99 (2)

Use of Force: Incentives, Capabilities, and the Prospect of Regime Change

Actual force may be directed both at capabilities and at incentives — as in the 1998 Operation Desert Fox, intended, it seemed, to force Iraqi compliance with UN weapons inspectors and to degrade Iraq's military capabilities (possibly also to weaken Saddam Hussein's domestic position). In that case, the specific objective was ambiguous enough to make discussion of success or failure somewhat moot. In most instances, however, fairly clear evaluations are possible.

Yugoslavia and Operation Allied Force

The comparative wealth of information on Yugoslavia and on the domestic impact of the NATO intervention makes this an especially fruitful subject for analysis. Although the air campaign was expected to be quick and successful, it lasted eleven weeks and involved thirty-eight thousand sorties. It was multiphased, beginning with attacks on anti-aircraft defense and command bunkers, proceeding to a destruction of Yugoslav infrastructure in Kosovo and southern Serbia, and culminating in the strategic bombing of Belgrade and northern Serbia — the last phase included attacks on economic facilities and utilities, with the purpose of weakening the civilian population's will to resist.

The war, according to President Clinton, was directed at both Yugoslav capacity and incentives: "To demonstrate NATO's seriousness of purpose . . . to deter an even bloodier offensive against innocent civilians in Kosovo, and, if necessary, to seriously damage the Serb military's capacity to harm the

people in Kosovo."[30] Beyond this, there was little doubt that a broader objective was to promote the demise of the Milošević regime. Many accepted
that "Overthrowing Milosevic was built into the rationale for [the] war . . .
that defeat in Kosovo would inevitably topple the Milosevic regime."[31] While
there was some expectation that popular unhappiness with the bombing
would be channeled toward the regime, it was also hoped that it would chip
away at support from elites whose own sources of wealth and power were
being destroyed by the bombing.[32] To what extent did the bombing advance
these purposes?

Policy Alteration   This clearly was produced by Operation Allied Force,
supporting the predictions of the IO model. Given the meaning Kosovo
held for most Serbs, the incentives to resist were strong; but some two months
into the bombing, the costs (coupled with the fear that NATO ground troops
would be sent into the fray) began to dominate popular feelings, and few in
Belgrade objected to NATO's terms that made Kosovo a de-facto UN pro-
tectorate, that forced the evacuation from Kosovo of virtually all Serbian
security forces, and that entrusted the region's internal security to NATO.

Serbian civilian dead have been estimated at five hundred by Human
Rights Watch, with several thousand wounded.[33] The economic consequences[34] were grave: much of the nation's infrastructure was destroyed,
including fifty highways and railroad bridges, two oil refineries, and a substantial portion of Serbia's POL stock. Destruction encompassed fourteen
major industrial facilities (some owned by Milošević cronies), nine of Serbia's major electric power-generating facilities, and a number of electric
power transmission towers.[35] The result was devastating to an economy already debilitated by years of isolation, and attacks on utilities caused deep
hardship, adding to the trauma of nightly bombing raids. Core instruments
of regime control also were destroyed, including the ministries of defense
and interior in Belgrade, as well as a twenty-three-story office building housing Milošević's Serbian Socialist Party and his wife's United Yugoslav Left
(JUL) Party.

Its initial bravado aside, the public became war-weary by late May.[36]
"The energy that had galvanized Serbs into an outpouring of popular rage
and defiance at the NATO bombing during the early weeks of the war had
dissipated into a struggle for personal survival."[37] Although the military
establishment remained defiant, the will to resist was being sapped from
economic rent-seekers, whose assets were being destroyed, from leaders
who may have feared for the regime's survivability, and from opposition

figures who had rallied round the regime during the early phases of the bombing.[38]

The outcome was nevertheless much harder to achieve than the Clinton administration and NATO war planners had expected. Ivo Daalder, of the National Security Council staff, reports that "all available evidence suggests that the betting was that Milosevic would soon capitulate."[39] As the bombing began, Madeleine Albright ventured that "I don't see this as a long-term operation. I think that this is something . . . that is achievable within a relatively short period of time"[40] This expectation rested on Milošević's proven pragmatism and on the experience of the NATO bombing of Bosnian Serb military installations around Sarajevo in 1995, to lift the siege of that city and to bring the Serbian side to the negotiating table. On that occasion, relatively light bombing achieved its objective. Viewed though "the lenses of Bosnia,"[41] NATO expected rapid capitulation. Why was this not achieved? The answer must be sought in the IR model: in incentives amplified by feelings of nationalism in the face of the external military assault, by the rally–effect, and by the constraints it placed on the political opposition.

NATO bombing propelled nationalist sentiment to levels not attained before the attack, as observed in virtually every report on the political climate in Serbia. According to one description of the situation, "A wave of stubborn patriotism swept through Serbia. For a time, political differences were forgotten. The country was under attack, and like Londoners during the blitz, Serbs exhibited a stubborn pride."[42] According to another, "Public fear and anxiety about the bombing clearly seemed to be outweighed by a growing outrage over the attacks, which triggered a surge of Serbian nationalist sentiment across the country."[43]

A leading Belgrade public opinion analyst confirmed that both pro- and anti-Milošević forces regarded NATO as their common enemy.[44] For much of the nation, distinctions between nation, regime, and leader were obscured by foreign bombing, no endorsement of which could be found within the opposition — some of which felt tainted by previously pro-Western leanings.[45] Even the independent media, usually critical of the regime, climbed on to the patriotic bandwagon.

Although the IO and IR dynamics operated at cross-purposes during the first two months of the bombing, fear and hardship ultimately trumped pride and defiance. By late May, attendance at anti-NATO demonstrations declined, significant troop desertions were reported,[46] there were antiwar demonstrations in several Serbian cities, and both opposition leaders and regime insiders began calling for a diplomatic solution. The IO logic prevailed eventually, but not without making capitulation and agreement less likely in the short run.

NATO Bombing and the Regime's Collapse   Claims to the contrary notwithstanding, no clear causal chain links bombing to regime overthrow. Had Milošević been ousted during the bombing, a connection could not be denied; had this occurred in the following weeks or months, it would have been quite plausible. Since, however, almost a year and a half separated the two events, the interval is too long for causation to be assumed, but not so long that it must be dismissed. To assume it, one would have to believe that the circumstances that ended the regime were set in motion by the military action, that, although they took some time to mature, they would not otherwise have materialized, and that, once they did mature, the outcome became inevitable or highly probable.

To argue this case, a causal mechanism connecting bombing to regime collapse would have to be found and traced through the intervening period. The mechanism would encompass developments that (a) led to the regime's toppling and (b) also are attributable to the bombing. Proceeding accordingly, a first task is to identify those developments that, according to the authors who most closely followed the regime's demise, caused Milošević's downfall. The second task is to find out whether they were rooted in the military action. On this basis, we may ask whether there is a credible case for linking the regime's demise to the intervention.

Three interrelated developments are included in most narratives of the conditions that produced the events of early October 2000 leading to the regime's collapse:[47] first, growing fissures within the regime — reflected in defections, purges, and a general demoralization — that prevented it from offering a unified resistance to forces arrayed against it; second, the ability of the opposition to overcome its internal differences and to mount a credible electoral challenge to Milošević; and third, the public's growing disillusion with its government and the emergence of nontraditional sources of resistance to the regime.

Fissures Within the Regime   In the interval between the NATO attacks and the regime's collapse, regime cohesion was breaking down with defections from Milošević's Socialist Party of Serbia (SPS) amid resentment at the growing influence of his wife's JUL Party (considered a club of cronies, rent-seekers, sycophants, and toadies) on regime policies.[48] Many Socialists also resented the presence within the government of Vojislav Šešelj's Serbian

Radical Party (SRS), a right-wing, ultranationalist organization that regime insiders despised.[49] There was also unhappiness within the military, a number of officers expressing "shock and disappointment" when Milošević accepted NATO's terms.[50] Although he placed a fellow indicted war criminal, Dragoljub Ojdanić, at the head of the military, frustration was apparent below the top tier of its hierarchy.[51] As the military declined to come to the regime's rescue in October 2000, its disaffection must be considered a cause of the ultimate outcome.

If internal fissures weakened the regime, we still must ask whether these stemmed from NATO's war and its outcome. Probably not, since significant rifts plagued the regime well before the military action. The JUL's influence on major matters of state had been apparent for some time. In October and November 1998, Milošević purged a number of regime figures no longer willing to back his policies,[52] most of whom were replaced by JUL loyalists and those acceptable to the regime's most hard-line elements. At the same time, Šešelj was assuming an increasingly influential position — to the dismay of regime moderates.

It could, therefore, be argued that pre-existing dissension within the regime, muted during the bombing, simply resurfaced as it came to an end. If international pressure contributed to fissures, it did so in another way. In May 1999, the European Union, in a display of "smart" sanctions, announced a list of 305 key people within the regime who were banned from doing business with, or traveling to, EU countries. This damaged the economic interests of Milošević allies and JUL fellow travelers, leading some to question the value of continued loyalty. "The list sowed dissent among the senior ranks of the Milosevic regime, by hitting key figures in their pockets, and humiliated them by refusing them visas."[53] At the same time, Milošević's indictment on May 27 for war crimes fueled fears among many of his associates that they would be next. Several reportedly contacted the International Criminal Tribunal for the Former Yugoslavia (ICTY), offering cooperation and testimony.[54]

Thus, international punishment probably sowed dissent within the regime, but this does not imply that the *war* did.

A Consolidated (and Expanding) Opposition   A frequently emphasized cause of Milošević's downfall was the readiness of a previously fragmented opposition to make common cause behind a viable candidate in the September 2000 presidential election, and to present a united front when the regime tried to steal the election by falsifying its results. Absent a unified opposition, the regime may well have survived, but it is improbable that unity was a product of NATO bombing.

One might argue that the war and its outcome undermined Milošević's standing, and that this vulnerability encouraged antiregime forces to coalesce in the hope that unity would enable them to prevail. Just how vulnerable Milošević was at that juncture will be assessed presently; a prior question is whether an opposition alliance was encouraged by NATO's military intervention. Two issues stand in the way of an affirmative answer: first, coalitions of opposition parties had existed well before the bombing; second, the Democratic Opposition of Serbia (DOS), which toppled the regime, exhibited no more unity than its predecessors.

The first major prewar coalition, the Democratic Movement of Serbia (DEPOS) appeared in 1992, ahead of that year's presidential and parliamentary elections. It included Vuk Drašković's Party of Serbian Renewal (SPO), the New Democracy Movement for Serbia, the Serbian Peasants Party, Vojislav Koštunica's Democratic Party of Serbia (DSS), and the Civic Alliance (GSS). It did not, however, include one leading antiregime party — Zoran Djindjić's Democratic Party (DS). In the event, the governing coalition of Milošević's Socialist Party of Serbia and the ultranationalist Serbian Radical Party handily carried the vote. The next notable opposition partnership, Zajedno ("Together"), encompassing the SPO, DS, GSS, and DSS, emerged to contest the 1996 elections. It did not prevail in the federal elections, but it did quite well in the local elections, and, when the regime declined to recognize the outcome, mass demonstrations, lasting three months, were organized.

Thus, while an opposition coalition was a necessary condition for the regime's removal — initially at the ballot box, and, when the results were dismissed by the regime, through massive street action — such partnerships had appeared in the past, making it hard to believe that, without NATO's armed intervention, a movement like DOS would not have appeared in 2000. In any case, the SPO (one of the strongest of the opposition parties) did not participate in the alliance, so the show of unity was no greater than with DEPOS, and, arguably, lesser than with Zajedno. Accordingly, neither the fact nor the scope of DOS can be attributed to the military action.

It could be argued at least that new sources of opposition to the regime emerged at this juncture. A movement that contributed to the regime's overthrow was the group Otpor ("Resistance"), comprised of intensely committed college and high school students. With its symbol of a clenched fist and its slogan Gotov Je ("He's Finished"), Otpor was steeped in principles of nonviolent resistance.[55] Its effectiveness was recognized by some $3 million worth of U.S. assistance[56] and by the brutal repression directed at its members.[57] Nevertheless, and although Otpor's power increased with growing antiregime feeling, it was founded in 1998, well before the NATO bombings.[58]

Growing Public Disillusionment   A decline in support both for Milošević and the SPS had become apparent at the time of the 2000 electoral campaign, and the question is whether this can be linked to NATO's military action. It can, according to General Wesley Clark, the NATO supreme allied commander at the time of the bombing. In his view, "NATO bombing contributed to this in an important way because it brought home to the Serb people the consequences of Milosevic and his leadership."[59] Given the associated destruction and de facto loss of Kosovo, the action should have hurt public support for the regime and its leader, but this is not the conclusion to which the data lead.

Figure 6.1 traces Milošević's popular ratings before and after the bombing. It indicates that favorable opinion declined between the two surveys bracketing the intervention. But it also shows support trending downward since 1993 — making the 1999 decline appear as a continuation of the previous trend, not as a discontinuity coincident with the bombing. In fact, approval ratings increased during the next eight months, possibly because of Milošević's association with reconstruction efforts, contradicting the view

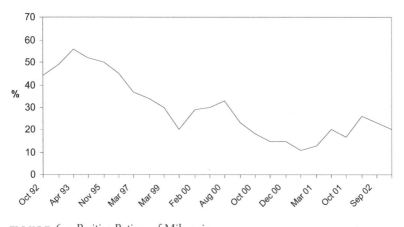

FIGURE 6.1 Positive Ratings of Milosevic
Source: *Centar Za Politikološka Istraživanja i Javno Mnenje,* Institut Za Društvene Nauke, Beograd

that war-induced dissatisfaction had taken over. His standing declined again only when the election campaign got underway — as, for the first time, the opposition presented the electorate with an appealing alternative to Milo-šević. Unlike Vuk Drašković, Vojislav Koštunica had never joined the ruling coalition; unlike Zoran Djindjić, he had remained in Yugoslavia during the bombing. Most importantly, and unlike the regime's incumbents, he led a modest existence (driving a Yugo, living in a small apartment) and had earned a reputation for impeccable integrity. Also, he had amply demonstrated his nationalist credentials (lambasting NATO and the United States during his campaign) without the chauvinistic extremism of Milošević and Šešelj. As the campaign progressed, his popularity soared, reaching approximately 80 percent approval ratings by the time of the election.

Milošević was defeated because, in a situation of popular despair, the opposition came up with a candidate whom most Serbs deemed a desirable alternative to their current leader: a development endogenous to Serbian politics, not one caused by the bombing. It could still be argued that the bombing must have diminished Milošević's standing because he was held accountable for the associated trauma and the loss of Kosovo. But this is doubtful. To begin with, many did not regard the final settlement as a clear-cut defeat because Yugoslavia retained a theoretical sovereignty over Kosovo. A survey conducted by the weekly *NIN* just after the peace settlement found that a plurality of 46 percent of Serbs felt that their country had won the war, while only 20.5 percent deemed NATO the victor (26.5 estimated that there was no winner).[60]

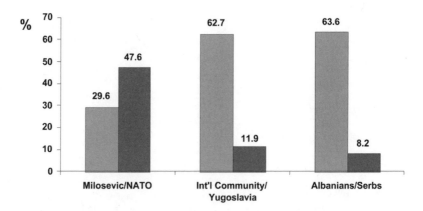

FIGURE 6.2 Who Is Responsible for NATO's Intervention?

Although they had come to dislike and distrust Milošević, only a minority of Serbs considered him responsible for their military ordeal. A poll asking whom the respondents deemed responsible for the bombing (paired questions) found that only 29.8 percent blamed the regime's policies, whereas 55.2 percent said it was prompted by the economic or the political interests of the West.[61] Asked, further, whether major responsibility for the NATO intervention rested with (a) Milošević or NATO, (b) Yugoslavia or the international community, or (c) the Albanians or the Serbs, most respondents considered the international community more culpable than Yugoslavia, Albanians more responsible than Serbs, and NATO more at fault than Milošević.[62]

Since Milošević escaped much of the blame for the bombing, it is unlikely to have cost him the election. Feelings toward the regime reflected diffuse anger and dissatisfaction that had been festering for several years, and that was temporarily mitigated by a rally-effect and the regime's reconstruction efforts. Both of the latter were occasioned by the military action, without which development of the dissatisfaction may have progressed in an uninterrupted manner.[63]

NATO strikes suggest that military action of considerable scope, even if limited to air attacks, may endanger the renegade's instruments of coercion and cause great trauma to regime insiders and the general population,[64] and that this may cause desired shifts in regime policy. But the Yugoslav case provides little support for the expectation that military coups or popular revolts follow such coercion, as the IR logic often trumps the costs and trauma of military punishment.

The goals of the 1986 raids against Libya and of Operation Desert Storm against Iraq bear some similarity to NATO's purpose in Yugoslavia. In both cases, the immediate aim was to alter regime policy: to curb Libyan-sponsored terrorism and to force Iraq's unconditional withdrawal from Kuwait. It also was hoped that the action would spur popular opposition to the government and discontent within the military and security forces — raising the possibility of the regime's ouster. These two interventions also provide a valuable comparative reference since, in one case, the scope of the intervention was far slighter than in Yugoslavia (involving a concerted but brief raid on a limited number of targets), and, in the other, far greater (including a ground invasion encompassing several hundred thousand allied troops). The three cases encompass action against three types of renegade behavior: massive ethnic cleansing (Yugoslavia), sponsorship of terrorist activity (Libya), and outright territorial aggression (Iraq).

Libya, 1986

Qaddafi's support of terrorism (and other misbehavior) had excited the ire not only of the United States, but also of much of the Arab world and Western Europe. U.S. economic sanctions were not having a restraining effect. The Reagan administration determined to deal forcefully with Libya. The failure of the intimidation measures in the Gulf of Sidra was reflected in the April 5 bombing of a West Berlin discotheque, killing three people (two Americans) and traced, via intercepted communications, to Tripoli. The day after the bombing, President Reagan ordered air strikes (Operation El Dorado Canyon) on Libya. This involved attacks on five targets in Libya and two in Benghazi. The strikes were launched from U.S. naval air units and F-111 bombers operating from British soil. All five Libyan targets were hit, although their destruction was not, in every case, as complete as had been hoped.[65]

The primary objective was to force Qaddafi to stop sponsoring terrorism by denting both his incentives and his ability to do so,[66] but it is not clear that this was achieved. The U.S. State Department reported that although detectable Libyan involvement in terrorist activity declined in 1986 and 1987, Qaddafi showed no credible signs of reforming.[67] In 1988 the State Department labeled Libya the third most active state sponsor of terrorism. It has, moreover, been questioned whether the lull in Libyan terrorist activity was attributable to the raids, several other explanations offering themselves. The decrease could have been due to the regime's greater care to disguise its involvement.[68] Also, soon after the air strikes, many European nations adopted stricter measures against Libya, curtailing the number of Libyan diplomats in their countries while tightening surveillance of those who remained.[69] This complicated the logistics of planning and executing terrorist operations. Finally, it has been suggested that Qaddafi's military difficulties in Chad in 1986 and 1987 (in which as many as three thousand Libyans were killed) decreased his enthusiasm for risky foreign ventures.[70]

Another purpose of the air strikes was to weaken (fatally, it was hoped) Qaddafi's hold on power. The most obvious way in which Qaddafi could have been removed was by killing him. This may not have been a primary aim of the attack on his compound, but the thought that he might perish did occur to war planners.[71] According to President Reagan, although the United States was not "dropping these tons of bombs, hoping to blow that man up," nevertheless "I don't think any of us would have shed tears if that had happened."[72]

At the very least, the Reagan administration expected the attacks to weaken Qaddafi's hold on power. A popular revolt among a largely apolitical population was not anticipated, but it was hoped that the bombing might encourage a military coup. Secretary of State Shultz claimed that there was "considerable dissidence" within the Libyan armed forces, and that a goal of the air raids was to encourage Qaddafi's overthrow. The strikes on his compound were partly intended to convey to regime insiders their own physical vulnerability under Qaddafi.[73] The strikes were also intended to demonstrate to the Libyan military that some of its most valued equipment could be destroyed,[74] increasing their resentment of the regime. However, the goal of increased domestic anger at Qaddafi was not attained.

One analysis of the aftermath of the air raids concludes that the jolt counterproductively strengthened Qaddafi vis-à-vis his opponents.[75] Partly, this was because the Libyan military's standing suffered from its performance during the raids. Libyan anti-aircraft artillery opened fire only after the strikes began, when most of the U.S. planes had already begun their trip home, and a Libyan newspaper castigated military officials who apparently abandoned their posts at the crucial hour.[76] The armed services were discredited within the corridors of government, diminishing the prospect of a coup. Simultaneously, the position of Qaddafi's revolutionary committees — shock troops of ideological loyalists inserted within all levels of organized activity (including the military) — was strengthened.[77] The U.S. attacks also provided Qaddafi with considerable fodder for mobilizational rhetoric. At a time of growing economic difficulties, due largely to falling oil prices and economic mismanagement, it was reported that the bombing had, in the short term at least, increased his nationalist public support.[78] If the verdict on the air strikes' impact on Libyan support of terrorism is mixed, the judgment on their contribution to regime change is not — they were unsuccessful at best, counterproductive at worst.

Iraq, 1991

By early January it was clear that the only way to ensure Saddam's withdrawal from Kuwait was by military force. On January 17 Operation Desert Storm was launched: a multistage operation beginning with air strikes against Iraqi military positions and the regime's coercive apparatus. On February 24 a coalition of U.S. and allied forces attacked across the Saudi–Kuwait border in the direction of Kuwait City.

Undeniably, Operation Desert Storm accomplished its military objectives. Within a mere two days of ground war, Iraqi forces were routed and Saddam announced their complete withdrawal. However, a corollary intent was to prompt Saddam Hussein's ouster. Apart from the possibility that he would be killed or incapacitated by a direct hit on one of his palaces or bunkers, the bombing was expected to weaken the security structure that constituted the "central nervous system" through which the regime controlled the country. It was especially hoped that significant destruction of Republican Guard units and facilities might undermine Saddam's grip on power.[79] And it was expected that a decisive and mortifying defeat would generate pressure for a coup d'état within the Baathist apparatus — [80]most likely from within the military establishment. The assumption was that "dealing Saddam another battlefield defeat would shatter what support he had within the military, which probably would then topple him."[81] Some hopes of a popular uprising also were entertained.

This confidence was quickly dashed. The expectation that the civilian hardship attending the destruction of Iraq's power grid, along with the inconvenience caused by destroying the bridges between the Tigris and Euphrates rivers in Baghdad, would rouse the population against Saddam was chimeric. Dropping messages urging the people to "rise up . . . for the overthrow of Saddam and his supporters"[82] produced no result. Although the lives of many Iraqis were disrupted by the war, the motivation to risk action that, in all likelihood, would be brutally crushed was nowhere evident.

There also was little to show for U.S. efforts to instigate an insurrection by military and other security forces. The regular army suffered considerably, but the Republican Guards and Special Republican Guards were not badly hurt. Similarly, the bombing of security headquarters did not meaningfully degrade the police, intelligence, and other security forces. In any case, their loyalty was firm: recruited from favored Sunni tribal groups, handsomely rewarded for their service, and commanded by members of Saddam's own family and tribe (al-Bu Nasir), they had little reason to turn against him.[83] Nor did the humiliation of defeat do the job. President Bush was bemused: "I thought, when the war ended, that he could not survive the humiliating defeat. . . . We did not believe that he would stay in office."[84]

The revolts that erupted were of a sectarian nature — among the Kurds in the North and the Shiites in the South — and they were brutally quashed by Saddam's forces. In any case, independence for either was discouraged by the international community's norm-setters, including the United States, which wanted a unified Iraq as a bulwark against fundamentalist Iran. The safe-haven later established to protect the Kurds, and the no-fly zone bene-fiting the Shiites, did weaken the regime's control of a significant portion of Iraqi territory, but its grip on the rest of the country may have strengthened after the war.[85]

These cases represent major instances of attempts to alter the delinquent policies of renegade regimes by offsetting their incentives and degrading their capabilities. In each case, the hope was that the pain and destruction would counter the benefits to the regime's position that the policies were expected to furnish; that popular and elite pressure would work toward that end. Although not the principal professed objective, some assumption that the intervention would hasten the regime's downfall — either by mass revolt or by military coup — was present in each of the three cases.

The record of success is ambiguous. With regard to capabilities, it was never evident how the targets damaged in Libya were instrumental to ter-rorism, while the military capacity destroyed in Yugoslavia was quite modest. In Iraq, however, the armed force occupying Kuwait was decisively routed. One implication is that renegade capacity cannot easily be jeopardized by air power alone. With regard to incentives, the verdict is also mixed. Al-though destruction and the threat of more to come did affect the motivations of both Saddam Hussein and Slobodan Milošević, it is less probable that they severely dented Muammar Qaddafi's — the obvious conclusion being that, when it comes to incentives, the amount of destruction matters.

The record provides least encouragement with regard to regime change: not one of the regimes was toppled by pressures rooted in the interventions. Some claims to the contrary notwithstanding, there is little evidence that Milošević's downfall owed anything to the NATO operation, and it is hard to argue that Qaddafi's and Saddam's positions were adversely affected by the military action directed against them.

Regime Change by Military Force: The Lessons of Afghanistan and Iraq

Where renegade policies cannot be quelled by military threats or actions aimed at capabilities and incentives, and where there is little likelihood of a domestically sparked overthrow, the regime may be directly removed and replaced by one more palatable. Such was the fate of the Taliban and the Saddam Hussein regime.

Afghanistan, 2001, and Iraq, 2003

Following the Taliban's refusal to meet U.S. demands, attacks began on October 7, 2001, with air strikes against Taliban air defenses and key towns under its control, amplified by gunship attacks on adversary ground positions and operations by U.S. special forces behind enemy lines. With U.S. air support, opposition units in the South (the Southern Alliance) scored major victories. As the battleground shifted to the North, a similar coalition of anti-Taliban forces took the battle to Kabul, after whose fall the bulk of the fighting focused on the mountainous areas where Taliban and al-Qaeda remnants sought refuge. By March an interim government led by Hamid Karzai assumed office, the adversary was substantially defeated, and the process of regime leadership transition moved from its military to its political phase.

The U.S. offensive in Iraq began on March 18 with a cruise missile attack followed by bombings and advances by U.S. and British troops northward from Kuwait, soon taking the city of Basra. Nine days after the start of the action, U.S. forces landed in the North, acting in concert with insurgent Kurdish forces. Overcoming initial setbacks, coalition forces advanced rapidly, capturing Baghdad on April 9. On May 1 President Bush declared the war pretty much over, as efforts moved toward establishing a political authority headed by the United States in the form of the Coalition Provisional Authority and a legitimizing, but essentially powerless, Iraqi Governing Council appointed by the United States.

In both the Afghan and Iraqi cases, the major military phase was conducted quickly and successfully. Even so, substantial pockets of resistance remained, whereas the political transition to a new and stable regime proved more difficult than initially reckoned. These words are being written while the situation in both countries is in flux, but the clearest appreciation of the problems following initial military success sometimes is gleaned while they are being encountered and addressed. Although far more has been invested in Iraq than Afghanistan, in terms of both military effort and economic assistance, similar problems appear.

Given its history and circumstances, it would have been unreasonable to expect rapid political success in Afghanistan, and three and a half years later, indicators are mixed. The level of conflict is reduced, a constitutional convention (the Loya Jirga) has taken place, and elections were conducted in October 2004. At the same time, the government's writ does not extend much beyond Kabul, while the situation in the countryside, where local

militia commanders control much of the political landscape, remains precarious.[86] Functioning as warlords, they often struggle over control of land and
water (an even scarcer resource), and these struggles are sometimes complicated by ethnic differences.[87] One major warlord, Gulbuddin Hekmatyar,
has claimed to lead a "holy war" against the Karzai government and U.S.
forces.[88] Opium production has soared. Despite steps at disarming the militias,[89] local security remained precarious three years after the U.S. intervention. According to a report by a UN Security Council mission to
Afghanistan, terrorism, drug-related crime, and factional fighting have hin-
dered rebuilding and transition to democracy.[90] There was soon evidence of
resurgent Taliban activity,[91] extending into the summer of 2004, while a
leaked memo of Secretary of Defense Rumsfeld complained of mixed results
with al-Qaeda, wondering whether recruitment of terrorists in madrassas
outpaced the rate at which they could be captured or killed, and predicting
a "long, hard slog" in both Afghanistan and Iran.[92]Despite elections, prospects for the government's control of the country beyond Kabul are
uncertain.

Although less time has elapsed since the invasion of Iraq, parallels are
apparent. Resistance there has been far more virulent than in Afghanistan,
with a continuing pattern of well-organized attacks on U.S. forces and their
Iraqi allies. U.S. soldiers are routine victims of car bombs, mortar attacks,
and small gunfire. A suicide bomber struck the headquarters of the International Red Cross, wounding at least 224 people.[93] The UN headquarters
in Baghdad were bombed, killing Sergio de Mello, the UN representative
in Iraq, and 17 other people, and wounding 100.[94] Several political figures
were assassinated, as were hundreds of Iraqis working for the new government; a large number of foreigners were kidnapped, some gruesomely be-
headed. April 2004 saw particularly high levels of violence in Falluja as well
as the eruption of a full-scale Shiite insurgency centered on Najaf. Security
forces collaborating with the United States have been targeted with particular vigor. The insurgency continued to gain momentum, especially in
Sunni-held areas, leading to another major U.S. invasion of Falluja in November 2004, which, in turn, prompted reinvigorated rebellion in several
other cities. The future political structure remains entangled in distrust between Sunnis (traditionally dominant) and Shiites, who for the first time in
the country's history are in a position to claim a share of power commensurate with their dominant demographic size, and who might find growing
common cause with Iran. Iraq's Kurds are intent on as much autonomy as
possible from Baghdad. Jihadis sometimes find common cause with deposed

Baathists. The appointment of the first Iraqi government, in April 2005, was accompanied by a significant surge in insurgent attacks.

Stumbling Toward Political Transition The problems following the initial flush of military victory highlight the problems of regime change by military intervention. Here, we slip away from our theoretical concerns, which bear on the shaping of a renegade's policy preferences (the military ouster of a regime has little to do with its preferences). Although the issue is not fully encompassed by our analytic framework, several of its assumptions apply to our current concerns, particularly those dealing with the conditions of regime stability and the way this may be conditioned by the actions of foreign powers.

Attempts to set up palatable regimes in Afghanistan and Iraq have encountered the challenges confronting military occupiers trying to install governments to their liking in a social context not wholly receptive to their aims. The bedrock condition for a successful government is its willing embrace by those it seeks to govern, whereas feelings toward a new regime cannot be disentangled from the opinion in which its sponsor, the foreign intervener, is held. Several circumstances impair the prospects for a benevolent attitude.

The first barrier to the occupier's domestic acceptance is the continued existence of pockets of resistance to the occupation. After the initial battles are won, remaining rebels are often those most intensely committed to the fight and to the old order because of their identification with its ideational aims or the benefits in terms of political position and wealth it provided. Logistically, too, this residue often is hardest to defeat: the Taliban in the geographically inhospitable mountains of Afghanistan and Iraqi insurgents entrenched in politically hospitable urban areas. The latter's resistance has been more dramatic than the fighting in remote Afghan regions, but both demonstrate the difficulty of meeting the central challenge of political authority — furnishing security to those it professes to govern. In addition, the perception of vulnerability fostered by a continued resistance discourages wholehearted commitment to the new authorities and their goals. Consequently, the struggle to alter the form of political rule is entangled with the battle against the residual resistance. This fight increasingly focuses the attention and tries the patience of the occupier, whose measures may become increasingly harsh, thrusting deeply into the country's society, often alienating the very people whose acceptance is sought, and jeopardizing acceptance of the transitional authority whose position it is, in principle, defending. Complete military victory is essential to the political goals, but this prospect may be undermined by the very fact of its determined pursuit.

Domestic perception of the intervener is altered when it becomes the occupying power, or at least the coercive pillar of a transitional authority. This perception is further shaped by the fact that the military measures required to root out insurgents differ from those involved in the initial victories. It is no longer a matter of bombing anti-aircraft defenses or battling regular forces, but of extirpating a resistance firmly imbedded in the country's physical and social tissues. Armed force is used in a manner that is more and more intrusive, penetrating deeply into the fabric of society. Two consequences follow. The first is the inevitable, and often poignant, destruction of civilian life and property. The considerable deaths of Iraqi civilians following U.S. raids against neighborhoods and houses suspected of harboring resistance forces engendered, in many parts of that society, a bitterness not evident in the early days of the liberation, as did accidental military damage to mosques. Air strikes in Afghanistan have left a legacy of wrenching incidents such as the killing of nine Afghan children followed, shortly thereafter, by the death of six more in another attack.[95] Apart from the collateral damage, the directly witnessed (but sometimes unavoidable) brutality makes it harder to think of the occupying force as a liberator. Sometimes, the consequences of intrusive military coercion are appalling: as with instances of abuse and humiliation, by U.S. military intelligence units, of Iraqi prisoners. In any case, the ugliness of desperate attempts to root out the enemy leaves its mark. Civilian fear and humiliation may begin eclipsing gratitude. Searching and destroying homes suspected of harboring insurgents and imprisoning their relatives violates, in both countries, deeply held social norms and fuels predictable bitterness. As one Iraqi police officer blurted out, "I hate Americans. They don't respect us. They throw us to the ground and put their boots at the back of our heads."[96] Attempts to control the movements of potential insurgents in Iraq led to the cordoning off of entire villages behind barbed wire with access requiring passes,[97] with results reminiscent of the politically disastrous consequences of the Diem regime's Strategic Hamlets in South Vietnam. In Afghanistan, the bombings and aggressive searches of U.S. Special Forces[98] have, in many areas, had counterproductive effects, officials conceding that a sense of alienation and resentment encouraged the regrouping of Taliban.[99]

The risk is that the occupiers may narrow their vision of the society they seek to transform — it becomes less a political system whose transition must be nurtured than a society bristling with enemies, and perceptions of the host society adjust to the logic of the evolving challenge. As one U.S. officer explained, "You have to understand the Arab mind. The only thing they understand is force—force, pride, and saving face."[100] In response, sullen resentment often settles within the population, encouraging sympathy for insurgents; this causes the occupiers' conception of their mission to tilt even more heavily toward military than political objectives. As sentiments harden, the legitimacy of the transitional political authorities, allied to this military force, becomes precarious.

As the problem is defined in military terms, an offsetting realization of the misplaced stress is also evident. Discomfort with the emphasis may be felt even in quarters traditionally sympathetic to the virtues of military strength. Thus, even an exasperated Newt Gingrich declared that "The real key here is not how many enemy do I kill. The real key is how many allies do I grow. And that is an important metric that [U.S. decision makers] just don't get."[101]

The pains of reconstruction magnify the problem. Countries such as Afghanistan and Iraq have suffered the economic consequences of misman-agement, foreign sanctions, and war, and what the population most ardently desires is an improvement in the quality of its life. Following liberation, there is an expectation of a dramatic surge in economic conditions, but appreciation of obstacles is shallow. The technological might demonstrated by foreign forces in armed action, the ability to destroy barriers that stand in the path of military aims, sparks expectations of comparable prowess in economic reconstruction. Referring to both Kabul and Baghdad, one jour-nalist mused that "The inhabitants of both cities watch with amazement as U.S. troops go on duty with their futuristic equipment, advanced techno-logical resources and efficient logistics that provide them with plentiful food and bottled water. They wonder why these supermen are incapable of con-necting water supplies for everybody else, getting the phones to work, and guaranteeing electricity supplies."[102] As economic goals are not quickly at-tained, the goodwill rather than capacity of the occupier is questioned, add-ing to resentment and distrust.

In turn, feelings toward the occupying force shape those toward the tran-sitional national authority, which, in many cases, bears something of a for-eign stamp: partly because it is more closely linked to foreign beliefs and practices, and also because its leaders have often spent much of their life abroad whereas foreign intervention has brought them to power. Starting with this handicap, the political authority's future acceptability hinges largely on the opinion in which the foreign military power is held: if it is considered an oppressive and humiliating presence, the transitional government suffers the reflected antipathy.

When the foreign occupiers are disliked, the police and military forces they create tend also to be distrusted. There has been evidence of this in both Afghanistan and Iraq, where security forces trained, equipped, and directed by the United States are not always perceived as servants of the people rather than agents of an occupying force.[103] The political authorities struggle with the added difficulty of identification with distrusted foreigners — a problem increasing in direct proportion to the extent of the foreigners' political intrusiveness. Thus, the Iraqi governing authority carried the stigma of its U.S. sponsorship, influential Afghanis resented America's influence on Afghanistan's Loya Jirga, and so forth. In Iraq, this forced the Bush administration to seek the help of the previously scorned United Nations with the political transition, as well as of former Baathist military officers.

I am not arguing against the possibility of successfully ousting a renegade by force and replacing it with a stable regime operating in harmony with international norms, but, as witnessed in Afghanistan and Iraq, the road to success can be unexpectedly bumpy once the "heroic," purely military, phase is over. As the quest to bolster its domestic position may lead a regime to renegade behavior, so the prospect of replacing it with one more desirable depends on the domestic acceptance it is granted.

Two types of situations are conceivable. In the pessimistic scenario, the use of force discredits both the occupier and the local political authority. The insurgency maintains momentum. A period of indeterminate duration is entered wherein neither success nor failure can credibly be claimed but where the dominant sentiment is anxious frustration. Outright failure is unlikely as long as sufficient military force is committed, but an extended period of precarious transition to a somewhat unsatisfactory political outcome must be expected. In the optimistic scenario, resistance is decisively defeated, with minimal collateral damage, before the political consequences of failing to do so appear irreversible. There is no further need for intrusive coercion, and the emphasis shifts toward the political challenges of ushering in a new regime. Military action is replaced by amply financed reconstruction efforts entrusted to a widely respected international authority, resentment is replaced by an appreciation of the improved circumstances, and the new regime is enthusiastically embraced by its people and by the elites without whose support its stability cannot be assured.

In any case, the removal of regimes by military coercion carries implications beyond the country in question. The possibility that this might have

a sobering influence on other, present and future, renegades must be con-
fronted with the contingency that those not participating in the global normative order may feel besieged, encouraging their further radicalization.
There is also the chance that the costs and frustrations attendant upon the
transition to a politically acceptable regime, which always seem to exceed
initial expectations, might deter similar action in the future.

To Summarize

Military force has only exceptionally been used against renegade regimes;
when it has, the results disappointed more often than not. In fact, the likelihood of attaining objectives has not been appreciably better here than with
economic sanctions. Thus far, threats have rarely worked, generally because
their targets have failed to take the threatener's intent seriously enough or
because they expected no more than light consequences from intervention.
Still, the future may not mimic the past. The two most vigorous instances
of military intervention (Afghanistan and Iraq) occurred toward the end of
the period covered here, suggesting that they — rather than, say, the experiences of Haiti or Somalia — are apt to shape the perceptions of future
renegades.

On the basis of what we have seen here, actual coercion, particularly if
its is substantial, can be expected to force specific policy changes on a renegade, but not to alter its disdain for generally accepted standards of behavior.
And force designed to alter policies cannot be expected to provide the corollary benefit of inciting the regime's overthrow. If the aim is to oust a renegade, this can be achieved with massive military action, but the transition
to an acceptable new regime is more difficult than typically anticipated, and
the broader international consequences are uncertain.

Interestingly, threats of force and its limited use do not generate as predictable rally effects or as much opportunity for the regime to demonize the
opposition as do comprehensive economic sanctions. Military action, short
of outright campaigns to remove the regime, rarely has the *counterproductive*
effect of bolstering its position: when it fails to achieve its goals, this is because it does not offset the regime's stake in deviance, thus success depends
on a readiness to commit the force needed to do this and to absorb the
corresponding costs. Ultimately, the criteria for the success or failure of military force are simpler than those determining the effectiveness of economic
sanctions.

7   Closing Thoughts

      I argued in chapter 1 that it is time to narrow the gap between the evolving character of international relations and the concerns of those who analyze it, to move away from models of power politics toward a greater emphasis on international deviance. This study is a step in that direction. It suggests a framework for the analysis of international deviance based on assumptions regarding the driving incentives of renegade regimes, the distinction between primary and secondary renegades, and the relative roles of direct and indirect links between regime goals and internationally transgressive policies. The study highlights the causal importance of legitimacy based on goals and values deemed both radical and exceptionally elevated, and on claims that foreign forces harbor inimical intents toward the national community. It accounts for the relative unconcern of primary renegades at the prospect of economic retaliation, and it illuminates the circumstances under which subsequent sanctions may or may not be effective. It examines how military coercion may affect renegade incentives and capabilities, and it discusses the prospects for efforts to replace such regimes with structures of political authority more compatible with basic tenets of international behavior. Significance for policy is very much entangled with theoretical implications.

Some Theoretical Implications

The Issue of Endogeneity

It is important that the structure of domestic interests and preferences to which renegades react is not exogenous to the international responses their behavior calls forth. This means that those seeking to punish or reward renegades should not assume that they can simply add behavioral incentives or disincentives to the regimes' decisional calculus, since their interests and preferences usually are reconfigured by the external pressures. It is very much as if, in a microeconomic model of consumer behavior, incentives or disincentives in the form of adjustments to a product's price had to contend with the fact that price changes also modify consumer tastes. Or, in a different sort of example, that misbehavior might seem more attractive to a wayward child when punished for it. The fact that the interests and preferences on which regime support depends are endogenous to international responses makes the situation especially complex and dynamic. This need not mean that the consequences of various policies must be less predictable, but it does mean that these consequences are less simple, and that effective policy instruments must be correspondingly sophisticated. In any case, the mental models on which our analyses of policy rest must be improved to the point of an adequate recognition of the endogeneity issue.

Ideas and Material Forces

A second important implication concerns the relative causal priority of ideas and material forces in shaping the genesis and trajectory of renegade regimes. The comparative importance of the two types of influences has long been debated among international relations scholars; within recent decades, however, material forces have been accorded clear primacy. This has been so, I think, for four reasons. The first is the theoretical ascendancy of realism, especially structural realism, as the dominant doctrine of international relations. Realists have always been preoccupied with insecurity as the primary concern of states and with the primordial role of power in managing insecurity. Power, in turn, has been viewed as the ability to coerce, ultimately by brute material force. Ideology, psychology, values, emotions, and such were considered irrelevant — a distraction at best, a delusion at worst. A second reason has been the relative parsimony of the theoretical models that could be built on the assumption of power-seeking and insecurity — wishing to emulate the deductive elegance of the harder sciences, particularly economics, political scientists were loathe to entertain notions that detracted from that quest. a third (somewhat related) reason resides in the fact that the components of hard power — i.e., military and economic resources — could, in principle, be measured, encouraging the use of sophisticated statistical techniques, and allowing political scientists to make seemingly objective statements on causality, akin to those made in the exact sciences. Yet a fourth reason might be that idealism, implying belief in the primacy of ideas, is easily confounded with idealism in the sense of wooly headed utopianism, with which few scholars wish to be associated.

But not all political scientists jumped on the realist-materialist bandwagon, and a variety of perspectives, including liberal-institutionalism and theories of the democratic peace, have emerged to argue that political outcomes, even the structure of material forces, cannot be grasped without reference to the role of ideas, i.e., beliefs about value, structure, and causation. There is even a strand in the literature — one that enjoys increasing academic respectability — asserting that political decisions cannot be understood if the emotions by which they are animated are ignored, whereas emotions, at the aggregate societal level, cannot easily be abstracted from the beliefs in which they originate.[1] Most important, a sophisticated and increasingly influential body of literature has begun to address the role of norms and shared knowledge in shaping social behavior, observing that analysis can reach much further when it is appreciated how *meaning* shapes political interaction.[2]

At the level of this study, the question of the respective weight of ideas and material circumstances turns into the issue of how either shapes regime behavior — that is, how they determine the regime's commitment to a certain course of action, where this commitment is assumed to depend on the behavior's impact on the regime's political position. Viewed from this perspective, our analysis suggested that the genesis and trajectory of renegade regimes hinges on both ideational and material circumstances. Nationalism, religion, and political ideology provide a foundation on which renegades argue their right to rule, and it is largely on such bases that those whose support matters determine where their own interests should lie, and thus whether or not to support the regime. Without this ideational foundation, the justification for the regime and the impetus for its policies might be absent. An expectation of material consequences may influence the regime's expectations of future support but, at the primary stage, political vulnerability to foreign reaction often depends on the strength and substance of the ideational program. When other nations begin responding, economically or militarily, the ideational basis for regime support may continue to encourage resilience to such pressures, but only in the short to medium term. This is because, in the long run, material factors generally triumph, and the causal weight one chooses to assign to either category depends primarily on how long an interval one considers relevant.

Policy Implications

Given the theoretical premises on which this study rests, what can be said about the malleability of the conditions that determine the emergence and subsequent course of renegade regimes; specifically, what impact can the policies of other nations be expected to have? The answer depends on whether the aim is to prevent the emergence of primary renegades or to deal with the policies of secondary renegades.

The Challenges of a Secondary Renegade   Once a regime has been labeled a renegade, how can the international community alter its character or expedite its removal? As most such regimes rely on an ideational basis for societal mobilization, which typically includes claims of egregious wrongs done by others to the community's values and aspirations, we ask whether such claims can be challenged at the ideational level — i.e., without resort to threats or bribes.

If an attempt to influence another society's cognitions is pursued as a matter of explicit policy, it comes under the general rubric of "public diplomacy," which, in a bilateral context, is the business of seeking to influence the beliefs and perceptions of foreign audiences in order to encourage sympathy for the national interest of one's own country.[3] While the effectiveness of most public diplomacy is questionable even when its objectives are thus cast, in the present context doubts multiply because a much vaster objective is involved. It is no longer a matter of trying to sell the character or interests of a specific country, it is a matter of countering an argument about the way a people or a religion have been treated, and about the culpabilities involved. It is a matter of altering an interpretation of history, one that is rooted in abstract arguments and historical claims that, by their nature, cannot easily be refuted; they may be deeply rooted in a people's myths and advanced by politicians who spring from these people and act as ideational entrepreneurs. Not only does the nature of the argument make it hard to falsify (its claims resting as much on an emotional as on a factual basis), but foreigners trying to disprove it often operate from a position of presumptive insincerity — since candor cannot be expected from alien and guilty parties. Thus, an argument from leading norm-setters that Islam has not been threatened — from the crusades to current policies toward the Middle East — or, say, that Serbs had not been mistreated by their enemies, would encounter the most stubborn skepticism.

Because little can realistically be expected from attempts to discredit the assumptions behind these ideational programs with externally formulated counterarguments and counterpropaganda, we must ask whether *material* responses can counter the secondary renegades' incentives to continue acting on the assumptions implied by ideational programs?

We saw that, as a rule, economic sanctions do little to mitigate delinquent policies, which may in fact be entrenched by particularly comprehensive sanctions. The long run (a period generally exceeding a decade, sometimes several decades) favors a waning of ideational zeal and weariness with economic hardship, encouraging erstwhile renegades to seek reintegration into the international community. But even this is more likely (as some of our cases confirm), where the country's middle class has not been decimated by international economic isolation, where powerful rent-seeking interests have not taken root, where the international community is not perceived as the nation's enemy, and where vested interests desire readmission into the international community. It is not that economic pressure is futile, but that measures that punish a whole society are counterproductive, and problems are compounded when the target is a renegade.

Beyond the fact that sanctions should be measured, effectiveness requires considerable flexibility in their application — pressure has to be adapted to changes in the target regime's policy: loosened when behavior starts to improve, tightened in the case of backsliding. An all-or-nothing approach is not likely to work. Thus, for example, in the case of Vietnam, U.S. sanctions were generally responsive to the degree of the regime's compliance with U.S. demands, including assistance with the Cambodian peace process and progress on soldiers who were missing in action. Sanctions were incrementally lifted with evidence of cooperation; by 1995 diplomatic relations were restored, and, in 2000 the first trade agreement between the two countries was signed.[4] Vietnam, however, was not treated as a renegade or powerfully vilified during this period — the desire to put that chapter of U.S. history

firmly in the past probably accounts for the firm yet nonhistrionic and pragmatic manner with which Hanoi was dealt. The deep stigma attached to
most renegades and the occasionally extreme politicization of measures
taken against them makes it hard to reward incremental improvements in
behavior with corresponding relaxations of punitive measures (and the con-
verse), encouraging a generally ineffective all-or-nothing approach.

If flexible adjustments are especially difficult when the targets have violated core norms of international behavior, it is important that the design of
the sanctions not be ill conceived at the outset. A solution may lie in the
practice of what have been called "smart" or "targeted" sanctions, directed,
not at an entire society, but at those responsible for the objectionable policies
and at their main supporters. They flow from the recognition, expressed by
UN Secretary General Kofi Annan, that, in the case of comprehensive sanctions, "Those in power not only transfer the costs to the less privileged, but
perversely often benefit from such sanctions by their ability to control and
profit from black market activity, by controlling the distribution of the limited resources, and by exploiting them as a pretext for eliminating domestic
sources of political opposition."[5]

The purpose of smart sanctions, then, is to cause costs to be borne by the
regime itself, providing it with an incentive to abandon its objectionable
ways; ensuring that, by analogy with "smart weapons," the end is attained
with minimal collateral damage, and, in this case, without politically counterproductive consequences. Put another way, the purpose of smart sanctions
is to ensure the operation of an IO, not IR, logic. Experience with targeted
sanctions is not very extensive, but thought has been devoted to the conditions of their effectiveness.

As the intent is to hurt the regime's leadership and supporters, they must
be denied that which, economically, they most desire. This may require
restrictions on access to luxury goods—a measure whose effectiveness is
inversely proportional to the ease with which the restrictions can be circum-
vented (e.g., through smuggling). Other categories of goods to be denied
include military and police equipment, and also various types of commu-
nication equipment—weakening the regime's ability to coerce. It has also
been suggested that restrictions on the travel of elites and their families were
effective in the case of the Milošević regime. Travel restrictions not only
impose deprivation on those affected (e.g., inability to educate their children
abroad) but, as a symbol of international scorn, may also be domestically
delegitimizing.

The most effective form of smart sanctions probably involves targeted financial sanctions — since financial resources are the foundation of the elite's personal economic interests and, in many cases, their ability to rule. The aim is to localize and freeze the assets of specific individuals and entities on the world financial markets, an enterprise fraught with generally surmountable technical challenges.[6] While comprehensive sanctions are a blunt instrument requiring little specialized knowledge about the details of the target economy, targeted financial sanctions demand a detailed and deeper grasp of the financial and economic profile of the targeted elites and their institutional connections to the outside world: information about trading associates, the manner in which commercial operations are financed, investment partners, correspondent banks, and so forth. World financial markets are complex, but globalization and reliance on computerized electronic transfers make it theoretically possible to monitor the movement of funds and track the identity of the owners. Experience tackling money-laundering operations may be useful. In fact, smart financial sanctions present a more manageable challenge, since their targets are a restricted number of individuals and companies, while money laundering may involve an open-ended set of individuals and companies.

Still, two main difficulties confront targeted financial sanctions. First, it often is difficult to impose sufficient pain on the culpable leaders and elites to cause a reevaluation of their priorities. Second, it is hard to avoid situations where targeted sanctions shade into comprehensive sanctions, causing undesired collateral economic damage and encouraging the emergence of interests linked to continued isolation. The problem arises where it is difficult to make a sharp distinction between regime assets and the national economy, since companies owned or controlled by the state allow individuals or entities to circumvent sanctions through the transactions conducted by these companies, whereas targeting the companies themselves would amount to comprehensive sanctions.

What of armed force? Although chapter 6 cast serious doubt on the effectiveness of military threats, perhaps the past sheds a distorting light on the future: since the U.S.-led invasions of Afghanistan and Iraq may have heightened the values of subsequent threats by displacing Vietnam and Somalia as models of U.S. resolve and increasing the perceived likelihood that threats would be carried out. The counterargument, however, is that the costs and frustrations of these interventions could lead future renegades to deem it unlikely that the United States would wish to repeat the experience. Accordingly, it is not entirely clear what lessons would be drawn.

As far as the actual use of force is concerned, the international community cannot renounce its right to excise from its midst, coercively if necessary, regimes that violate its most essential norms — especially as it is increasingly recognized that sovereignty does not shield certain transgressions. But if the purpose is to promote a world without renegades, military action should follow the collective decision of those who are institutionally empowered to act on behalf of the international community — generally, the United Nations Security Council. The alternative, in post–Cold War international conditions, has been for the United States to act unilaterally. Unilateral action is not undesirable just because it is less likely to achieve the regime's removal, but because it is less likely to result in its replacement by a stable, domestically legitimate, and internationally compliant regime. There are three reasons for this concern.

The first is that the task of "state building" is more effectively undertaken as a multilateral venture, whereas the participation of others often assumes their involvement in the initial decisions. The task of establishing internal security during the transition period is, as seen in Afghanistan and Iraq, often beyond the abilities of even the most powerful state. The financial burden of reconstructing an economy devastated by misrule and mismanagement, and further ravaged by military destruction, is a process both long and expensive, one whose costs are more often underestimated than overestimated. The U.S need to call on the assistance of foreign donors to help underwrite the costs of Iraqi reconstruction illustrates the problem, but it is understandable that other countries should be disinclined to bear a major financial burden for a war they were not a party to and whose initiation they may have regarded with misgivings. Also, the task of rebuilding a country's administrative machinery (again, as seen in Afghanistan and Iraq) is immensely complex, especially if it is neither feasible nor desirable to build it entirely in the image of the intervening country's own administrative structure. A diversity of potentially applicable models requires a diversity of administrative experience, which cannot easily be solicited from those who were not party to the decision to use force.

Beyond practical considerations, it is harder to establish the domestic legitimacy of new institutions and leaders when neither they nor the process that produced them have been collectively endorsed, not even by the system's major norm-setters. Thus, it is not surprising that, in Iraq, Shiite clergy opposed U.S. plans for the indirect selection of a Provisional Assembly, calling instead for direct elections; and it is understandable that they agreed to rescind the call only when the United Nations, not the United States, declared elections unfeasible. As the London *Economist* observed with regard to Iraq, "If there is one factor that just about all the rivals for power in Iraq acknowledge, it is that the United Nations must play a big part in giving legitimacy to whoever rules the country."[7] In the absence of a broad international endorsement, the new regime and the manner of its creation are considered as umbilically linked to the United States, opening them to charges of being U.S. puppets. In most cases, regime legitimacy benefits substantially if it is grounded in broad multilateral action. It is for that reason, in part, that the legitimacy of the post-Saddam Iraqi regime is wobbly.

Finally, unilateral military intervention demonstrates that the regime is objectionable to the intervener (notably, the United States), but not necessarily to the rest of the world. Under the circumstances, the principle that core international norms have been violated and must be defended is not established, perpetuating their vulnerability to challenge by future renegades. Principles regarded as U.S. principles, and renegades perceived mainly as U.S. adversaries, do not evoke strong feelings and commitments from other societies.

The Challenges of Primary Renegades   The difficulty of dealing effectively with secondary renegades implies that it is best to discourage their initial emergence. As the genesis of primary renegades is linked to a quest, by nondemocratic regimes, for a basis for legitimacy involving claims of wrongs done by others to the community's values and aspirations, one can attempt to undermine, more generally, the foundation for such claims, making it less likely that they would be made at the outset. Another possibility, if legitimacy continues to rest on these claims, is to sever the link between such assumptions and transgressive behavior. In other words, even if it continues to be believed that the community has been the victim of a grievous injury, try to make it less likely that the result would be the sort of behavior that qualifies a regime as a renegade (terrorism, for example). The difference between the policies involved here and those applicable to secondary renegades is that, in this case, the international community, at least its leading members, is not reacting to the misbehavior of specific states — instead, it is discouraging the emergence of renegade pathologies within a broad category of regimes. In the former case, action was directed at an *agent*; in the present case, it aims to reshape the *structure* of ideational beliefs.

The structure of ideational beliefs: If a characteristic basis of renegade mobilizational efforts is a claim of wrongs at the hands of others — generally norm-setters or countries associated with them — then the apparent solution is to decrease the domestic political value of such claims by undermining their overall plausibility. Here, it is not a matter of countering arguments about specific wrongs (this usually would assume secondary renegades, and I have indicated that such arguments rarely produce much effect); it is a matter of making it generally unproductive to make such claims because their likely targets enjoy a presumption of benign intent. A number of policy orientations could strengthen such presumptions. These include a consistent regard for the welfare of less privileged nations, a concern not easily imputable to self-interest, and also genuine evidence of commitment to the values on which core international norms rest. Nothing is less conducive to the kind of reputation desired here than double standards and assumptions of national exceptionalism. It may be argued that, in a context of self-interested realpolitik, this places unrealistic expectations on the world's norm-setters, which may be true. In any case, clear evidence of laudable character and intent must be offered for a long time before it is thoroughly absorbed, and the issue may be too pressing to place exaggerated expectations in the model behavior of powerful countries.

If the argument of a wrong cannot always be dealt with by undermining its credibility, another solution might be to make these claims irrelevant, in the sense that, even if in principle credible, they have little mobilizational force. This assumes a political culture that is sufficiently de-ideationalized to make it unprofitable to seek legitimacy on such foundations. One possibility is that the values and symbols in which renegade behavior is grounded might find themselves in a losing competition with those of Western consumer culture, making it futile to mobilize national wrath via ethno-nationalism, religion, or political ideology. Some view this as the welcome product of economic globalization[8] whose cultural corollaries will be embraced by significant portions of societies that would otherwise be vulnerable to renegade pathologies. Moreover, it has been suggested that Western, especially U.S., culture may represent a source of "soft" power[9] — soft because it flows from attraction, not coercion, from the pull of a value system others wish to be a part of. Identifying with this culture, people are unlikely to support regime policies that vilify its source. Cultural attraction was, for example, a considerable basis of U.S. and Western power during the Cold War, due to its appeal to the masses enduring the drabness of life within the Soviet bloc. Soft power is structural — it creates patterns of internationally shared values, and it stands to perform its function enduringly. It is not directed toward a particular target for a particular reason, it shapes the motivations of major segments of international society, and it does so relatively unobtrusively.

But the benefits of cultural globalization are uncertain. While connotations of affluence and enjoyment explain its lure, the danger of backlash cannot be ignored.[10] This culture competes with the values and traditions that gave its people a sense of belonging and location and that were laden with emotional content. Clashing cultural identities and a guilty sense of disloyalty toward one's own society's values are painfully experienced, sometimes producing hostile reactions to the encroaching culture and its source. Resentment is exacerbated where intimations of affluence and enjoyment collide with the reality of squalor and the unlikelihood that it will be alleviated, heightening the sense of deprivation and bitterness toward those who will never experience these hardships, a bitterness that is deepest when rich and powerful nations appear indifferent to the plight of others.

Because resentments channeled into the ideational premises of renegade regimes may not be defused from the outside, we must ask whether delinquent policies can be discouraged even where such belief systems remain a foundation of regime legitimacy? This implies that the regime's basis of legitimacy can be delinked from the behavior it often implies. Thus, for example, a regime wishing to affirm its position by righting past wrongs or elevating the community to a loftier position within international society would do so without, say, seeking weapons of mass destruction or territorial aggrandizement. Similarly, a regime claiming ethno-nationalist injuries would, nevertheless, not seek redress by harming its ethnic rivals, and so forth. In short, the behavioral implications drawn by the regime from the grievances that animate its ideational program would be less inconsistent with international norms.

Several possibilities should be considered. The first is that the regimes might be deterred from acting in a transgressive manner, i.e., from becoming primary renegades, because of how other renegades have been dealt with by the international community in the past. Although we have not found punitive measures especially effective at changing the behavior of the targeted regime, their main benefit may lie in the deterrent effect they have on potential emulators. A generalized expectation that renegade behavior will be met by decisive punishment should be considered a structural feature of the international system, deterring the genesis of delinquent regimes. But this is not a necessary consequence of frequent and harsh retaliatory measures because, as we have seen, external pressure often benefits the regime's domestic position, presumably decreasing the measures' ability to intimidate and deter others. Thus, if one regime witnesses rally-round-the-flag benefits within a comparable regime besieged by hostile foreign forces, the consequences of such pressure might be less feared. If the regime finds that domestic commitment to ideational agendas is reenergized in such circumstances, it may, again, discern the silver lining. If punishment directed at one renegade does little to deter the emergence of others, this may be because of an expectation that IR effects will prevail; if it does deter, the IO model could be considered operative.

Even if one suspected that deterrence worked, the belief could not reliably be confirmed. When we impute the absence of an outcome to some cause, we cannot be sure of the casual relationship unless we are in a position to observe what happens both when the cause is present and when it is absent. This is done regularly in experimental settings conjured by natural scientists, but it is outside the reach of most international relations scholarship.

If renegade behavior flows largely from a domestic political calculus, then the genesis of renegades is best discouraged by ensuring that the desired political benefits would not materialize. The aim is to have core international normative tenets penetrate nations so thoroughly that incompatible policies stand to hurt, rather than help, the regime's position; but it is not always apparent how this can be fostered. As observed in chapter 1, the best students of the subject argue that international norm propagation is a three-stage "life cycle," where behavioral implications differ between the stages.[11] Beginning with "norm emergence," when norm "entrepreneurs" call attention to critical issues and situate them within appropriate cognitive frames, the process enters a "tipping point" as a critical mass of states adopt the implied norms and become norm leaders. Following this, the stage of "norm cascades" sees a rapid norm contagion, as states adopt the norms to affirm their identity as members of international society. Finally, "internalization" of norms causes them to be taken for granted as their justification no longer needs to be argued. For the four categories of norms whose flouting defines renegades, it may be said the "cascade" phase is behind us and the phase of internalization well underway. Because several societies have, so far, resisted the process, we must ask how the most recalcitrant states may be brought to internalize these norms to the point where "citizens make judgments about whether their government is better than alternatives by looking at those alternatives (in the international and regional arena) and by seeing what other people and countries say about their country."[12]

The point is not to convince other societies of the blamelessness of those who are suspected of having injured them, a difficult matter at best; rather, the objective is to make them adopt generally accepted conceptions of what is right and wrong. This is partly a matter of having them *wish* to belong to the broader international society, a wish experienced at a variety of levels.

Relatedly, it is a matter of discrediting the behaviors via which renegades seek domestic legitimacy. If these endeavors are successful, it is less likely that renegades would emerge; should they nevertheless do so, their longevity becomes doubtful. A growing, systemwide expectation that the legitimizing strength of norm-compliance trumps that of norm-defiance becomes a feature of the international system, but this requires that the appeals of the former outrun those of the latter.

If the attractiveness of renegade ideational programs is to fall short of the desire for membership in international society, this may simply be the unintended effect of the former's invariably disastrous consequences. Much as communism's demise was as much (or even more) attributable to its internal failings as to the West's Cold War policies, the senselessness of most renegade programs ensures, in the medium to long term, thorough societal disillusionment, the contagion of which may shape the expectations of other potentially vulnerable societies. Whether or not Libya endured economic sanctions, the fatuous premises of Green Book economics or the implausibility of Qaddafi's messianic pretensions would, in all likelihood, have produced bitter disenchantment, making emulation elsewhere correspondingly unlikely. Similarly, the bloodletting and economic devastation associated with Milošević's ethnic wars translated into a national trauma enhancing revulsion in other multiethnic societies at such purposes and policies. Thus, some progression toward normative expectations incompatible with renegade programs might be expected simply because they always end so badly, even independently of external responses.

At the same time, there is little doubt that major normative reassessments occur in countries whose aims are not only catastrophically costly but also decisively defeated from the outside. For example, it is significant that "Ideas and norms most associated with the losing side in a war or perceived to have caused an economic failure should be at particular risk of being discredited, opening the field for alternatives."[13] The task, then, from the international community's perspectives is to help expedite the discrediting of renegade agendas without producing counterproductive (IR) consequences. If others do not anticipate these consequences, delinquent behavior loses some of its luster to politicians seeking to buttress their domestic position. Accordingly, campaigns, economic or otherwise, to bring down delinquent regimes should emphasize measures that punish those associated with the regime rather than entire nations, measures that powerfully convey international distaste for the regime's behavior but that cannot be interpreted as external assaults on a community's beliefs and sense of identity.

Since acquiescing in the international community's norms is a condition for acceptance into its midst, as many nations as possible should covet membership and internalize the norms. Apart from the direct economic benefits of membership (commercial and investment relations with the rest of the world), a number of symbolic gratifications come with belonging to a global community of nations — including the sense of self-worth attendant on being a member of a society that others welcome into their midst. This, however, assumes that the international community is considered highly estimable and this, in turn, generally assumes that it has three features. The first is that membership encourages a sense of self-respect, not of humiliation. People are less likely to be enticed by a community thought to have unfairly scorned and punished them, rather than just the guilty regime. Generalized resentment discourages internalization of the system's norms, implying a need for discrimination in the targeting of punishment and suggesting the desirability of a balance of punishment and inducements, of sticks as well as carrots. Thus, and although the inducements were offered for self-serving reasons, Pakistan was brought into a state of at least partial compliance by the considerable financial rewards tendered by the United States in the wake of September 11 to convince the regime to shift from participation in anti-Indian terror to an endorsement of the war on terror. Rewards may not be as politically palatable to norm-setters as punishments, but they erect fewer barriers to better behavior.

Further, an international community that citizens would not wish to alienate is one that relegates no member to clearly second-class status. This means that the voice of the weak should be solicited along with the voice of the strong. It also assumes that the tools by which the weak pursue their national interests — mainly diplomacy and institutional methods — are not irrelevant because predictably defeated by the tools of the strong — especially military and economic coercion. As John Ikenberry has cogently argued, the most stable international orders are those within which there is minimal return to force and maximal return to institutions; whereas, "When political orders are organized in ways that constrain the ability of one actor or group to dominate or to wield power arbitrarily or indiscriminately, other actors and groups are more likely to abide by the rules and outcomes that the political order generates at the moment."[14]

As it is hard to be enticed into an order considered unjust or unfair, the international system, as defended by leading norm-setters, should not be so perceived. From the perspective of the weak and underprivileged, this implies a conviction that the system is not designed to perpetuate their inferiority, inasmuch as the resentments underlying many renegade ideational programs, from *Juche*, to the Third Universal Theory, to the Mustakberin-Mustazesin dichotomy of radical Islam, rest on that very assumption. Transcending these beliefs requires, at a minimum, a conviction that principal norm-setters care enough about the plight of poor nations to do something tangible about it. In this respect, a study of indicators of commitment to the development of poor countries[15] compared the performance of the countries richest nations, finding that the United States ranked next-to-last, while Britain and France (also members of the UN Security Council) were in the lower half of the distribution (Japan was last). This is not a picture that flatters the norm-setters or, by implication, the type of international society they advocate. Moreover, awareness that the principal norm-setter allocates approximately forty times as much to military outlays as to foreign aid (half of which, in any case, goes to only two countries — Egypt and Israel) may indicate to many that security through coercion is prized far more highly than security based on the conception many poor societies hold of distributive justice. If societies, otherwise vulnerable to renegade suasion, are to place greater value on international norms than on the visions offered by such regimes, foresight must trump fear as the basis of an international order, norm setters cannot be viewed as self-serving powers intent on creating a world designed to serve their own needs, not those of the dispossessed.

Finally, it is crucial that the system's leaders' commitment to the norms not appear an instrument for the pursuit of their own national interest nor be advocated chiefly when compatible with those interests — it is hard for others to internalize norms that appear in that light. Thus, it might be argued that democratic norms would have penetrated a number of societies more thoroughly during the Cold War if the United States and some of its allies had not condoned authoritarian rule when this suited a geopolitical purpose.

In any case, the objective is a structure of international relations based on norms more attractive to most people than those at the forefront of most renegade agendas. This cannot be achieved just by convincing potential renegades of the dire consequences of their behavior; the emerging international community also must appear as worthy to others as it does to its norm setters.

At the moment, the number of renegade regimes has declined with respect to the beginning of the period examined in this study, but it would be overly sanguine to assume that major deviance from core international norms is a thing of the past. Expanding opportunities for ideational mobilization around extreme and wrathful beliefs may emerge — possibly springing from anger at some of the harsh and alienating consequences of globalization. Nationalism shows no sign of withering, and regimes may discover neoteric, radical, and rage-based forms of religion to embrace. Moreover, growing consensus on new internationally consequential norms, possibly involving protection of the environment, may emerge — expanding the ways in which regimes may become renegades. Concern with renegades will wax and wane, but the altered international system described in chapter 1 will persist through the foreseeable future. In the meantime, it is important that international relations scholarship close the distance that separates it from the world it seeks to account for.

Notes

1. From Power Politics to International Deviance

1. For example, Klaus Knorr, *The Power of Nations: The Political Economy of International Relations* (New York: Basic Books, 1975); Jack H. Nagle, *The Descriptive Analysis of Power* (New Haven: Yale University Press, 1975); Jacek Kugler and William Domke, "Comparing the Strength of Nations," *Comparative Political Studies* 19, no. 1 (April 1986): 39–69.

2. The major advocate of a bipolar system is, of course, Kenneth Waltz, in *Theory of International Politics* (Reading, Mass.: Addison-Wesley, 1979). Proponents of the virtues of multipolarity include Karl W. Deutsch and J. David Singer, "Multipolar Systems and International Stability," *World Politics* 16 (April 1964): 390–406. For a position midway between the two, see Richard N. Rosecrance, "Bipolarity, Multipolarity, and the Future," *Journal of Conflict Resolution* 10 (September 1966): 314–327.

3. Leading authors include Samir Amin, *Accumulation on a World Scale* (New York: Monthly Review Press, 1974); Fernando E. Cardoso and Enzo Faletto, *Dependency and Development* (Berkeley: University of California Press, 1979); Andre Gunder Franck, *Dependent Accumulation and Development* (New York: Monthly Review Press, 1980).

4. Major theorists include Robert Gilpin, *War and Change in World Politics* (New York: Cambridge University Press, 1981), and Robert Keohane, *After Hegemony* (Princeton: Princeton University Press, 1984). For critical perspectives, see Duncan Snidal, "The Limits of Hegemonic Stability Theory," *International Organization* 39, no. 4 (Autumn 1985): 579–614; and Isabelle Grunberg, "Ex-

ploring the Myth of Hegemonic Stability," *International Organization*.44, no. 4 (Autumn 1990): 431–477.

5. This assumption is at the core of neorealist thinking, especially Kenneth Waltz, *Theory of International Politics* (Reading, Mass.: Addison-Wesley, 1979). It is also at the heart of the variant of the theory called "offensive realism." See John J. Mearsheimer, *The Tragedy of Great Power Politics* (New York: Norton, 2001). For critiques of realist views of anarchy, see Helen Milner, "The Assumption of Anarchy in International Relations Theory: A Critique," *Review of International Studies* 17 (1991): 67–85, and Alexander Wendt, "Anarchy Is What States Make of It: The Social Construction of Power Politics," *International Organization* 46 (1992): 335–370.

6. See the discussions in Joseph Grieco, Robert Powell, and Duncan Snidal, "The Relative Gains Problem for International Cooperation," *American Political Science Review* 85, no. 4 (December 1991): 729–743; John C. Matthews III, "Current Gains and Future Outcomes: When Cumulative Relative Gains Matter," *International Security* 21, no. 1 (Summer 1996): 112–146; Duncan Snidal, "International Cooperation among Relative Gains Maximizers," *International Studies Quarterly* 35, no. 4 (December 1991): 387–407.

7. Discussion of the security dilemma may be found in Robert Jervis, "Cooperation under the Security Dilemma," *World Politics* 30, no. 2 (January 1978): 186–214, and Charles Glaser, "The Security Dilemma Revisited," *World Politics* 50, no. 1 (October 1997): 171–201.

8. For a detailed development of the concept of soft power, see Joseph S. Nye, Jr., *Soft Power: The Means to Success in World Politics* (New York: Public Affairs, 2004).

9. For discussion of globalization, see George E. Stiglitz, *Globalization and Its Discontents* (New York: Norton, 2002), and Mark Rupert, *Ideologies of Globalization* (New York: Routledge, 2000).

10. The literature on the interdemocratic peace is extensive. Representative contributions include Zeev Maoz and Nasrin Abdolali, "Regime Types and International Conflict," *Journal of Conflict Resolution* 33, no. 1 (March 1989): 3–35; David Spiro, "The Liberal Peace, and Yet It Squirms," *International Security* 19, no. 3 (Spring 1995): 177–180; Erich Weede, "Some Simple Calculations on Democracy and War Involvement," *Journal of Peace Research* 29, no. 4 (November 1992): 649–664; Bruce M. Russett, *Grasping the Democratic Peace*(Princeton: Princeton University Press, 1993); John R. Oneal and Bruce M. Russett, "The Classical Liberals Were Right: Democracy, Interdependence, and Conflict, 1950–1985," *International Studies Quarterly* 41, no. 2 (1997): 267–294.

11. For a stimulating exchange of views on what the term "international community" implies, see the collection of essays entitled "What Is the International Community," *Foreign Policy*, no. 132 (September/October 2002): 28–47.

12. Samuel Huntington, "The Clash of Civilizations?" *Foreign Affairs* 72, no. 3 (Summer 1993): .27.

13. Robert Axelrod, *The Evolution of Cooperation* (New York: Basic Books, 1984).

14. Robert O. Keohane and Joseph S. Nye, *Power and Interdependence: World Politics in Transition*, 2nd edition (Glenview, Ill.: Scott, Foresman, 1989).

15. For a discussion of U.S. responses to the Bolshevik Revolution and its early years, see Miroslav Nincic, *Anatomy of Hostility* (San Diego: Harcourt, Brace, Jovanovich, 1989), pp. 86–98.

16. Gertrude Atherton, "Time as a Cure for Bolshevism," *New York Times*, March 16, 1919, p.3.

17. A good examination of the Soviet-Yugoslav break and subsequent Soviet-bloc pressures against Yugoslavia is Vladimir Dedijer, *The Battle Stalin Lost* (New York: Grosset and Dunlap, 1971).

18. Department of State, Office of the Spokesman, "Secretary of State Madeleine K. Albright Address before the Council on Foreign Relations, September 30, 1997." http://secretary.state.gov/www/statements/9770930.

19. Robert Litwak, *Rogue States and U.S. Foreign Policy* (Baltimore: Johns Hopkins University Press, 2000), pp. 65–66.

20. "How Afghanistan Went Unlisted as Terrorist Sponsor," *Washington Post*, November 5, 2001.

21. Wayne Merry, "Greek Terror," *Washington Post*, November 9, 1999.

22. "Nepad Plans to Crack Down on Rogue States," *Sunday Times*, November 10, 2002.

23. Pered Calvert, ed., *The Process of Political Succession* (London: Macmillan, 1987), p. 248

24. Stephanie Lawson, "Conceptual Issues in the Comparative Study of Regime Change and Democratization," *Comparative Politics* 25, no. 2 (January1993): 183–205.

25. Ibid., p. 185.

26. See Joseph Lepgold and Miroslav Nincic, *Beyond the Ivory Tower: Scholarship and Statesmanship in International Relations* (New York: Columbia University Press, 2001), and Miroslav Nincic and Joseph Lepgold, eds, *Being Useful: The Policy Relevance of International Relations Theory* (Ann Arbor: University of Michigan Press, 2000).

2. *The Logic of Renegade Regimes: A Theoretical Framework*

1. For an inventory of definitions of the concept "norm," see Jack P. Gibbs, *Norms, Deviance, and Social Control* (New York: Elsevier, 1982), chapter 1. See also Gregory A. Raymond, "Problems and Prospects in the Study of International Norms," *Mershon International Studies Review* 41, no. 2 (November 1997): 205–245.

2. John G. Ruggie, *Constructing the World Polity: Essays on International Institutionalization* (New York: Routledge, 1998), p. 105.
3. Edward Hallett Carr, *The Twenty Years Crisis 1919–1939: An Introduction to the Study of International Relations* (London: Macmillan, 1962 [1939]).
4. Alexander Wendt, *Social Theory of International Politics* (Cambridge: Cambridge University Press, 1999), and Martha Finnemore, *Defining National Interests in International Society* (Ithaca: Cornell University Press, 1996).
5. Ann Florini, "The Evolution of International Norms," *International Studies Quarterly* 40, no. 3 (September 1996): 363–389. See also Robert Axelrod, "An Evolutionary Approach to Norms," *American Political Science Review* 80, no. 4 (December 1986): 1095–1111.
6. See, for example, Martha Finnemore and Kathryn Sikkink, "International Norm Dynamics and Political Change," *International Organization* 52, no. 4 (Autumn 1998): 887–917, and Cass Sunstein, *Free Markets and Social Justice* (New York: Oxford University Press, 1997).
7. Wendt, Social Theory; Nicholas G. Onuf, *World of Our Making: Rules and Rule in Social Theory and International Relations* (Columbia: University of South Carolina Press, 1989); Vendulka Kublakova, Nicholas Onuf, and Paul Kowert, eds., *International Relations in a Constructed World* (Armonk, N.Y.: M. E. Sharpe, 1998).
8. James D. Fearon, "What Is Identity (As We Now Use the Word)?" ms., University of Chicago, 1997.
9. Finnemore and Sikkink, "International Norm Dynamics," pp. 891–892.
10. Axelrod, "An Evolutionary Approach," p. 1096.
11. Finnemore and Sikkink, "International Norm Dynamics," p. 903.
12. Emile Durkheim, *The Division of Labor in Society* (Glencoe, Ill.: The Free Press, 1947[1893]).
13. By one definition "deviance refers to behavior and conditions that people so define. The basis of such definitions is the definer's interests, which are felt to be jeopardized or threatened in some way by these acts or conditions." Edwin H. Pfuhl Jr., *The Deviance Process*, 2nd ed. (Belmont, Calif.: Wadsworth Publishing, 1986), p. 21.
14. Desmond Ellis, *The Wrong Stuff* (New York: Macmillan, 1987), p. 15.
15. See, for example, Erving Goffman, *Asylums* (Garden City, N.Y.: Doubleday, 1961).
16. The definition of deductive and inductive reasoning is as follows: deductive reasoning assumes that the premises of an argument fully (i.e., by logical necessity) support its conclusion; inductive reasoning assumes that the premises support the conclusion less than fully.
17. Yehezkel Dror, *Crazy States: A Counterconventional Strategic Problem* (Lexington, Mass.: Heath Lexington, 1971).
18. Herbert A. Simon, *Models of Man* (New York: Wiley, 1957).

19. See, for example, Robert Jervis, "The Drunkards Search," in *Explorations in Political Psychology*, ed. Shanto Iyengar and W. J. McGuire (Durham: Duke University Press, 1993): 336–360.

20. Howard S. Becker, *Outsiders: Studies in the Sociology of Deviance*, rev. ed. (New York: The Free Press, 1973), pp. 22–24.

21. Edwin Lemert, *Social Pathology* (New York: McGraw Hill, 1951).

22. Ibid., p. 82.

23. Clifford Geertz, "The Judging of Nations: Some Comments on the Assessment of Regimes in New States," *European Journal of Sociology* 18, no. 2 (1977): 251.

24. The position is that "Some degree of intimidation may make it possible for a regime to survive on a narrower base of support than would otherwise be feasible. When the voices of opposition are inhibited, the level of overt contention will be less and fewer active supporters will be required to sustain a regime." W. Howard Wriggins, *The Ruler's Imperative: Strategies for Political Survival in Asia and Africa* (New York: Columbia University Press, 1979), p. 176.

25. As Max Weber observes, although the state may claim a monopoly on the legitimate use of force, "force is certainly not the normal or the only means of the state." Max Weber, *Essays in Sociology*, ed. H. H. Gerth and C. Wright Mills (New York: Oxford University Press, 1946), p.88.

26. Robert W. Jackman, *Power without Force: The Political Capacity of Nation States* (Ann Arbor: University of Michigan Press, 1993), p. 98.

27. This view is developed in Walker Connor, *Ethnonationalism: The Quest for Understanding* (Princeton: Princeton University Press, 1994).

28. See the discussion in David Brown, *Contemporary Nationalism: Civic, Ethnocultural, and Multicultural Politics* (London: Routledge, 2000), especially chapter 3, and Michael Ignatieff, *Blood and Belonging: Journeys into the New Nationalism* (New York: Farrar, Strauss and Giroux, 1993), especially chapter 1.

29. Jeffrey R. Seul, "'Ours Is the Way of God': Religion, Identity, and Intergroup Conflict," *Journal of Peace Research* 36, no. 5 (September 1999): 558.

30. On this subject, see Rose McDermott, *Political Psychology in International Relations* (Ann Arbor: University of Michigan Press, 2004), chapter 6.

31. Seymour Martin Lipset, "Some Social Requisites of Democracy: Economic Development and Political Legitimacy," *American Political Science Review* 53, no. 1 (January 1959): 69–105.

32. One of the most influential developments of this view was Barrington Moore Jr., *The Social Origins of Democracy and Dictatorship* (Boston: Beacon Press, 1966).

33. Evelyne Huber, Dietrich Rueschmeyer, and John D. Stephens, "The Impact of Economic Development on Democracy," *Journal of Economic Perspectives* 7, no. 3 (Summer 1993): 71–85.

34. Adam Przeworski and Fernando Limongi, "Modernization: Theory and Facts," *World Politics* 49, no. 2 (January 1997): 155–183.

35. John D. Londregan and Keith T. Poole, "Poverty, the Coup Trap, and the Seizure of Executive Power," *World Politics* 42, no. 2 (April 1990): 151–183.

36. For example, Marc Lindenberg, "World Economic Cycles and Central American Political Instability," *World Politics* 42, no. 3 (April 1990): 397–421; Thomas H. Johnson, Robert A. Slater, and Pat McGowan, "Explaining African Military Coups, 1960–1982," *American Political Science Review* 78, no. 3 (September 1984): 622–640; Armando Razo, "Political Instability and Economic Performance: Evidence from Revolutionary Mexico," *World Politics* 51, no. 1 (October 1998): 99–143.

37. For example, Samir Amin, *Accumulation on a World Scale: A Critique of the Theory of Underdevelopment*, 2 vols. (New York: Monthly Review Press, 1974); Fernando Cardozo and Enzo Falleto, *Dependency and Development in Latin America* (Berkeley: University of California Press, 1979); Andre Gunder Frank, *Capitalism and Underdevelopment in Latin America* (New York: Monthly Review Press, 1967).

38. See, for example, Manuel Castells and Roberto Laserna, "The New Dependency: Technological Change and Socioeconomic Restructuring in Latin America," in A. Douglas Kinkaid and Alejandro Portes, *Comparative National Development: Society and Economy in the New Global Order* (Chapel Hill: University of North Carolina Press, 1994), pp. 57–83.

39. Broad discussions of globalization's pros and cons can be found in John Micklewaith and Adrian Wolldridge, *A Future Perfect: The Challenge and Hidden Promise of Delusions of Global Capitalism* (New York: The Free Press, 1998).

40. See, for example, Richard Haass, "Sanctioning Madness," *Foreign Affairs* 76, no. 6 (November/December 1997): 74–85.

41. These strategies may also help cushion the consequences of limited military reprisals.

42. For a closer discussion of the concept, see Miroslav Nincic, "The National Interest and Its Interpretation," *Review of Politics* 61, no.1 (Winter 1999): 29–55.

43. Litwak, *Rogue States and U.S. Foreign Policy*, p. 112.

44. For example, this was largely the case with U.S. bombing campaigns against North Vietnam in the late 1960s and early 1970. For further discussion, see chapter 6.

45. Economic sanctions have other purposes as well. Even if there is no expectation that the economic pressure will alter the government's policies or cause its removal, it may nevertheless *deter* other nations from emulating the objectionable policies. Additionally, sanctions may produce a welcome *domestic* effect — demonstrating to those within the nation who feel most strongly about the renegade's behavior that their government is not passive in the face of that conduct.

46. See Miroslav Nincic and Peter Wallensteen, "Economic Coercion and Foreign Policy," in *Dilemmas of Economic Coercion: Sanctions in World Politics*, ed. Nincic and Wallensteen (New York: Praeger, 1983); James M. Lindsay, "Trade Sanctions as Policy Instruments: A Reexamination," *International Studies Quarterly* 30, no. 2 (1986): 153–173.

47. This logic is related to that of import-substitution industrialization.

48. See Zachary Selden, *Economic Sanctions as an Instrument of Foreign Policy* (Westport, Conn.: Praeger, 1999), p. 66.

49. Rent-seeking may be defined as "behavior in institutional settings where individual efforts to maximize value generate social waste rather than social surplus." James M. Buchanan, "Rent-seeking and Profit-seeking," in *Toward a Theory of the Rent-Seeking Society*, ed. James Buchanan, Robert Tollison, and Gordon Tullock (College Station: Texas A&M University Press, 1980), p. 4.

50. Elizabeth D. Gibbons, *Sanctions in Haiti: Human Rights and Democracy under Assault* (New York: Praeger, 1999).

51. David M. Rowe, *Manipulating the Market: Understanding Economic Sanctions, Institutional Change, and the Political Unity of White Rhodesia* (Ann Arbor: University of Michigan Press, 2001), p. 126.

52. Ibid., p. 127.

53. The manner in which this was to be done is conveyed in Wallace J. Thies, *When Governments Collide: Coercion and Diplomacy in the Vietnam Conflict* (Berkeley: University of California Press, 1980).

54. On this issue, see Daniel Byman and Matthew Waxman, *The Dynamics of Coercion: American Foreign Policy and the Limits of Military Might* (Cambridge: Cambridge University Press, 2002), chapter 3.

55. The purpose was retaliatory as well, since Sudan was assumed to have supported Osama bin Laden's attacks against U.S. diplomatic facilities in Kenya and Tanzania earlier that year. There is some doubt whether the United States was correct in claiming that the chemical plant was involved in weapons production.

3. *Recognizing Renegades*

1. Abraham Kaplan, *The Conduct of Inquiry* (San Francisco: Chandler, 1964), pp. 187–189.

2. Charles C. Ragin, *Fuzzy-Set Social Science* (Chicago: University of Chicago Press, 2000), p. 58

3. Of course, any list thus established would be subject to revision, since international norms evolve. For example, although no nation (with the possible exception of Iraq at the time of the 1991 Gulf War) has engaged in wanton and massive environmental discussion, should this occur, and should the in-

ternational responses be those one might expect, the list of renegade behaviors would have to be expanded.

4. Barry Rubin, "U.S. Foreign Policy and Rogue States," *Middle East Review of International Affairs* 3, no. 3 (September 1999): 72.
5. Anthony Lake, "Confronting Backlash States," *Foreign Affairs* 73, no. 4 (March/April 1994): 45–55.
6. Paul D. Hoyt, "'Rogue' States and International Relations," paper presented at the fortieth annual conference of the International Studies Association, Washington, D.C., February 1999, p. 7.
7. To this list, some add the category of radiological weapons.
8. See the discussion in Jonathan B. Tucker, "From Arms to Abolition: The Evolving Norm against Biological and Chemical Warfare," in *The New Terror: Facing the Threat of Biological and Chemical Weapons*, ed. Sidney D. Drell et al. (Stanford, Calif.: Hoover Institution Press, 1999), pp. 159–226.
9. Richard Price, "A Genealogy of the Chemical Weapons Taboo," *International Organization* 49, no. 1 (Winter 1995): 73–104.
10. Many of the definitional quandaries are discussed in Bruce Hoffman, *Inside Terrorism* (New York: Columbia University Press, 1998), chapter 1.
11. Paul R. Pillar, *Terrorism and U.S. Foreign Policy* (Washington, D.C.: Brookings Institution Press, 2001), p. 13.
12. This contrast is drawn in Gordon Graham, *Ethics and International Relations* (Oxford: Blackwell, 1998), pp. 123–124.
13. Moreover, as one author observes, "the threat of a terrorist attack is itself terrorism." Pillar, *Terrorism and U.S. Foreign* Policy, p. 14.
14. For a discussion of just war principles, see Michael Walzer, *Just and Unjust Wars*, 2nd ed. (New York: Basic Books, 1977).
15. See Steven L. Burg and Paul S. Shoup, *The War in Bosnia-Herzegovina: Ethnic Conflict and International Intervention* (Armonk, N.Y.: M. E. Sharpe, 1999), pp. 169–170.
16. Donald Peterson, *Inside Sudan: Political Islam, Conflict, and Catastrophe* (Boulder, Colo.: Perseus Books, 1999), p. 29.
17. A one-year period will be adopted here.
18. External aggression is considered if it occurred during this period or if, assuming it had occurred earlier, it continued to involve territorial occupation during this period.
19. In 1996, for instance, the State Department charged Iran with at least eight assassinations of dissidents outside Iran. See U.S. Department of State, *Patterns of Global Terrorism, 1996* (Washington, D.C.: Government Printing Office, 1996).
20. Ibid. (1995).
21. Although the U.S. State Department accused Cuba, in May 2002, of having a capability to conduct research on offensive biological weapons, it did not sug-

gest that such research had been conducted or that Cuba had acquired such weapons. See, for example, "Carter and Powell Cast Doubt on Bioarms in Cuba," *New York Times*, May 14, 2002.

22. U.S. Department of Defense, *Proliferation: Threat and Response 2001* (Washington, D.C., Government Printing Office, 2001), p. 35.

23. See note 21.

24. U.S. Director of Central Intelligence, *Unclassified Report to Congress on the Acquisition of Technology Related to Weapons of Mass Destruction and Advanced Conventional Munitions, July 1 through December 31, 2000*. Washington, D.C.: CIA.

25. See note 21.

26. Anthony Cordesman, "Creeping Proliferation Could Mean a Paradigm Shift in the Cost of War and Terrorism," http://www.csis.org/mideast/stable/3h.html.

27. BBC, "The World's Nuclear Arsenal," http://news.bbc.co.uk.

28. "North Korea, Displeased, Said to Review Missile Pact," *New York Times*, June 5, 2001.

29. See, for example, "Tehran Rebuffs U.S. with Call for Nuclear File to Be Closed," *Financial Times*, March 8, 2004.

30. In December 2003 Qaddafi officially renounced Libyan nuclear programs, inviting international inspection of compliance.

31. The list is based on Dan Smith, "Counting Wars: The Research Implications of Definitional Decisions," paper presented at the Euroconference: Identifying Wars — Systematic Conflict Research and Its Utility in Conflict Resolution and Prevention," Uppsala, June 8–9, 2001.

32. See, for example, *BBC News (Online)*, "Lesotho and Its Big Brother," September 22, 1998, and Suzanne Daley, "Tiny Neighbor Gives South African Army Rude Surprise," *New York Times*, September 23, 1998.

33. A good overview of the complex situation in Congo during these years is provided in René Lemarchand, "The Crisis in the Great Lakes, " in *Africa in World Politics: The African State System in Flux*, ed. John W. Harbeson and Donald Rothchild, 3rd ed. (Boulder, Colo.: Westview Press, 2000), pp. 324–352.

34. See Mihailo Crnobrnja, *The Yugoslav Drama*, 2nd ed. (Montreal: McGill-Queens University Press, 1996), pp. 236, 276.

35. Ultimately, U.S. forces moved into northern Iraq and a no-fly zone was established over Kurdistan, allowing a large number of refugees to return.

36. For a discussion of the issue of Sudan's refugees, see U.S. Committee for Refugees, *World Refugee Survey 2002* (Washington, D.C.: U.S. Committee for Refugees, 2002).

37. An account of the background of the massacres, and of the genocide itself, is provided in Human Rights Watch, *Leave None to Tell the* Story (Washington,

D.C.: Human Rights Watch, 1999), and Linda R. Melvern, *A People Betrayed: The Role of the West in Rwanda's Genocide* (London: Zed Books, 2000).

38. For discussion of the regime's political tactics, see Robert Thomas, *Serbia under Milošević: Politics in the 1990s* (London: Hurst, 1999).

39. For an examination of the Iranian political system as it developed following the 1979 revolution, see Mohammed Amjad, *Iran: From Royal Dictatorship to Theocracy* (New York: Greenwood, 1989).

40. U.S. Department of State, *Patterns of Global Terrorism, 2001*, p. 67.

41. UN sanctions against Libya were lifted in September 2003.

42. U.S. Department of State, *Patterns of Global Terrorism, 2004*, p. 68.

43. "Musharraf Declares War on Extremism," *BBC News (Online)*, January 12, 2002.

44. Barbara Geddes, "How the Cases You Choose Affect the Answers You Get: Selection Bias in Comparative Politics," *Political Analysis* 2 (1990): 131–152, and Gary King, Robert O.Keohane, and Sidney Verba, *Designing Social Inquiry: Scientific Inference in Qualitative Research* (Princeton: Princeton University Press, 1994), pp. 129–132.

45. David Collier and James Mahoney, "Insights and Pitfalls: Selection Bias in Qualitative Research," *World Politics* 49 (October 1996): 56–91

46. See, for example, Douglas Dion, "Evidence and Inference in the Comparative Case Study," *Comparative Politics* 30, no. 2 (January 1998): 127–145.

47. John Stuart Mill, *A System of Logic* (Toronto: University of Toronto Press, 1967 [1843]).

48. To use our distinction between two types of conditions in this context, covariation is, at least, a necessary condition for causation.

49. King, Keohane, and Verba, *Designing Social Inquiry*, pp. 124–128.

50. Ragin, *Fuzzy-Set Social Science*, p. 60.

51. As Ragin also explains, "the search for causal commonalities shared by positive cases . . . provides important clues regarding *necessary* conditions for the phenomenon under investigation." Ibid., p.59.

52. Again, this is logically different from the reasons why others worry more when such behavior is engaged in by authoritarian and totalitarian states than by democracies, suggesting that a nondemocratic political system is also a defining feature of those labeled renegades.

53. See, in particular, Han S. Park, *North Korea: The Politics of Unconventional Wisdom* (Boulder, Colo.: Lynne Rienner, 2002), especially chapter 3.

54. This was expanded to a five-party system under Husni Mubarak.

4. Primary Renegades and the Genesis of Deviance

1. See Thomas Hosuck Kang, *Why the North Koreans Behave as They Do?* (Washington, D.C.: Center for Dao-Confucianism, 1994), pp. 120–124.

2. Han S. Park, *North Korea: The Politics of Unconventional Wisdom* (Boulder, Colo.: Lynne Rienner, 2002), p. 18.
3. Ibid., p. 32.
4. Adrian Buzo, *The Guerilla Dynasty: Politics and Leadership in North Korea* (New York: I. B. Tauris, 1999), p. 27.
5. Park, *North Korea*, p. 171.
6. Elaine Sciolino, *The Outlaw State: Saddam Hussein's Quest for Power and the War in the Gulf* (New York: Wiley, 1991), p.39.
7. W. Thom Workman, *The Social Origins of the Iran-Iraq War* (Boulder, Colo.: Lynne Rienner, 1994), pp. 150, 151.
8. Quoted in Ofra Bengio, *Saddam's Word: Political Discourse in Iraq* (New York: Oxford University Press, 1998), p. 146.
9. "Nuclear Anxiety in Pakistan: Complex Pressures, Dominated by Islam, Led to Testing," *New York Times*, June 1, 1998.
10. Ibid.
11. See, for example, "Pakistani President at the Fulcrum of Crisis," *New York Times*, May 31, 2002.
12. Shiren T. Hunter, *The Future of Islam and the West* (Westport, Conn.: Praeger, 1998): 132.
13. Ronald Bruce St. John, *Qaddafi's World Design: Libyan Foreign Policy, 1969–1987* (London: Saqi Books, 1987), p. 21.
14. Ibid, p.27
15. Ibid, p.26
16. In fact, after World War II, one plan that was not actually implemented called for a UN trusteeship over Libya with separate administrative responsibilities for the provinces: British in Cyrenaica, Italian in Tripolitania, and French in Fezzan.
17. Hervé Bleuchot, "Les fondements de l'idéologie du Colonel Mouammar el-Kadhafi," *Megreb* 46 (March/April 1974): 21–27.
18. Slovenia and Croatia partake of an essentially Central European culture, are Catholic, and, by Yugoslav standards, were rather wealthy republics. Serbia, Montenegro, and Macedonia are Orthodox, use the Cyrillic rather than Latin script, identify with the Balkans, and are considerably poorer.
19. Since the late mid-1980s, between 200,000 and 300,000 Serbs had left Kosovo, many of them forced out by Albanian extremists. Aleksa Djilas, "A Profile of Slobodan Milošević," *Foreign Affairs* 72 , no. 2 (Summer 1993): 82.
20. See, for example, the discussion in Vesna Pešić, *Serbian Nationalism and the Origin of the Yugoslav Crisis* (Washington, D.C.: United States Institute of Peace, 1996).
21. Milošević observed, in one speech, that "Borders, as you know, are always dictated by the strong, they are never dictated by the weak. Therefore it is basic for us to be strong. We simply believe that the legitimate right and interest of

the Serbian people is to live in one state. And if we have to fight, God help us we will" (ibid., p. 9).
22. Once called Nubia, a large part of what is now Sudan had a history dominated by Egyptian influence. Although substantially converted to Christianity in the sixth century A.D., the northern part, increasingly infiltrated by Egypt, became Muslim, while the southern part espoused a combination of Christianity and traditional African beliefs. Two ideationally and geographically sharp divisions came to characterize the country; they further gelled during the Anglo-Egyptian condominium (1899–1955), which established distinct administration for the two regions and kept northerners out of the South. Thus, the country's bifurcation was its dominant feature upon independence in 1956. Religious and ethnic differences largely overlap: Arabs represent most of the population of the North (where the next largest group are the Nile Nubians); most of the South's population are non-Muslim Niolitic peoples, among which the largest ethnic groups are the Dinka and Nuer, followed by the Shilluk.
23. Robert Shaloub, "War, Development, and Identity Politics in Sudan," *Middle East Report* 26, no. 3 (July–September 1996): 32.
24. For a good discussion of the Taliban, see Peter Marsden, *The Taliban: War and Religion in Afghanistan* (New York: Zed Books, 2002).
25. Martha Neff Kesler, *Syria: Fragile Mosaic of Power* (Washington, D.C.: National Defense University Press, 1987), p. 15.
26. The country once covered an area encompassing, in addition to its present territory, much of present-day Lebanon, Israel, and Jordan, and part of Turkey.
27. The ruling Alawis theoretically are a Shiite sect, but one whose distinct character places it on the very fringes of Islam. Moreover, Christians make up 10 percent of the population, there is a Druze minority, and close to a million Palestinians live permanently in Syria.
28. See, for example, Rouhollah K. Ramazani, *Revolutionary Iran: Challenge and Response on the Middle East* (Baltimore: The Johns Hopkins University Press, 1986), pp. 19–22.
29. Hunter, *The Future of Islam*, pp. 132–133.
30. Ibid., p. 133.
31. According to Ahmed Rashid, "The Taliban are poorly tutored in Islamic and Afghan history, knowledge of the Sharia and the Koran and the political and theoretical developments in the Muslim world during the twentieth century." *Taliban* (New Haven: Yale University Press, 2000), p. 93.
32. See William Malley, "Interpreting the Taliban," in *Fundamentalism Reborn: Afghanistan and the Taliban*, ed. Malley (New York: New York University Press, 1998), pp. 14–15.
33. Sciolino, *The Outlaw State*, p. 99.
34. Bengio, *Saddam's Word*, p. 182.
35. "Iraq Rediscovers Religion," *The Economist*, February 14, 1998.

36. See, for example, "Pakistani Militants' Ties to Military Make Radicals Hard to Dislodge," *New York Times*, May 27, 2002.

37. Ibid.

38. Most Libyans belong to the Sunni branch of Islam and adhere to its Malikite school, holding that the only valid sources of religious truth are the Koran and the *hadith* (the sayings of the Prophet Mohammed), but not, as accepted by other Sunnis, consensus of religious authorities (*ijma*) and analogy (*qijas*).

39. St. John, *Qaddafi's World Design*, pp. 33–39.

40. The Party of the United Left, led by Milošević's wife, Mirjana Marković, was also a successor to the former Communist Party.

41. However, a number of Milošević's ultranationalist rivals for power, such as Vojislav Šešelj and Vuk Drašković, did invoke symbols of Serbian Orthodoxy.

42. See, for example, Hunter, *The Future of Islam*, pp. 128–130.

43. Khomeini cited in Ramazani, *Revolutionary Iran*, p. 21.

44. For a discussion, see Adbelwahab El-Affendi, *Turabis' Revolution: Islam and Power in Sudan* (London: Grey Seal, 1991).

45. Quoted in Mohammed Elhachmi Hamdi, *The Making of an Islamic Political Leader: Conversations with Hasan al-Turabi* (Boulder, Colo.: Westview Press, 1998), p. 122.

46. A Taliban spokesman explained that "the [Taliban] Movement may represent a strong force that will . . . resume the role of liberating the Islamic lands from the Atheistic, faithless American tyranny. Particularly, after Muhajid Usama bin Laden declared war on the Crusade existence in the Arab regions." "The Islamic Movement and the Dangers of Regional Assimilation, Interview with Taliban Spokesman," *Nidaul Islam* (April–May 1997): 3.

47. For discussions of *Juche*, see Han Shik Part, "*Chuch'e*: The North Korean Ideology," in *Journey to North Korea: Personal Perceptions*, ed. C. I. Eugene Kim and B. C. Koh, Research Papers and Policy Studies no. 8 (Berkeley: Institute of East Asian Studies, 1983), and Adrian Buzo, *The Guerilla Dynasty*, especially chapter 2.

48. Park, *North Korea*, p. 91.

49. Ibid., p. 47.

50. See Ruth First, *Libya: The Elusive Revolution* (Middlesex, UK: Penguin Books, 1974).

51. Lenard J. Cohen, *Serpent in the Bosom: The Rise and Fall of Slobodan Milošević* (Boulder, Colo.: Westview Press, 2002), p. 102.

52. Ibid.

53. Dubravka Stojanović, *The Balkans, War, and Textbooks: The Case of Serbia* (Belgrade, Yugoslavia: Belgrade Association for Social History, 1999), p. 168.

54. See J. Devlin, The *Ba'th Party: A History from Its Origins to 1966* (Stanford, Calif.: Hoover Institution Press, 1976).

55. Efraim Karsh and Inari Rautsi, *Saddam Hussein: A Political Biography* (New York: The Free Press, 1991), pp. 12–14.

56. Martina Neff Kessler, *Syria: A Fragile Mosaic of Power* (Washington, D.C.: National Defense University Press, 1987), pp. 49–50, 58–59.

57. Park, *North Korea*, p. 87.

58. Kim Il-Sung, "On Some Theoretical Problems of the Socialist Economy," *Selected Works*, vol. 5 (Pyongyang: Foreign Languages Publishing House, 1972), p. 302.

59. The reference is to the Chongsanri agricultural cooperative, where the method was first initiated.

60. It was introduced at the Taean Electric Machinery Plants.

61. See, for example, William O. Beeman, "Images of the Great Satan," in *Religion and Politics in Iran*, ed. Nikki R. Keddie (New Haven: Yale University Press, 1983), p. 192.

62. Mohammed Elhachmi Hamid, *The Making of an Islamic Political Leader* (Boulder, Colo.: Westview Press, 1999), p. 120.

63. M. J. Gohari, *The Taliban: Ascent to Power* (Oxford: Oxford University Press, 1999), p. 68.

64. Muammar Qaddafi, *The Green Book* (London: Martin, Brian, and O'Keefe, 1976), part 2.

65. This emphasis was confirmed by Fifth Plenum of the Central Committee.

66. Sciolino, *The Outlaw State*, p. 99.

67. See Cohen, *Serpent in the Bosom*, pp. 130–132.

68. Benaiah Yongo-Bore, "Sudan's Deepening Crisis," *Middle East Report* 21, no. 172 (September–October 1991).

69. Dilip Hiro, *Iran under the Ayatollahs* (London: Routledge and Kegan Paul, 1985), p. 151.

70. See First, *Libya*, chapter 9.

71. See Rashid, *Taliban*, chapter 9.

72. Hiro, *Iran under the Ayatollahs*, p. 138

73. Ibid., p. 137.

74. Sepehr Zabih, *Iran Since the Revolution* (London: Croom Helm, 1982), p. 148.

75. See, for example, David Blundy and Andrew Lycet, *Qaddafi and the Libyan Revolution* (London: Weidenfeld and Nicholson, 1987), p. 86.

76. "Libyan Chief Pessimistic on Arab Cause," *New York Times*, April 18, 1973.

77. Karsh and Rautsi, *Saddam Hussein*, p. 99.

78. Cohen, *Serpent in the Bosom*, p. 144.

79. Ibid., p. 166.

80. Robert Thomas, *The Politics of Serbia in the 1990s* (New York: Columbia University Press, 1999), p. 131.

81. See "Islamic Fervor from Iran Puts Azerbaijan on Alert after Unrest," *New York Times*, February 4, 2001.

82. See Michael R. J. Vatikiotis, *Indonesian Politics under Sukarno* (London: Routledge, 1993), pp. 121–129, 132–138.

83. Robert Cribb and Colin Brown, *Modern Indonesia: A History since 1945* (London: Longman: 1995), p. 115.

84. These are belief in God, national unity, humanitarianism, people's sovereignty, and social justice and prosperity.

85. See, for example, Raymond A. Hinebusch Jr., *Egyptian Politics under Sadat*, (Boulder, Colo.: Lynne Rienner, 1988), p. 303.

86. For a discussion of the economic predicament and its political ramifications, see International Crisis Group, "Algeria's Economy: The Vicious Circle of Oil and Violence," *Africa Report* (October 2001).

87. See, for example, "Azerbaijan's Economic Upturn Blighted by Corruption," *Agence France Press*, March 12, 1998.

88. For a discussion of the corruption of the Suharto regime see Hamish McDonald, *Suharto's Indonesia* (Honolulu: University Press of Hawaii, 1981), chapter 6; see also Cribb and Brown, *Modern Indonesia*, pp. 145–147.

89. For a discussion, see Paul Adams, "Reign of the Generals," *Africa Report* (November–December 1994): 27–29.

90. Oladimeji Aborisade and Robert J. Mundt, *Politics in Nigeria* (New York: Longman, 2002), p. 201. See also "Nigerian Military Empties Coffers as End of Rule Nears," *Guardian Unlimited*, May 19, 1999.

91. Suharto's massacre of Indonesian communists is described in John Hughes, *Indonesian Upheaval* (New York: David McKay, 1967), passim.

92. For a discussion of the odds-ratio and its properties, see Joseph L. Fleiss, *Statistical Methods for Rates and Proportions* (New York: Wiley Interscience, 1973), chapter 5.

5. Secondary Renegades and Nonmilitary Responses

1. Discussions of the aims and impact of economic sanctions can be found in David Baldwin, *Economic Statecraft* (Princeton: Princeton University Press, 1989); James M. Lindsay, "Trade Sanctions as Foreign Policy Instruments," *International Studies Quarterly* 30, no. 2 (1988): 91–111; Miroslav Nincic and Peter Wallensteen, *Dilemmas of Economic Coercion* (New York: Praeger, 1983); Zachary Selden, *Economic Sanctions as Instruments of American Foreign Policy* (Westport, Conn.: Praeger, 1999); and George Tsebelis, "Are Sanctions Effective?: A Game Theoretic Analysis," *Journal of Conflict Resolution* 34, no.3 (1990): 3–28.

2. See, for example, Baldwin, *Economic Statecraft*; Margaret Doxey, *International Sanctions in Comparative Perspective* (New York: St. Martin's Press, 1987); Gary

Hufbauer, Jeffrey Schott, and Kimberly Elliot, *Economic Sanctions Reconsid-ered: History and Current Policy*, 2nd ed. (Washington, D.C.: Institute for International Economics, 1990); Robert Pape, "Why Economic Sanctions Do Not Work," *International Security* 22 (1997): 90–136.

3. D. Kahneman and A. Tversky, "Prospect Theory: An Analysis of Decisions under Risk," *Econometrica* 47 (1979): 263–291, and "Choices, Values, and Frames," *American Psychologist* 4 (1984): 341–350.

4. For an application of this theory, see Miroslav Nincic, "Loss Aversion and the Domestic Context of Military Intervention," *Political Research Quarterly* 50 (March 1997): 97–120.

5. Susan Woodward, *Balkan Tragedy: Chaos and Dissolution after the Cold War* (Washington, D.C.: Brookings Institution, 1995), p. 291.

6. Veran Matić, "Strangling Serbia's Democrats," *New York Times*, January 12, 1994.

7. See Mirjana Vasović "Opravdanost Sankcija," in *Ekonomske Sankcije UN: Uporedna Analiza I Slučaj Jugoslavije*, ed. Miroslav Prokopijević and Jovan Teokarević (Belgrade: Institut za Evropske Studije, 1998), pp. 141–152.

8. Peter Marsden, *The Taliban: War and Religion in Afghanistan* (New York: Zed Books, 1998), p.98.

9. Park, *North Korea*, p. 99.

10. Kim Jong-Il, "The Historical Lesson in Building Socialism and the General Line of Our Party," quoted in Hy-Sang Lee, *North Korea: A Strange Socialist Fortress* (Westport, Conn.: Praeger, 2001), p. 217.

11. "Iraq's Rising Forces of Faith Create Fears for Future," *Washington Post*, March 15, 2003.

12. Ibid.

13. "Attitudes Altered in Iraq as Hussein Solidifies Standing," *Washington Post*, September 22, 2002.

14. As one observer judged the situation, "In many ways, the Islamic Republic was destined to face serious challenges. Its use of religion as a political idiom produced utopian expectations that no state — much less a developing country, even a major oil producer — could ever hope to achieve." Robin Wright, *The Last Great Revolution: Turmoil and Transformation in Iran* (New York: Knopf, 2000), p. 62.

15. Ibid., especially chapters 2 and 7.

16. According to one survey, only 15 percent of the voters deemed it important to confront the West's "cultural onslaught" and resist détente with the United States. See Stephen C. Fairbanks, "Theocracy versus Democracy: Iran Considers Political Parties," *Middle East Journal* 52, no. 1 (Winter 1998): 18.

17. Tim Niblock, *Pariah States and Sanctions in the Middle East: Iraq, Libya, and Sudan* (Boulder, Colo.: Lynne Rienner, 2001), p. 90.

18. "Musharraf Condemns Religious Hardliners," *BBC News (Online)*, June 5, 2001.

19. Quoted in "Sudan's Fake Muslim Reformers," *Baltimore Sun*, March 6, 1996.

20. Quoted in "God, Oil, and Country: Changing the Logic of War in Sudan," International Crisis Group, *Africa Report* 9 (January 2002): 213. For the increasingly pragmatic turn, see also Abdel Salam Sidahmed, *Politics and Islam in Contemporary Sudan* (Richmond, UK: Curzon, 1997), pp. 212–226.

21. See Bijan Khajehpour, "Iran's Economy: Twenty Years after the Islamic Revolution," in *Iran at the Crossroads*, ed. John Esposito and R. K. Ramazani (New York: Palgrave, 2001), p. 104.

22. Ibid., p. 113.

23. Japeh Youssefi, "Trade Mafia: U.S. Sanctions Helping Corrupt Businesses in Iran," *The Iranian*, May 25, 2001.

24. Lenard Cohen, *Serpent in the Bosom: The Rise and Fall of Slobodan Milošević* (Boulder, Colo.: Westview Press, 2001), p. 132.

25. Randolph Ryan, "Stranglehold Sanctions on Serbia Squeeze Middle Class More than Milošević," *The World Paper*, October 1999.

26. See, for example, "Fatal Fight over Spoils by Insiders in Belgrade," *New York Times*, November 9, 1997.

27. These interests were active even after the return to democracy and were held accountable for the murder of Prime Minister Zoran Djindjić in 2003.

28. "Palaces and Oil Smuggling," International Information Programs, U.S. Department of State.

29. "Political Forces," *The Economist Intelligence Unit*, October 6, 2000.

30. See, for example, "Oil Suppliers Gave Hussein Kickbacks," *Washington Post*, May 7, 2003.

31. See, for example, "Iraq's Elite Living Large: Smugglers Make Fortunes amid Nation's Squalor," *San Francisco Chronicle*, January 15, 2003; "How Hussein Gets Anything He Wants," *Los Angeles Times*, November 23, 2002.

32. Frederick Balfour, "Dark Days for a Black Market," *Business Week*, October 2001, p. 38.

33. Ahmed Rashid refers to "the biggest smuggling racket in the world [which has] enmeshed the Taliban with Pakistani smugglers, transporters, drug barons, bureaucrats, politicians and army officers." Rashid, *Taliban*, p. 189.

34. As Dirk Vandewalle observed, "There is extremely little evidence of financial corruption. This is perhaps the most striking fact considering Libya's rapid development under Qaddafi." "Libya's Revolution Revisited," *Middle East Report*, no. 143 (November–December, 1986): 34.

35. See, for example, Dirk Vandewalle, "The Libyan Jamahiriyya since 1969," in *Qadhafi's Libya, 1969–1994*, ed. Dirk Vandewalle (New York: St. Martin's Press, 1995), pp. 3–46.

36. Ray Takeyh, "The Rogue Who Came in from the Cold," *Foreign Affairs* 80, no. 3 (May/June 2001): 77.

37. Ibid., p. 79.

38. Niblock, *Pariah States*, p. 72.

39. See, for example, "'Heroin Trail Leads to North Korea," *Washington Post*, May 12, 2003.

40. See Volker Perthes, *The Political Economy of Syria under Assad* (London: Taurus, 1995), especially chapter 2.

41. Raymond A. Hinnebusch, "Liberalization in Syria: The Struggle of Economic and Political Rationality, " in *Contemporary Syria: Liberalization between Cold War and Cold Peace*, ed. Eberhard Kienly (London: British Academic Press, 1994), pp. 107–110.

42. An interesting variant of this view can be found in Fred H. Lawson, *Why Syria Goes to War: Thirty Years of Confrontation* (Ithaca: Cornell University Press, 1996).

43. M. Sarkees and S. Zunes, "Disenchantment with the 'New World Order': Syria's Relations with the United States," *International Journal of Middle Eastern Studies* 49, no. 2 (April 1994): 361.

44. Neil Quilliam, *Syria and the New World Order* (Reading, UK: Ithaca Press, 1999), p. 162.

45. "Bush Opposes U.S. Sanctions on Syria," *BBC News (Online)*, September 4, 2002.

46. As Meghan O'Sullivan notes, "On average, Sudan sold only 3.8 percent of its total exports to the United States between 1990 and 1997." *Shrewd Sanctions: Statecraft and State Sponsors of Terrorism* (Washington, D.C.: Brookings Institution Press, 2003), p. 249.

47. International Crisis Group, *God, Oil, and Country: Changing the Logic of War in the Middle East* (Brussels: International Crisis Group Press, 2002), p. 72.

48. According to Susan Woodward: "While the sanctions undercut the prospects of democratic and anti-war pressures, they increased the ability of the ruling party and nationalist militants to Milošević's right." Woodward, *Balkan Tragedy*, p. 293.

49. Ryan, "Stranglehold Sanctions," p. 4.

50. Ibid.

51. Reported in Srbobran Branković, "Sankcije I Stav Zapada Prema Srbiji," in *Ekonomske Sankcije UN*, pp. 88–122.

52. See Louis J. Sell, *Slobodan Milosevic and the Destruction of Yugoslavia* (Durham, N.C.: Duke University Press, 2002), p. 203.

53. Ibid., p. 214

54. See R. K. Ramazani, "Iran's Foreign Policy: Both North and South," *Middle East Journal* 33 (Summer 1992): 393–412.

55. Fairbanks, "Theocracy versus Democracy," p. 18.

56. International Crisis Group, "Iran: The Struggle for the Revolution's Soul," *Middle East Report* (August 2002).
57. "Reform Faction in Iran Hurt by 'Evil' Label," *Washington Post*, February 15, 2002.
58. "Iranian Abandons Push to Improve U.S. Ties," *Washington Post*, May 30, 2002.
59. "Bush's Support for Reformers Backfires in Iran," *Washington Post*, August 3, 2002.
60. "Desire for Empowerment a Uniting Factor in Iran," *Washington Post*, November 14, 2004.
61. Selig S. Harrison, *Korean Endgame: A Strategy for Reunification and U.S. Disengagement* (Princeton: Princeton University Press, 2002), p. 31.
62. Ibid., p. 33.
63. Ibid., chapter 18.
64. U.S. Department of State, *Patterns of Global Terrorism, 2004*, p. 68.
65. See, for example, "Through a Glass Darkly," *The Economist*, March 11, 2004.
66. International Crisis Group, "Voices from the Iraqi Street," *Iraq Briefing*, December 4, 2003, pp. 2–4.
67. Litwak, *Rogue States and U.S. Foreign Policy*, p. 146.
68. Taliban spokesperson , "The Islamic Taliban Movement and the Dangers of Regional Assimilation," *Nida'ul Islam*, no. 18 (April–May 1997): 2.
69. Francois Burgat, "Qadhafi's Ideological Framework," in *Qadhafi's Libya*, ed. Vandewalle, p. 54.
70. Ibid.
71. Niblock, *Pariah States*, p. 213.
72. See, for example, William Safire's view, "Qaddafi's Surrender, Bush's Success," *International Herald Tribune*, December 23, 2003.
73. Quoted in "Two Decades of Sanctions, Isolation Wore Down Gaddafi," *Washington Post*, December 20, 2003. See also "Secret Diplomacy Won Libyan Pledge on Arms," *New York Times*, December 21, 2003.
74. "Libyan Stagnation a Big Factor," *New York Times*, January 8, 2004.
75. Ibid.
76. "Why Did Qaddafi Surrender?" *Africa News*, December 29, 2003, and "New Faces Herald Hopes for New Libya: Ministers under Gaddafi Signal Reforms Meant to End Isolation," *Washington Post*, January 3, 2004.
77. Quoted in "Has Gaddafi Reformed?" *Washington Post*, August 19, 2003.
78. "Le Nouveau Kadhafi," *Le Monde*, January 8, 2004.

6. The Value of Military Coercion

1. Daniel Byman and Matthew Waxman, *The Dynamics of Coercion: American Foreign Policy and the Limits of Military Might* (New York: Cambridge University Press, 2002), pp. 68–69.

2. Of course, regime capacity can merely be threatened, with the hope of altering its incentives; but when we move to the operational use of force, it is not
   motivations that are targeted but the material foundations of renegade
   policies.
3. For a historical perspective, see Miranda Vickers, *Between Serb and Albanian:
   A History of Kosovo* (New York: Columbia University Press, 1998).
4. The United States, Russia, Britain, Germany, and France.
5. Quoted in Ivo H. Daalder and Michael E. O'Hanlon, *Winning Ugly: NATO's
   War to Save Kosovo* (Washington, D.C.: Brookings Institution Press, 2000), p.
   33.
6. Cited in Louis Sell, *Slobodan Milosevic and the Destruction of Yugoslavia* (Durham, N.C.: Duke University Press, 2002), p. 303.
7. Slobodan Reljić, "NATO Nije Dobrodošao, *NIN*, March 18, 1999.
8. Cohen, *Serpent in the Bosom*, p. 301.
9. Michael J. Mazaar, Don M. Snider, and James Blackwell Jr., *Desert Storm: The
   Gulf War and What We Learned* (Boulder, Colo.: Westview Press, 1993), pp.
   39–40.
10. Ibid, p. 467.
11. Rick Atkinson, "What Were Saddam's Miscalculations?" PBS interview, http:/
    /www.pbs.org/wgbh/frontline'shows/iraq/interviews/ross.html. See also Richard
    Hermann "Coercive Diplomacy and the Crisis Over Kuwait," in *The Limits of
    Coercive Diplomacy*, ed. Alexander George and William E. Simons (Boulder,
    Colo.: Westview Press, 1994), pp. 234–239.
12. Steve A. Yetiv, *The Persian Gulf Crisis* (Westport, Conn.: Wesport Press, 1997),
    p. 78.
13. Mazarr, Snider, and Blackwell, *Desert Storm*, p. 53.
14. Ibid., p. 65.
15. The year before, in a February 1990 speech, pointing to U.S. retreat from
    Lebanon several years earlier, after the bombing of the U.S. Marine barracks,
    he maintained that "The United States has been defeated in some combat
    arenas for all the forces it possessed, and it has displayed signs of fatigue, frus-
    tration, and hesitation." Ibid., p. 80.
16. He "seemed to conclude that Iraq would realize its greatest political leverage,
    and thus be in a position to drive its best deal, only if it took the crisis all the
    way to war." Herrmann, "Coercive Diplomacy," p. 255.
17. See, for example, President Bush's State of the Union address: "State of the
    Union: The Iraq Issue; Bush Enlarges Case for War by Linking Iraq with Ter-
    rorists," *New York Times*, January 29, 2003.
18. "Blix Says He Saw Nothing to Prompt a War," *New York Times*, January 31,
    2003.
19. See, e.g., "Blunt Diplomacy: Powell Attacks the Validity of the Work by Weap-
    ons Inspectors in Iraq," *New York Times*, March 6, 2003.

20. "The President Readies U.S. for Prospect of Imminent War," *New York Times*, March 7, 2003.
21. See, for example, "Iraq Said to Have Tried to Reach Last Minute Deal to Avert War," *New York Times*, November 6, 2003.
22. Daniel Byman, *Confronting Iraq: U.S. Policy and the Use of Force since the Gulf War* (Santa Monica, Calif.: RAND, 2000), p. 56.
23. Elaine Sciolino, "Kuwait Crisis," *New York Times*, October 11, 1994.
24. Brian Davis, *Qaddafi, Terrorism, and the Origins of the U.S. Attack on Libya* (New York: Praeger, 1990), p. 89.
25. Ibid., p. 108
26. Joseph T. Stanik, *El Dorado Canyon: Reagan's Undeclared War with Qaddafi* (Annapolis, Md.: Naval Institute Press, 2003), p. 46.
27. "President Bush's Address on Terrorism before a Joint Meeting of Congress," *New York Times*, September 21, 2001.
28. "Mullah Omar—In His Own Words," *The Guardian*, September 26, 2001.
29. The inverted positions of 0 and 1 in the rows of the two tables is due to the fact that we associate IO = 1 with success, but IR = 1 with failure of the threat. This maintains the expectation that data in the diagonal cells would indicate a positive relation.
30. Quoted in Sell, *Slobodan Milosevic*, p. 304.
31. Stratfor.com, "Toppling Milosevic: The Carrot Instead of the Stick," *Global Intelligence Update*, June 26, 2000.
32. "NATO Said to Focus Raids on Serb Elite's Property," *Deutsche Press-Agentur*, April 19, 1999.
33. "Civilian Deaths in the NATO Air Campaign," *Human Rights Watch* 12, no.1 (February 2000): 4.
34. For an analysis of the economic consequences, see Mladjan Dinkić, ed., *Final Account: Economic Consequences of the NATO Bombing* (Belgrade: Stubovi Kulture, 1999).
35. Steven Hosmer, *The Conflict over Kosovo: Why Milosevic Decided to Settle When He Did* (Santa Monica, Calif.: RAND, 2001), pp. 66–68.
36. "Belgrade's People Still Defiant, but Deeply Weary," *New York Times*, May 24, 1999.
37. Hosmer, *The Conflict over Kosovo*, p. 53.
38. Ibid., pp. 71–76.
39. Daalder and O'Hanlon, *Winning Ugly*, p. 91.
40. Inrterview, PBS, *Newshour with Jim Lehrer*, March 24, 1999, http://www.pbs.org.
41. Cohen, *Serpent in the Bosom*, p. 320.
42. Adam LeBor, *Milosevic: A Biography* (London: Bloomsbury, 2002), p. 289.
43. Hosmer, *The Conflict over Kosovo*, p. 50.
44. Reported in Cohen, *Serpent in the Bosom*, p. 334.

45. Hosmer, *The Conflict over Kosovo*, p. 51.

46. "Hundreds of Yugoslav Troops Said to Desert," *New York Times*, May 20, 1999.

47. The authors involved are Cohen, *Serpent in the Bosom*; Sell, *Slobodan Milosevic*; LeBor, *Milosevic*; and Dragan Bujošević and Ivan Prodanović, *The Fall of Milosevic: The October 5th Revolution* (New York: Palgrave, 2003).

48. As former SPS leader Radovan Raka Radović complained (referring to the first couple), "One marriage and the state of that marriage had become the condition on which the fate of the spouses, their immediate and possibly extended families, but also a huge number of people, the members of both parties, and almost the whole nation depended." *BETA Radio*, January 13, 2000.

49. LeBor, *Milosevic*, p. 300.

50. Sell, *Slobodan Milosevic*, p. 310.

51. According to Louis Sell, "Lower-level officers had long resented Milosevic's lack of financial support for the army, and now they seethed over his bootless policy of launching them into a war with NATO and then forcing them to withdraw from Kosovo without — in their view — having been defeated" (ibid., p. 311).

52. Jovica Stanišić, head of the internal security apparatus, had become critical of Milošević and was fired, along with his closest associates. Just before this, Milorad Vučelić, a pragmatic member of the SPS and, like Stanišić, much despised by the JUL, was also removed. Also sacked were General Ljubiša Veličković, commander of the air force and air defense, who had criticized Milošević, and, even more important, General Momčilo Perišić, the chief of staff of the Yugoslav Army, who had counseled a conciliatory position toward NATO.

53. LeBor, *Milosevic*, p. 294.

54. Ibid., p. 296.

55. Sell, *Slobodan Milosevic*, p. 339.

56. "Who Really Brought Down Milosevic?" *New York Times*, November 26, 2000.

57. "Student Group Emerges as Major Milosevic Foe," *New York Times*, May 22, 2000.

58. Cohen, *Serpent in the Bosom*, p. 302.

59. Clark interview, PBS, *Newshour with Jim Lehrer*, October 6, 2000. http://www.pbs.org/newshour/bb/europe.july-dec00/yugo.

60. Batić Banević,"Mirova Pobeda," *NIN*, June 16, 1999.

61. Strategic Marketing and Media Research Institute (SMMRI).

62. Ibid.

63. Reflecting on the impact of foreign pressure on the ultimate ouster of the regime, Aleksa Djilas, a leading Serbian historian and political analyst, reminded the *New York Times* correspondent of a dedication by the novelist P. G. Wodehouse to his daughter, "without whose never-failing sympathy and encouragement the book would have been finished in half the time." The

analogy cannot be rejected peremptorily. "Did US Bombs Help or Hinder?" *New York Times*, December 25, 2000.

64. In the Yugoslav case, these effects were amplified by a conviction that a ground invasion was also being contemplated. See Hosmer, *The Conflict over Kosovo*.

65. Operation El Dorado Canyon is discussed in Davis, *Qaddafi*.

66. As Reagan explained, "preemptive action against his terrorist installations will not only diminish Colonel Qaddafi's capacity to export terror, it will provide him with incentives and reasons to alter his criminal behavior." "Transcript of Address by Reagan on Libya," *New York Times*, April 15, 1986.

67. U.S. Department of State, *Patterns in Global Terrorism, 1987*, p. 36.

68. Tim Zimmerman, "The American Bombing of Libya: A Success for Coercive Diplomacy," *Survival* 29, no. 3 (May–June 1987): 219.

69. Stephen T. Hosmer, *Operations against Enemy Leaders* (Santa Monica, Calif.: RAND, 2001), p. 30.

70. Zimmerman, "The American Bombing of Libya," p. 219.

71. While Qaddafi was not hurt, his adopted daughter apparently was killed, and his wife and two sons were injured.

72. "Reagan Denies Libya Raid Was Meant to Kill Qaddafi," *New York Times*, April 19, 1986.

73. "Shultz Expresses Hopes for a Coup to Oust Qaddafi," *New York Times*, April 18, 1986.

74. Hosmer, *Operations against Enemy Leaders*, p. 6.

75. Edward Schumacher, "The United States and Libya," *Foreign Affairs* 65, no. 1 (Winter 1986–87): 336.

76. Special Correspondent, "U.S. Raid Haunts Libya," *Middle East Report*, July–August 1986, p. 36.

77. In addition to acting as informants, they began supplanting the police and courts as the regime's coercive pillars, becoming a "virtual parallel government." Schumacher, "The United States and Libya," p. 338.

78. "Qaddafi's Troubled Economy," *New York Times*, May 2, 1986. See also Special Correspondent, "U.S. Raid Haunts Libya," p. 37.

79. Hosmer, *Operations Against Enemy Leaders*, p. 67.

80. Litwak, *Rogue States and U.S. Foreign Policy*, p. 124.

81. George Bush and Brent Scowcroft, *A World Transformed* (New York: Knopf, 1998), p. 433.

82. Hosmer, *Operations Against Enemy Leaders*, p. 69.

83. On the loyalty of Saddam's security forces, see Amatzia Baram, *Between Impediments and Advantage" Saddam's Iraq* (Washington, D.C.: United States Institute of Peace, June 1998).

84. "The Survival of Saddam Hussein," CNN.com, Specials 2001.

85. For example, Steve A. Yelive, *The Persian Gulf Crisis* (Westport, Conn: Greenwood Press, 1997), and Roger Hilsman, *George Bush vs. Saddam Hussein: Military Success, Political Failure* (Novato, Calif.: Lyford Books, 1997).

86. See, for example, "Afghan Warlords Thrive beyond Official Reach," *New York Times*, September 24, 2003.
87. These problems are discussed in International Crisis Group, *Peacebuilding in Afghanistan*, Asia Report no. 64 (September 29, 2003); also, "Northern Afghan Region Still Roiled by Rivalries and Fighting," *New York Times*, September 24, 2002
88. See "Profile: Gulbuddin Hekmatyar," *BBC News (Online)*, January 28, 2003.
89. International Crisis Group *Disarmament and Reintegration in Afghanistan*, Asia Report no. 65 (September 30, 2003), "Mixed Signals on Afghan Stability," *Washington Post*, December 10, 2003.
90. "'Rule of Gun' Said to Imperil AFGHAN Democracy Efforts," *New York Times*, November 11, 2003.
91. "Taliban Pouring into Afghanistan," *CBS News.Com*, September 7, 2003.
92. "Rumsfeld Sees Need to Realign Military Fight against Terror," *New York Times*, October 23, 2003.
93. "Baghdad Terror Blask Kills Dozens," *BBC News* online, October 27, 2003.
94. "Huge Suicide Blast Demolishes UN Headquarters in Baghdad," *New York Times*, August 20, 2003.
95. "Afghan Villagers Torn by Grief after US Raid Kills 9 Children," *New York Times*, December 8, 2003.
96. "2 US Fronts: Quick Wars but a Bloody Peace," *New York Times*, September 19, 2003.
97. Signs around the villages read, "This fence is here for your protection. Do not approach or try to cross or you will be shot." "Tough New Tactics by US Tighten Grip on Iraqi Town," *New York Times*, December 7, 2003.
98. Human Rights Watch has complained that U.S. forces operating in Afghanistan have arbitrarily detained civilians, used excessive force during arrests of non-combatants, and mistreated detainees. "Enduring Freedom: Abuses by U.S. Forces in Afghanistan," *Human Rights Watch*, March 8, 2004.
99. Ibid.
100. Ibid.
101. John Barry and Evan Thomas, "Dissent in the Bunker," *Newsweek*, December 15, 2003, p. 36.
102. "Waves of Chaos," *Le Monde Diplomatique*, September 2003.
103. As *Newsweek* observed with regard to Iraq, "The Iraqis in uniform today are seen by too many Iraqi citizens as foreign collaborators." Barry and Thomas, "Dissent in the Bunker," p. 36.

7. Closing Thoughts

1. On this topic, see George E. Marcus, W. Russell Neuman, and Michael Mackuen, *Affective Intelligence and Political Judgment* (Chicago: University of Chicago Press, 2000).

2. No note can do justice to this literature. Nevertheless, representatives include Alexander Wendt, *Social Theory of International Politics* (Cambridge: Cambridge University Press, 1999); Nicholas G. Onuf, *World of Our Making: Rules and Rule in Social and International Relations* (Columbia: University of South Carolina Press, 1989); Martha Finnemore, *Defining National Interests in International Society* (Ithaca: Cornell University Press, 1996); Ann Florini, "The Evolution of International Norms," *International Studies Quarterly* 40, no. 3 (September 1996): 363–389; Robert Axelrod, "An Evolutionary Approach to Norms," *The American Political Science Review*. 80, no. 4 (December 1986): 1095–1111; Gregory Raymond, "Problems and Prospects in the Study of International Norms," *Mershon International Studies Review* 41, no. 2 (November 1997): 205–245; Jeffrey Legro, "Which Norms Matter? Revisiting the Failure of Institutionalism," *International Organization* 51 (Winter 1997): 31–63.

3. For discussions of the future of public diplomacy, see Carnes Lord, "The Past and Future of Public Diplomacy," *Orbis* 42, no. 1 (Winter 1998): 49–72; Rosaleen Smyth, "Mapping U.S. Public Diplomacy in the 21st Century," *Australian Journal of International Affairs* 55, no.3 (2001): 419–433.

4. For a discussion of flexibility in the Vietnam case, see Meghan L. O'Sullivan, *Shrewd Sanctions: Statecraft and State Sponsors of Terrorism* (Washington, D.C.: Brookings Institution Press, 2003), pp. 288–289.

5. Introductory remarks to the International Peace Academy's "Seminar on Sanctions," April 17, 2000. http://un.org/News/Press/docs/2000/2000417.sgsm7360.doc.html.

6. The most extensive discussion of practical issues surrounding such sanctions is in the proceedings of the two Interlaken seminars on targeted UN financial sanctions. See http://www.smartsanctions.ch/papers/Ag2.pdf. See also Peter Wallensteen et al., eds., *Making Targeted Sanctions Effective: Guidelines for the Implementation of UN Policy Options* (Uppsala University, Department of Peace and Conflict Research, 2003).

7. "Democratizing in Iraq," *The Economist*, January 24–30, 2004, p. 44.

8. See David Rothkopf, "In Praise of Cultural Imperialism," *Foreign Affairs*, no. 107 (Summer 1997): 38–53.

9. The most complete treatment of soft power is Joseph S. Nye Jr., *Soft Power: The Means to Succeed in World Politics* (New York: Public Affairs, 2004).

10. Benjamin Barber, *Jihad vs. McWorld: How Globalism and Tribalism Are Reshaping the World* (New York: Ballantine Books, 1996).

11. Martha Finnemore and Kathryn Sikkink, "International Norm Dynamics and Political Change," *International Organization* 52, no. 4 (Autumn 1998): 887–917.

12. Ibid, p. 903.

13. Ibid, p. 909.

14. G. John Ikenberry, *After Victory: Institutions, Strategic Restraint, and the Rebuilding of Order after Major Wars* (Princeton: Princeton University Press, 2001), p. 266.

15. The overall index is based on whether their trade, aid, immigration, investment, peacekeeping, and environmental policies help or hurt poor countries. "Ranking the Rich: Who Really Helps the Poor?" *Foreign Policy*, no.136 (May–June, 2003): 56–66.

Index

Abbas, Abu, 54
Abu Nidal organization, 54, 143
Ad Bellum principles, 51
Afghanistan, 55, 64, 65, 69, 79, 81, 82,
  84, 113, 118, 125, 144, 145,
  159–66, 174; Northern Alliance, 44,
  125; sanctions against, 125;
  Southern Alliance, 44, 160; Taliban
  regime, 12, 113, 144; U.S. led inva-
  sion of, 173; U.S., war aims in, 121
Aggression, international consensus on,
  51; territorial, 15, 34, 86, 155
Agreed Framework, 58, 124
Air India, flight hijacking of, 55
Akazu, 63
Alawi faith, 82
Albania, 137
Albanians, 78, 136, 155; ethnic cleans-
  ing of, 61
Albright, Madeleine, 12, 125, 149
Algeria, 71, 95, 96, 98, 99
Algerian regime, 96
Aliyev, Ilham 97
Aliyev regime, 71, 95, 96
Alliance for Change, 138
Annan, Kofi, 172

Arab Islamism, 70
Arab-Israeli war (1967), 77
Arabic identity, 82
Arabism, 79
Arabization, 96, 98
Armenia, 59
Army Mechanized Task Force, U.S.,
  142
Arusha Accord, 63
Assad, Bashar, 120, 126
al-Assad, Hafez, 12, 70, 90, 94
Assad regime, 94
Austrian Anschluss, 10
Axelrod, Robert, 8, 20
Axis of Evil, 12, 123, 125
Azerbaijan, 59, 71, 95, 98, 99; Mus-
  lims, 96; State Oil Company, 99

Baath ideology, 70, 114
Baath Party, 120
Baathism, 81, 86, 93
Baathist regimes, 70, 162
Baghdad, 89, 158, 160, 161, 164
al-Bakr, Ahmad Hasan, 70
Bani-Sadr, Abol Hassan, 92
Bank of Sudan, 90

al-Bashir, Omar Hassan Ahmad, 54, 55,
   62, 70
Bashir regime, 52, 62, 78, 90, 94
Bashir-Turabi regime, 90
Basque ETA terrorists, 55
Basra, 160
Bazargan, Mahdi, 92
Becker, Howard, 26
Beirut, attack on U.S. embassy in, 144
Belgrade, 137, 147, 148
Ben Bella, Ahmed, 97
Benghazi, 156
Benjedid, Chadli, 71, 97
Berlin discotheque, bombing of, 143,
   156
Berlin Wall, fall of, 16, 53
Bhutto, Benazir, 76, 126
bin Laden, Osama, 12, 44, 54, 55, 65,
   121, 144, 145
Biological and Toxin Weapons Conven-
   tion, 50
Black markets, 41, 112, 117–19, 121,
   122
Blix, Hans, 142
Bonahar, Muhammad Reza, 92
Bolshevik regime, 10
Bolshevik Revolution, 10
Bosnia, 77, 78, 137; war in, 86, 122
Bosnian Croats, 61
Bosnian Serbs, 61
Bourgeoisie, 116, 119, 120, 121, 122
Britain, 10, 142, 143
Brzezinsky, Zbigniew, 92
Bush, George H. W., 54, 121, 124,
   158, 160; Iraqi plot to assassinate, 54
Bush, George W., 12, 40, 58, 125, 139,
   141, 160; administration of, 123,
   140, 142, 144, 165

Capitalism, global, 5, 85; and communism, conflict between, 4
Carr, Edward H., 19

Carter, Jimmy, 92
Causality, 47, 66–69, 102; Links, direct
   and indirect, 91–100, 102, 105,
   106; necessary and sufficient condi-
   tions, 66–69, 95, 104, 105, 169
Center for Defense Information (CDI),
   56
Central Intelligence Agency, 92
Chad, 52, 156
Charisma, leadership/authority, 29, 71,
   144
Chemical and biological weapons
   (CBW), 1, 6, 17, 49, 50, 56, 57, 64,
   72
Chemical Weapons Convention, 50,
   56, 57
China, Peoples Republic of, 5, 70
Chongsanri method and spirit, 88
Christians, African, 79; Maronite, 79
Civic Alliance (GSS), 152
Clark, Wesley (General), 153
Class structure, 33
Clinton, Bill, 147; administration of,
   12, 123, 125, 138, 149
Coalition Provisional Authority, 160
Cohen, Lenard, 117
Cold War, 3, 5, 10, 11, 15, 17, 49, 50,
   51, 53, 59, 61, 63, 113, 176, 179,
   181; post-Cold War era/period, 6,
   16, 17, 20, 49, 53, 60, 72, 133
Collectivism, 86
Colonialism, 86
Communism, 80, 85, 93; collapse/de-
   mise of, 5, 51, 71, 85, 179
Compliance, stakes in, 25, 27, 28, 37,
   38, 39, 98, 108, 133, 136; see also
   Deviance, stakes in
Congress of Vienna, 10
Conoco, 123
Consumer behavior, microeconomic
   model of, 168
Contact Group, 137

Covenant of the League of Nations, 51
Croatia, 77, 78
Cuba, 12, 55
Culture: French, 96; Libyan, 82; politi-
    cal, 6; Sunni, 79; U.S., 176; U.S.
    popular, 4; Western, 88; Western
    consumer, 176
Czechoslovakia, 10

Daalder, Ivo, 149
Darfur, 52, 61, 62, 65
Dar-ul-Islam and Dar-ul-Harb, 83
Dayton Accords, 61, 117
Declaration of Pillnitz, 9
Democracy, 5, 6, 25, 33, 41, 46, 47, 63,
    64, 71, 85, 98
Democratic movement of Serbia (DE-
    POS), 152
Democratic Opposition of Serbia
    (DOS), 152
Democratic Party (DS), 152
Democratic Party of Serbia (DSS), 152
Democratic peace, theories of the, 169
Democratic Republic of Congo, 60, 62
Deobandism, 81; neo-Deobandism, 81
Dependency: literature, 33; theory of,
    33
Deterrence: Incentives-Offsetting type,
    143; nuclear and conventional, 3
Deviance, 12, 15, 18, 20, 21, 22, 26,
    contingencies of, 23, 48, 110; inter-
    national, 2, 167; international con-
    cept of, 11; primary and secondary,
    26; sociological literature on, 26;
    stakes in, 25, 28, 37, 39, 42, 43, 74,
    91, 98, 108, 112, 133, 136, 144,
    166; see also Compliance, stakes in
Diem regime, 163
Diplomacy, "public," 170
Djindjić, Zoran, 152, 154
Drašković, Vuk, 152, 154
Durkheim, Emile, 20

Economic interdependence, 5, 7, 8, 30
Economist, 174
Ecuador, 59
Egalitarianism, 88, 89
Egypt, 71, 95, 98, 99,
Endogeneity, issue of, 168
Environmental protection, interna-
    tional, 20
Eritrean-Ethiopian conflict, 59
Ethnic cleansing, 1, 22, 35, 43, 61, 69,
    134, 137, 138, 155
Ethnic repression, 72
Ethnic/nationalist identification, 31
Ethnonationalism, 31, 34, 74, 83, 112
Ethnonationalist policies, 36
European Union, 151
Exceptionalism, national/political, 86,
    97, 176
Expected utility theory, 111

Faisal Islamic Bank, 121
Falluja, U.S. invasion of, 161
Faqih, 80
Fascism, 31
Al Fateh University, 132
FIS, 96
Fourteen Points (Woodrow Wilson), 51
France, 10, 142
FRAPH, 42
French Assembly, 10
French colonialism, 96
French Revolution, 9, 35

Gasani, Anastase, 63
General Popular Congress, 97
Genocide, 58, 62, 63; ethno-nationalist
    goals of, 7
George Washington (U.S. aircraft car-
    rier), 142
Germany, 10; unification of, 93
Ghanem, Shokri, 132
Gibbons, Elizabeth, 41

Gingrich, Newt, 164
Glaspie, April, 140
Globalization, 33, 173, 181, 182; cultural, 176; economic, 5, 33, 176
Government, 13, 88
Greece, 13
Green Book, 32, 88, 179
Gulf of Sidra, 43, 143, 144, 156
Gulf War (1991), 44, 58, 62

Habyarimana, Juvenal, 63
Habayarimana regime, 63
Hague, 65
Haiti, 41
Halabja, 62
Hamas, 54, 55
Hamurabi, 75
Haq, Zia-ul, 81
Harakat ul-Mujahidin, 55
Hekmatyar, Gulbuddin, 161
Hezbollah, 54, 55, 120, 144
Hitler, Adolf, 10, 51
Hitler regime, 10
Holbrooke, Richard, 137, 138
Human rights, 5, 15, 20
Human Rights Watch, 148
Hume, David, 67
Huntington, Samuel, 7
Hussein, Saddam, 54, 60, 61–62, 70, 75, 81, 89, 93, 114, 139, 140, 141–42, 147, 158, 159
Hussein regime, 118
Hutu extremists, 62, 63

Idealism, 169
Ideational entrepreneurs, 171
Ideational mobilization, 181
Ideology, legitimizing, 71
Identity, issues of, 7
Ikenberry, John, 180
Imams, 80, 96
Incentives offsetting (IO) model, 16,

28, 42, 44, 108–10, 130, 134, 145, 148, 178
Incentives restructuring (IR) model, 16, 28, 42, 44, 110–12, 126, 130, 132, 134, 136, 145, 149, 178
India, 76, 82
Indonesia, 71, 95, 97, 99
Infitah, 97, 98, 99
Interhamwe youth militia, 62, 63
International Atomic Energy Agency, 58, 124, 125
International community, 6–11; Afghanistan and, 79; chemical and biological weapons, opposition to, 50; international norms and, 48, 178, 179; Iraq and, 93, 139, 158; Kabul regime and, 125; Libya and, 119, 132, 143; Milošević regime and, 35, 61, 86, 93, 94, 122, 137, 138, 155; North Korea and, 84, 124; Pakistan and, 55; religion and, 80, 82
International Criminal Tribunal for the Former Yugoslavia (ICTY), 151
International Monetary Fund, 121
International Red Cross, Baghdad headquarters, bombing of, 161
International War Crimes Tribunal, 61
International relations, 1, 2, 5, 9, 14, 18; dependency school of, 3; deviance in, 9; models of, 4; realist and neorealist perspectives on, 19; scholars/scholarship, 2, 168, 178, 182; and theories of hegemonic stability, 3; three attributes of, 3, 4
Internet, 132
Investment, multinationalization of, 5
Iran, 40, 54, 63, 64, 69, 76, 77, 80, 82, 83, 90, 123, 124; American hostage crisis, 92; chemical and biological weapons, 56, 57; dialogue of civilization with U.S., 123; Islamic con-

stitution, 116; Islamic Revolution, 27, 40, 76, 80, 90, 92, 114, 116; Islamic Revolutionary Council, 92; minimum daily wage increase, 90; nationalization in, 90; privatization in, 116; redistributive policies, 91; sanctions against, 110, 117; state sector of economy, 116, 117; Trade Mafia, 117; uranium enrichment program, 124; U.S., relations with, 124

Iran-Iraq war, 61, 79, 82,

Iranian regime, 27, 91, 124

Iraq, 44, 54, 60, 64, 75, 79, 82, 86, 89, 93, 114, 125, 131, 135, 139–43, 147, 157–59, 162, 164, 165, 174, 175; arms/weapons inspectors, UN, 141, 142, 147; invasion of, U.S. led, 120, 139–43, 160, 161, 173; "Iraqi man" identity, 75; Kurds in, 61, 62, 125, 158, 159, 161; Kuwait, invasion of, 60, 81, 139–43; nuclear facilities, 58; Oil for Food Program, 118, 125; Oil Ministry, 118; oil smuggling in, 118; Osirak nuclear reactor, Israeli bombing of, 44; Provisional Assembly, 174; Republican Guard, 139, 142, 158; sanctions against, 108, 125; Shiite insurgency, 161; Shiite minority in, 62; Sunni elite in, 118; WMDs, destruction of, 56

Iraqi Governing Council, 160

Iraqi prisoners, abuse of, 163

Iraqi reconstruction, 165, 174

Islah Party, 97

el-Islam, Saif, 132

Islam: fundamentalist and secular, 98; Mustakberin-Mustazesin dichotomy of radical, 181; radical, 88

Islamic: fundamentalists, 27, 76, 97; Guardian Council, 64; hierarchy,

86; Republic, 69; Republican Party, 92; Revolution, 27, 40, 76, 80, 90, 92, 114; Revolutionary Council, 92; World Government, 80

Islamism, 71, 115, 116

Islamist ideology, 83

Israel, 79, 93, 120, 140, 141; chemical weapons capability, 57

Jacobin manifesto, 10

Jadid regime, 70

Jamaat Islami, 76

Janjaweed militias, 52

Japan, 113

Javanese, 95

Jihad, 114

Jihadists, 81, 82, 114, 161

Juche, 32, 70, 74, 84, 87, 111, 113, 181

Justice, distributive, 181

Kabul, 160, 161

Kabul regime, 125

al-Kadhim, Imam, 114

Karbala, 89

Karzai, Hamid, 160

Kashmir, 55, 76, 82

Kashmiri terrorists, 65

Keohane, Robert, 8

Khartoum, 79

Khatami, Mohammad, 54, 115, 117, 123, 124

Khomeini, Ayatollah Ruhollah, 27, 36, 40, 54, 69, 80, 83, 84, 85, 88, 90, 92, 123

Khrushchev, Nikita, 70, 84

Kim Jong-Il, 114

Kim Il-Sung, 32, 70, 74, 84, 87, 94

Kimongi, Fernando, 33

Korean unification, 87

Kosovar Albanians, 60

Kosovo, 78, 134, 136–38, 147, 153, 154

Kosovo Liberation Army, 137
Koštunica, Vojislav, 152, 154
Krajina, ethnic cleansing of Serbs in,
    138
Kremlin, 11
Kucan, Milan, 78
Kurdish Democratic Party of Iran, 54
Kurdish Workers Party (PKK), 54
Kurdistan People's Party (PKK), 55
Kurds, Iraqi, 61, 62, 125, 158, 159, 161
Kuwait, 139–43, 155, 157, 159, 160;
    invasion of, 60, 81, 139–43
Kuwait City, 157

League of Communists, 82
Lebanon, 79, 120
Lemert, Edwin, 24
Lesotho, 59, 60
Liberal-institutionalism, 169
Libya, 43, 54, 77, 85, 91, 93, 110, 115,
    119, 131, 132, 143, 144, 156, 157,
    179; air strikes against, U.S., 134,
    155; chemical, biological and nu-
    clear weapons, 56, 57, 58, 65; eco-
    nomic liberalization, 115, 119; egal-
    itarian ideology of, 115; electronic
    perestroika in, 132; ideological ex-
    ceptionalism, 85; land redistribu-
    tion, 91; privatization in, 119, 132;
    sanctions against, 115, 119, 156;
    Third Universal Theory, 85, 132;
    trade embargo against , U.S., 115
Libyan regime, 91
Libyan Revolution, 132
Lipset, Seymour Martin, 33
Litwak, Robert, 12
Lockerbie bombing, 65, 119
Londregan, John, D., 33
Loya Jirga, 160, 165

Macedonia, 61, 137
Madrassas, 81
al-Mahdi, Sadiq, 70

Mahdi, 80
Manichaeism, 82
Marine Expeditionary Unit, U.S., 142
Marxism, 70, 97
Marxist ideals, 35
Materialism, 98
Measurement, fundamental and de-
    rived, 47
Mello, Sergio de, 161
Messianism, 132
Middle class, 116, , 118, 119, 120, 171,
    122
Middle East peace process, 12, 54,
    126
Military force, objectives of, 133–36
Military intervention, unilateral, 175
Mill, John Stuart, 67
Millennial ideologies, 35
Milošević, Slobodan, 35, 36, 52, 70,
    78, 89, 93, 94, 96, 113, 122, 137,
    138, 139, 141, 146, 149, 150, 151,
    152, 153, 154, 155, 159; ethnic
    wars, 179; modernity, 81
Milošević regime, 52, 61, 63, 85, 89,
    111, 117, 148, 151, 172; collapse of,
    150–55
Modernization, 86
Mohammed, Prophet, 80, 114
Mohammad Reza Pahlavi, 27, 69
Mojahedin-e Khalq, 54
Money laundering, 173
Mujahedins, 81
Musharraf, Pervez, 76, 82, 86, 91, 115,
    126
Musharraf regime, 115, 121
Muslim Brotherhood, 93, 126
Muslim exceptionalism, 84
Muslim Nation, 80
Muslims, African, 79; Bosnian, 61, 77,
    78; Lebanese, 82; Sudanese, 79
Mustard gas, 56
Mustakberin and Mustazefin, 83
Mustazafin Foundation, 91

Nagorno Karabakh, 59, 98
Najaf, 89
Nasser, Gamal Abdel, 71, 77, 97
Nasserite regime, 71, 95, 96
Nation, primordialist view of, 30
National Democratic Party (Egypt), 72
National Islamic Front, 54, 62, 90, 121
Nationalism, 30, 70, 71, 74, 75, 78, 79,
    96, 100, 113, 169, 182; Arab, 71, 72,
    77, 115; civic or situationalist con-
    ception of, 30; ethno-, 31, 176; Ira-
    nian, 76; Iraqi, 75, 114; North Ko-
    rean, 74; Pakistani, 76; pan-Arab,
    96; and religion, 31, 83; Serbian,
    40, 82, 149 NATO, 13, 60, 61,
    134,136–39, 147–55
Naumann, Klaus, 137
Nazi Germany, 10
Nazism, 31
Nebuchadnezzar, 75
Neoconservatives, U.S., 131
Nepotism, 99
Netherlands tribunal, 54
New Democracy Movement for Serbia,
    152
New Partnership for Africa's Develop-
    ment, 13
Nidal, Abu, 143
Nigeria, 71, 95, 96, 99
Nimeiri, Gaafar, 80, 121
NIN, 138, 154
Noesu, 70
Norm cascades, 19, 20, 178
Norm entrepreneurs, 19, 20, 178
Norm-setters, 16, 21, 22, 27, 32,
    37–41, 43, 45, 48, 49, 56, 57, 63,
    64, 75, 83, 107, 136, 159, 171, 174,
    175, 176, 180, 181
Normative consensus, hierarchical na-
    ture of, 21, 22, 23
Normative order, international, 83
Norms: defined, 19; democratic, 181;
    of diplomatic immunity, 19; emer-

gence of, 178; evolutionary ap-
    proach to, 19; of freedom of the
    seas, 19; internalization of, 178; in-
    ternational, core, 2, 11, 12, 14, 15,
    18, 20, 22, 25, 27, 29, 35, 39, 45,
    46, 48, 49, 63, 69, 72, 74, 81, 87,
    95, 107, 120, 124, 165, 172, 175,
    176, 177, 181; life cycle of, 20; and
    renegades, 18–20; of sovereignty,
    19, 20
North Korea, 36, 70, 74, 75, 82, 84, 85,
    87, 88, 89, 113, 124, 125; Agreed
    Framework, 58, 124; chemical
    weapons program, 57; Chongsanri
    method and spirit, 88; as "chosen
    people," 75; Confucian legacy, 74;
    household ideology, 74; Japan, rela-
    tions with, 113, 114; Juche philoso-
    phy, 32, 70, 74, 84, 85, 87, 111,
    113, 181; missile program, 124; nu-
    clear facilities, IAEA inspection of,
    124, 125; nuclear weapons capabil-
    ity, 85, 124; purges of 1966, 94;
    Pyongyang, 58, 70, 113, 125; Rajin-
    Songbong free trade zone, 124;
    Seven Year Plan, 89; Soviet Union,
    relations with, 113; Taean method,
    88; Third Universal Theory, 181;
    United States, relations with, 113,
    125; Uranium enrichment program,
    125; Workers Party Central Com-
    mittee, 124
North Korean regime, 74, 111, 119
North Vietnam, 43
Nuclear arms race, 50
Nuclear deterrence, 49
Nuclear Non-Proliferation Treaty, 49,
    125
Nuclear weapons, 35, 69, 75, 76, 85
Nye, Joseph, 8

Odds-ratio, 102
Oil for Food program, 118, 125

Ojdanié, Dragoljub, 151
Omar, Mullah, 145
Operation Allied Force, 147–55
Operation Desert Fox, 138, 147
Operation Desert Shield, 134, 139
Operation Desert Storm, 134, 143, 155,
    157, 158
Operation Determined Falcon, 137
Operation El Dorado Canyon, 156,
    157
Opium trade, 91
Organization of the Islamic Confer-
    ence, 96
OSCE observers, 137
Osirak nuclear research reactor in Iraq,
    Israeli bombing of, 44
Otpor, 152, 153

Pancasila, 97
Pakistan, 55, 76, 81, 82, 86, 91, 115,
    118, 121, 126, 180; military and in-
    telligence service (ISI), 82; nuclear
    and missile programs, 35, 65; sanc-
    tions against, 121; U.S. aid to, 121
Pakistan Institute for Public Opinion,
    76
Palestine-General Command, 55
Palestine Islamic Jihad, 54
Palestine Liberation Front, 54
Palestinian Authority, 54
Pan Am flight 103, bombing of, 54
Pan-Arabism, 77, 79, 86, 132
Panić, Milan, 93–94, 122
Paris Club, 121
Party of Serbian Renewal (SPO), 152
Pashtun Talibans, 79
Pashtuns, 76, 79
Patterns of Global Terrorism, 53
Peru, 59
Philosophy of science literature, 67
Poland, 10
Political decisions and emotions, 169

Political ideology, 31, 32, 35, 169, 176;
    and religious doctrines, 35
Political interaction and meaning, 169
Political stability and economic perfor-
    mance, link between, 33
Political scientists, 169
Politics, power, 2, 5, 8, 9, 167; theories
    of, 1, 4
Pool, Keith T., 33
Popular Arab and Islamic Conference,
    55
Popular Congresses, 85
Power, 168; access to, 24; balance of ,
    9, 10; coercive, 13; measurement of,
    3; "soft," 4, 176
Pragmatism, 97
Prague Spring, 11
Presidential Guard, 62, 63
Prisoners' Dilemma, 8
Privatization, 89, 90
Proletarian internationalism, 70
Prospect theory, 111
Przeworski, Adam, 33
Punishments, See Sanctions
Pyongyang, 58, 70, 113, 125

Qaddafi regime, 91
Qaddafi, Muammar, 32, 54, 65, 77, 82,
    85, 88, 93, 119, 125, 131, 132, 143,
    144, 156, 157, 159, 179
al-Qaeda, 6, 12, 44, 55, 65, 79, 81, 136,
    141, 145, 161

Rafsanjani, Hashemi, 117, 123
Ragin, Charles, 68
Rally-round-the-flag effect, 25, 28, 37,
    92, 112, 177, 127, 134, 136, 145,
    149, 155, 166
Random selection, 68
Rational choice theory, 24
Rationality, limited information, 24
Reagan, Ronald, 144, 156

Reagan administration, 156, 157
Realism, structural, 168
Realists, 168
Realpolitik, 176
Recording industry, 14
Regime: capacity, 134; change, 134,
    135; incentives, 133, 134, 135, 136,
    143; legitimacy, 20, 29–32, 35, 37,
    40, 45, 69–72, 74, 79, 84, 87, 95,
    96, 98, 101, 102, 104, 115, 119,
    145, 175, 177; stability, 162
Regimes: attributes of, 13; coercion,
    role of, 29; economic objectives,
    87–91; internal fragmentation, 95;
    political ideology, 83–87, 97; reli-
    gion, impact of 80–83; security, 28,
    29; and social movements, 14; sup-
    port, ideational, 170; see also, Rene-
    gade regimes
Religion, 31, 32, 80–87, 97, 100,
    169, 182; as foundation of regime
    legitimacy, 96; ideology, fusion
    with, 84
Religious extremism, 36
Renegade regimes, 13, 18, 23, 25, 26;
    aggression and, 51, 52, 58–60; ag-
    gression, territorial, 15, 34, 86, 155;
    attributes of, 48, 49; democracy, re-
    jection of, 52, 53; and domestic re-
    pression, 60–63; incentives, punish-
    ment and, 27–29; non-, 68, 69, 73,
    100, 102; primary, 27, 29, 48, 72,
    89, 92, 99, 100, 104, 107, 167, 170,
    175, 177; primary, incentives of,
    73–95; primary, genesis/emergence
    of, 34–38, 46, 65, 73, 94, 100, 102,
    105, 175; primary, basis for legiti-
    macy, 175; secondary, 27, 29,
    38–45, 48, 65, 66, 92, 107, 170,
    175; as "soft" concept, 46, 47
Renegade status, necessary conditions
    for, 95

Rentier economy, 91
Rent-seeking elites/interests, 41, 111,
    112, 116–22, 119, 127–29, 131,
    132, 134, 146, 148, 171
Republican Guard, Iraqi, 139, 142, 158
Rhineland, 10
Rhodesian Front, 42
Rogue states, 12, 38
Rome airport, terrorist attack against,
    143
Rumsfeld, Donald, 161
Russia, 61
Rwanda, massacres/ethnic cleansing in,
    61–63, 137; Interhamwe youth mili-
    tia, 62, 63
Rwandan Patriotic Army, 63

Sadat, Anwar, 72, 77
Saddam Mosque, 81
Saddam Hussein's regime, 6, 125, 159
Saladin, 75
Saleh, Ali Abdulah, 97
Saleh regime, 71, 96, 97
Sanctions: comprehensive, 42, 108–10,
    112, 115, 116–20, 122–26, 127,
    129, 130–32, 172, 173; diplomatic,
    39, 126; economic, 16, 37–39,
    41–43, 87, 89, 91, 98, 102, 107,
    110, 120, 134, 145, 146, 166, 167,
    171, 172; impact of, 107–32; mili-
    tary, 43–45, 167; models of effec-
    tiveness, 108–16; partial, 108, 109,
    110, 115, 120–22, 126, 127, 129,
    130; selection effect of, 110; tar-
    geted or "smart," 151, 172
Sarajevo, 149
Sarin, 56
Saudi Arabia, 139, 140
Secular liberalism, 88
Secularism, 86
September 11, 2001, 6, 21, 50, 54, 65,
    86, 120, 132, 141, 180

Serbia, 36, 61, 70, 78, 86, 122, 136–38, 147–49; anti-war demonstrations in, 149; ethnic Hungarians in, 77; political parties, POL stock, 148; 152; sanctions against, UN, 122; Vojvodina region, 77, 78
Serbian Peasants Party, 152
Serbian Radical Party, 151, 152
Serbian Socialist Party, 148
Serbianism, 86
Šešelj, Vojislav, 150, 151, 154
Seven Year Plan, 89
Shagari, Alhaji Shehu, 71
Shah of Iran, 27, 69, 77, 91, 92
Shariah, 96
Sharif, Nawaz, 76, 81, 126
al Shifa pharmaceutical plant in Sudan, U.S. missile attack on, 44
Shiite Hazaras, 79
Shiites, 75, 76, 82, 89, 125, 158, 159, 161; clergy, 174
Shiite Islam, 81
Short, Michael, 138
Shultz, George, 157
Siberia, Japanese intervention against, 10
Simon, Herbert, 24
Slovenia, 78
Social constructivists, 20
Socialism, 4, 11, 72, 86, 97; Egyptian, 97; state/statist, 71, 86
Socialist Party of Serbia (SPS), 150, 152
Sociologists, functionalist, 21
Somalia, 173
South Africa, 59, 60
South Korea, 74; chemical weapons development, 57
Soviet Union, 4, 10, 11, 70, 113, 114, 132; de-Stalinization of, 84
Soviets, 81

Stalin, 70
Stalinism, 70
State, definition of, 13, 14; identity of, 20
State building, 174
States of concern, 12
Sudan, 51, 54, 55, 70, 78, 79, 90, 115, 116, 121, 134, 194n22; civil war, 62; coup in, 1989, 80; sanctions against, U.S., 126
Sudanese regime, 126
Sudetenland, 10
Suez Canal, nationalization of, 77
Suharto, Mohamed, 99
Suharto regime, 71, 95, 96, 97, 99, 100
Sukarno, 71
Sunnis, 75, 76, 79, 82, 125, 161
Syria, 12, 55, 82, 86, 120, 121, 126; chemical weapons stockpile, 56, 65; diplomatic relations with Britain, 120; economic liberalization, 90, 120; economic sanctions on, 108; Egypt, union with, 79; foreign policy, 120; redistributive policies, 90; sanctions against, European Community, 120
Syrian Accountability Act, 108, 121
Syrian regime, 90, 126

Taean method, 88
Taiwan chemical weapons program, 57
Taliban, 6, 44, 55, 65, 69, 79, 81, 82, 84, 88, 91, 94, 125, 136, 141, 145, 159, 160, 162, 163
Taliban regime, 12, 113, 144
Terrorism: defined, 50, 51; international, 21, 49, 54, 55, 65, 72, 83, 143; state-sponsored, 53
Third Universal Theory, 181
Treaty of Utrecht, 9
Treaty of Westphalia, 5

Tribalism, 71
Tripoli, 156
Tudjman, Franjo, 78
al-Turabi, Hasan, 62, 84, 88
Turabi regime, 78
Turkey, 61
Tutsis, 62, 63
Twelfth Imam, 80

Ulama, 64
Unilateral Declaration of Independence, 42
United Nations, 42, 122, 165, 174, 175; Charter of, 23; Convention for the Suppression of the Financing of terrorism, 124; Oil for Food Program, 118, 125; Security Council, 22, 56, 57, 60, 63, 139, 141–43, 161, 174; trade embargo on Iraq, 108
United States, 23, 39, 173; and Afghanistan, air attacks on, 121, 145; commitment to poor countries, 181; Department of State, 53, 55, 65, 124, 156; embassies, bombing of, 134; hostage crisis in Iran, 92; imperialism, 93; and Iran, 27, 36, 56, 80, 92, 116, 117, 123, 124; and Iraq, 75, 139–43, 157–59, 174, 175; and Iraq, invasion of, 6, 120, 139–43, 160, 161, 173; and Libya, 156, 157; military intelligence units, 163; Navy, 144; National Security Council, 149; and Pakistan, 121, 180; quasi-hegemony of, 4, 16; security forces, 165; Special Forces, 163; and Syria, 120, 126; and the Taliban, 12, 144; unilateral action of, 174
United Yugoslav Left Party (JUL), 148, 150, 151
Upper class, landed, 33
Uwilingiyimana, Agathe, 63

Values: ethno-nationalist, 30, 35; ideational, 29–32; material, 29; nationalist/ethnic, 30; religious, 35
Vienna airport, terrorist attack against, 143
Vietnam, 163, 171, 173; Cambodian peace process, 171; MIA issue, 171; sanctions against, U.S., 171; Strategic hamlets, 163

War on terror, 180
Weapons of mass destruction, 6, 15, 22, 34, 44, 49, 50, 52, 56–58, 64, 75, 81, 86, 121, 131, 132, 141, 142, 177
White Nile Tannery, 90
Wilson, Woodrow, 9, 51
World Trade Organization, 132

Xenophobia, 113

Yayasans, 99
Yemen, 71, 97, 98, 99, 100
Yemen regime, 95
Yongbyon nuclear facility, 58
Yugoslav Communist Party, 137
Yugoslavia, 61, 63, 77, 78, 82, 93, 94, 112, 136–39, 147–55, 159; Constitution (1974), 78, 136; Krajina, ethnic cleansing of Serbs in, 138; NATO action against, 60, 61, 134, 137, 138, 149, 159; post-Tito communist hierarchy, 82; Račak, civilian murders in, 137; Rambouillet, meeting in, 138; sanctions against, 11, 117, 122; Socialist Party, 82;

Zaire, See Democratic Republic of Congo
Zajedno, 152
Zinawi, Meles, 116
Zionism/Zionists, 75, 80, 92, 93, 125
Zwara Declaration of 1973, 93